ACCLAIM FOR

LEARNED PIGS & FIREPROOF WOMEN

"A delightful excursion into some of the most exotic regions of show business . . . It is not only its range that makes *Learned Pigs & Fireproof Women* an exceptional book, but its humor and its learning."
—John Gross, *The New York Times*

* * * * *

"An irresistible tome that details the rise, demise, fame, and shame of history's most gifted freaks, geeks, wizards, and quacks."
—*People* magazine

* * * * *

"Prescribed as an antidote for Mondays. This is an account of some of the most astounding novelty acts in show business history."
—*Chicago Tribune*

* * * * *

"A can't-put-it-down compendium of mind readers, performing animals, daredevils, rock eaters, and incombustible artists of both sexes."
—*Los Angeles Daily News*

* * * * *

"A perceptive celebration . . . What makes it such a joy is the author himself. The man seems incapable of writing a mundane line."
—*Circus Report*

* * * * *

"*The* book to give for Christmas is Ricky Jay's fascinating tome about unique and eccentric entertainers called *Learned Pigs & Fireproof Women.*"
—Liz Smith, New York *Daily News*

* * * * *

"A dizzying encyclopedia . . . a magician, lecturer, actor and library curator, Jay is the country's leading weirdologist."
—*Rolling Stone*

* * * * *

LEARNED PIGS & FIREPROOF WOMEN

RICKY JAY

FARRAR, STRAUS AND GIROUX

NEW YORK

This book is dedicated to
my wonderful friend
CHARLES EARLE MILLER
a unique, eccentric, and remarkable entertainer

Farrar, Straus and Giroux
19 Union Square West, New York 10003

Library of Congress catalog card number: 98-073819

First published in 1986 by Villard Books
First published in paperback in 1987 by Warner Books
First Farrar, Straus and Giroux paperback edition, 1998

Contents

Introduction

A nervous participant was ordered to aim and shoot a pistol at an East Indian man he had never even met. Reluctantly, he fired a shot. The Indian smiled, quickly moved his hand forward, and caught the bullet.

Triumphantly displaying the projectile, which had previously been examined and marked for identification, Khia Khan Khruse bowed to hearty applause in the Green Man Assembly Rooms, Blackheath, England, on March 18, 1822.

But this was not the conclusion of his performance. He followed his demonstration of invulnerability with a "grotesque Indian dance" and a second, more incomprehensible two-step—this time barefoot on a sheet of red-hot iron. Next, he rolled a smoldering bar over his body. Then, extending his tongue as if for some primitive communion, he had it anointed with boiling hot wax, from which he allowed spectators to take a seal with their own signet rings. Finally, a 700-pound stone was lifted and placed on his breast and smashed to pieces with a giant sledgehammer.

Earlier in his act, before appearing as a human target, Khruse had swallowed some pins and then extracted them from his eyes. He lifted a water bottle using only a common straw. He balanced seven glasses of wine on his forehead and an additional full glass on his chin and in this posture passed his body through a small hoop without upsetting his "cargo." He "ran a circular race" on the top of twenty ordinary drinking glasses; swallowed a case knife which, when magically transformed into a bell, was heard to ring in various parts of his body; walked on his hands with one of his feet in his mouth; changed a small ball into a large toad; and mysteriously fried eggs on a sheet of writing paper.

But the most remarkable thing about Khia Khan Khruse is that he was not remarkable enough to warrant a chapter in this book.

The individuals who pass in review within these pages were not the equivalents of an act opening the show at a modern-day rock concert, or fillers on a vaudeville bill of the 1920's. They were a remarkable group of men and women who excited special interest, whether they spouted water on the streets of London in the seventeenth century or wrote ten different numbers simultaneously by means of chalk extended from each finger only a generation ago.

What they shared in common is that they captured the public's imagination. Unlike Khruse, who merely (although with great versatility) mimicked the skills of his contemporaries, these people were pioneers or refiners of peculiar performance. Though mostly forgotten today, they once commanded the attention of the press, the study of scientists, or the patronage of royalty.

It seems that I've always been especially interested in unusual entertainers. As a child I was the youngest magician ever to appear on television. Since then I've shared the stage with mediocre midget accordion players, splendid soap-bubble blowers, and Japanese quick-change artists. I developed an act which consisted of throwing playing cards at ersatz chickens, through newspapers, and into watermelons.

I learned the rudiments of my craft from my grandfather, an accomplished exponent of sleight of hand. Through his friendship with many remarkable stage artists, I had the chance to meet and watch some of the world's foremost magicians, jugglers, and ventriloquists. My waking hours were consumed by a desire to absorb and practice the techniques of sleight of hand. Books supplemented my personal instruction and opened the door to the history of the art.

From this beginning my zeal in collecting the peculiar information to be found in the following pages surprises even me. I have accumulated books, posters, photographs, programs, broadsides, and, most important, data about unjustifiably forgotten entertainers all over the world. In preparation for this book, I have visited libraries and private collections in a dozen countries on five continents in search of material on peculiar, bizarre, phenomenal, fantastic, unbelievable, and outrageous entertainers. I have had a terrific time.

In Paris, between shows at the Moulin Rouge, Bob Bramson, the great hoop-rolling juggler, provided me with important information about his grandfather LaRoche. In an act called "The Bola Misteriosa," LaRoche created a sensation at the turn of the century by climbing to the top of a fifty-foot spiral tower. What made this extraordinary is that LaRoche's climb was done while imprisoned in a small steel ball powered *only* by his precisely shifting body.

In Shelton, Connecticut, I tried on the coat of Arthur Lloyd, which contained fifteen thousand items carefully catalogued in more than forty pockets. From it he could produce upon demand, and without looking, any specific one requested by his vaudeville audience.

In Japan I searched for the recent television exponent of musical flatulence. I failed—but was rewarded with information about a famous eighteenth-century performer who had exhibited the same formidable powers.

In California, I sat for hours beguiled by Ozzie Malini, son of Max Malini, the remarkable magician. "Did you hear what my father did to Mayor Brown of the Philippines?" he asked. "At an elaborate state dinner the mayor and guests tried to play a joke on my dad. Knowing he was Jewish, they decided to serve him a roast pig— complete with an apple in its mouth. Undaunted, my father covered the platter with his napkin and stared at the company. When he whisked the napkin away, the pig had vanished and a cooked chicken occupied its place."

I have relied, wherever possible, on primary source material for the information presented in this book. Eyewitness accounts, newspaper reviews, and performers' publicity have been especially useful; but all of these sources must be weighed and considered carefully. As Richard Altick has stated, "Of all the classes of documents that historians may be called on to deal with, none are more engagingly disingenuous or downright mendacious than show business publicity where honesty possesses neither virtue nor advantage."

I hope my fondness for the sensational, verbose, and often preposterous claims of my fellow entertainers has not led me astray, inasmuch as I have tried to present a realistic picture of their life and times. I wholeheartedly welcome corrections or additions to the material here presented.

When I started to work on this project ten years ago, I wanted only to share what I found attractive, exciting, and amusing with a reading public I believed I could interest in my passions. What occurs to me now as I finish this book is that people are fooled today in the same way and by the same things that fooled them four or five hundred years ago. We are as skeptical, and as credulous; as approving and as fickle now as we were then. Our capacity to marvel at the strange, wonderful, and peculiar accomplishments of our fellow human beings is undiminished, and an inspiration to new generations of beguiling performers.

HARRY KAHNE:
The Multiple
Mental Marvel

Sitting in front of a blackboard, Harry Kahne wrote five different words simultaneously with pieces of chalk held in each hand, each foot, and his mouth.

Next the words "idiosyncrasies," "Constantinople," and "Indianapolis" were chosen by the audience. Kahne was hoisted upside down over the blackboard. He requested a popular piece of poetry. Rudyard Kipling's *Gunga Din* was selected. He began writing the three words and reciting the poem at the same time. As he exultantly declared, "You're a better man than I, Gunga Din!" he dramatically stopped writing. The audience was impressed but confused by the unbroken, unintelligible line of letterforms on the blackboard. Kahne slowly deciphered the jumble. He had alternated the letters of each word, but "Indianapolis" was written right-side up, "idiosyncrasies" upside down, and "Constantinople" in mirror writing, upside down and reversed. To illustrate this unusual ability for a *Strand Magazine* reporter in 1925, Kahne used the following sentence:

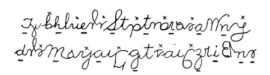

In another stunt, Kahne quickly glanced at a list of random nouns, numbered from one to twenty, written by a spectator in the audience. Next, a spectator suggested a three-digit number. Kahne began filling in a four-by-four square or grid with one- and two-digit numbers (never repeated): the resultant columns of this "magic square" were added vertically, horizontally, diagonally, or in any number of other ways, always totaling the original chosen figure. While he did this he would shout out the particular words previously numbered and suggested by the spectator. At one point, while reading a newspaper upside down, he transposed the letters, wrote upside down and backward, added five twelve-digit numbers, and divided another sum into five unequal parts. While he performed these functions Kahne pleaded with the audience to talk to him. He answered questions. ("What is the population of Manchester?" "735,551.") And he threw out quips. ("Are you married?" "No, it's my work that makes me act this way.")

9	6	3	16
4	15	10	5
14	1	8	11
7	12	13	2

These six distinct mental operations may have involved as many as fourteen separate processes of the brain, as Kahne claimed:

- Hearing questions
- Answering questions
- Reading a newspaper
- Transposing what is read
- Writing with the right hand
- Writing with the left hand
- Writing upside down
- Carrying six thoughts in mind
- Retaining questions
- Retaining figures for addition
- Retaining figures for division
- Proving his arithmetical working
- Controlling his physical actions

Perhaps he should be given credit for yet another mental operation. By all accounts, his act was not just interesting but marvelously entertaining. He played the world-famous Palace Theatre in New York five times, spanning some thirty years with his novel act.

Thea Alba, billed as "The Woman with 10 Brains," did an act much like Kahne's in Europe. Attending a dramatic school in her native

Thea Alba.

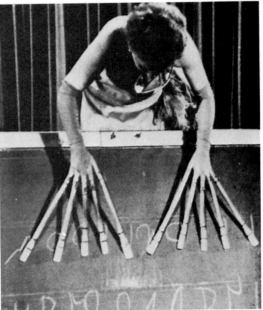

Writing with chalk extended from ten fingers.

Berlin in 1920, she effortlessly completed an acting exercise which involved moving her foot in perfect circles in a counterclockwise direction while writing, repeatedly, the numeral 3 with her right hand. Henry de Vry, the president of Germany's variety artists' association (Internationale Artisten-Loge), happened to be present and asked her to try writing different letters simultaneously with each hand. Although she accomplished this clumsily, de Vry urged the girl to practice, and within three weeks she made her debut "writing different sentences in French, German and English at the same time and ambidextrously drew a landscape in colored chalks." She developed quickly, learning to write with both feet and with her mouth. She also mastered the apparently unique stunt of writing ten different figures at the same time by using ten pieces of chalk mounted on long pointers attached to each of her fingers. In the course of a long career she exhibited for Maxim Gorky, Kaiser Wilhelm II, and Woodrow Wilson.

That such abilities could be taught no doubt inspired Kahne to write a book entitled *Kahnetic Mentalism* (1936). In this work Kahne stated that his was an "average brain made to perform certain tasks," and that intelligence was based on neither heredity nor education but was an "acquired trait." The book was much like today's self-help publications, but its premise was that the ability to write with either hand would lead to a happier, healthier, and more rewarding life.

Kahnetic Mentalism was never published. Perhaps the following paragraph explains why:

Fashioning different words with each foot and hand simultaneously.

I have had men and women tell me that the mental exercises and drills that I am here giving you have relieved them of such varied physical symptoms as shortness of breath, headaches, pains in the chest and abdomen, nausea, weakness in the back, spots before the eyes, stomach trouble, constant fatigue, palpitations of the heart—and faintness! Frankly, I was astonished as you probably are by their recitals—and as unbelieving. But they assured me that every word they uttered was true, which certainly leaves me with little to say.

Or me. Harry Kahne died at the age of 60 on February 16, 1955.

PORCINE PROPHETS
AND PIG-FACED LADIES

Sheet music for "The Wonderful Pig," circa 1785.

PORCINE PROPHETS

In 1785 a pig appeared in London. He (and his successors) inspired the attention, however fleeting, of Samuel Johnson, William Wordsworth, Pierce Egan, Mary Wollstonecraft, Thomas Rowlandson, Samuel Taylor Coleridge, and William Blake.

He was the subject of political satires, caricatures, and portraits. Robert Southey declared he was "a far greater object of admiration to the English nation than ever was Sir Isaac Newton."

Most likely this extraordinary pig was the property of a Scottish shoemaker, S. Bisset, who was born in Perth in 1721. Bisset moved to London, married a woman of some wealth, and, curious after reading about a "learned horse" at St. Germaine, tried his hand at animal training. His success was little short of remarkable. The former shoemaker had no trouble imposing his will on dogs and horses for simple acts of obedience. He next taught two monkeys an unusual routine. One danced on the tightrope while the second illuminated his brother's movements by holding a candle in one paw and providing musical accompaniment by playing on a barrel organ with the other. Bisset next turned his attention to domestic cats, a species notoriously uninterested in schooling. The results inspired one of the Pinchbeck family, the famous showmen and builders of automata, to persuade Bisset to perform publicly in London. Although Pinchbeck dropped out of the proceedings at the last moment, Bisset's "Cat's Opera" was an enormous success. After the parade of horses, dogs, and monkeys, three cats proceeded to play tunes by striking their paws on a dulcimer and squealing in different keys, producing some pleasing feline harmony, all the while staring intently at sheet music propped up in front of them. This performance garnered Bisset some £1,000 and encouraged his further efforts.

He taught canaries, linnets, and sparrows to spell by selecting appropriate alphabet cards, had a rabbit beat a drum with its hind legs (a stunt which goes back to at least the fourteenth century), and trained six turkeys to do a country dance (admittedly, he later confessed, by placing them on a heated floor—a spectacle which, alas, I saw many times in my youth in New York's Chinatown). He even taught a turtle to "fetch and carry" like a dog. After six months' training, the turtle, with blackened claws, scratched out any selected name on a chalk-covered floor! It was only after these successes and the additional accomplishment of training goldfish—to do exactly what, is never stated—that he applied his efforts to that beast of legendary stupidity and intractability—the pig.

Actually, a pig concert much in the manner of the Cat's Opera, but with a significantly less civil modus operandi, was provided for King Louis XI of France by the Abbot of Baigne in the fifteenth

Sparrows unable to speak Portuguese.

century. The king, noted for "caprices and humours which were very singular," requested of the musically inventive abbot a "consort of swine voices." Baigne responded with a "great number of hogs of several ages who were arranged beside an organical instrument." When the abbot played the organ keys, little spikes would prick the pigs to produce cries "in such order and consonance as highly delighted the king and all his company."

Bisset's attempts with a black suckling pig bought at Dublin market did not meet with immediate success. After sixteen months of patient training, the pig made his debut in August 1783, his repertoire consisting of spelling names, solving problems in arithmetic, telling time, and even pointing out words on flashcards—correctly selecting those thought of by the audience. Some days after his initial triumph Bisset moved to a location within the city at Dame Street. Although he exhibited with the permission of the magistrate, a lower-level official, outraged no doubt by the indignity of a pig in his domain, disrupted the show. He beat the exhibitor and threatened the life of the pig. "The agitation of mind Bisset experienced on this occasion threw him into a fit of illness from which he never recovered." A short time later, en route to London with his pig, he died in Chester.

"Perhaps," said the *Eccentric Mirror* (London, 1813), "no period ever produced a more singular character than Bisset: though in the age of apathy in which he lived, his merit was but little rewarded. At any former era of time, the man who could assume a command over the dumb creation, and make them act with a docility which far exceeded mere brutal instinct, would have been looked upon as possessed of supernatural powers. . . ."

A pig—or more than likely the same pig—arrived in London by way of a successful engagement at Scarborough and York in February of 1785. "The Amazing Learned Pig" at No. 55 the Admiralty, opposite Charing Cross, performed the stunts associated with Bisset's pig under the direction of a Mr. Nicholson. (According to Jacob Decastro, a learned pig appeared at the Royal Grove—established by Philip Astley, the founder of the modern circus—on May 25, 1784—another thorny problem in establishing pig precedence.) As Nicholson also featured (on his Scottish tour) a hare that beat the drum, a turtle that fetched, and six turkey cocks doing a country dance, one may assume something other than "independent invention." The London papers were favorably impressed with the pig, one stating: "A prodigy like this never

An American cartoon featuring the learned pig and many recognizable political figures, drawn by Bernhard Gillam for Puck, *1884.*

made its appearance amongst us before; and the most penetrating have frankly declared that neither the tongue of the most florid orator or the pen of the most ingenious writer can sufficiently describe the wonderful performance of that sagacious animal." Nevertheless, I shall continue. . . .

By the end of March the following "Impromptu on the Learned Pig" appeared in the *Morning Herald*:

> You men of genius and ye men of wit
> Who've sung the praises of your favorite Pitt
> In language pompous and in phrase more big
> Now hail a greater wonder in the—pig.

Prime Minister Pitt and his followers were also lampooned in a three-part political satire entitled "The Levee of the Wonderfull Pig." Some wags even suggested the pig be proposed for Parliament. A learned pig also appears in Samuel Collings' satirical print, *The Downfall of Taste and Genius* (1785), and *The Theatrical War* by James Gilray (1787). Thomas Rowlandson featured one in an eighteenth-century engraving, and as late as the 1890's learned pigs can be found as the subject of political cartoons.

The pig's prominence did not go unnoticed by Samuel Johnson, who, although he died shortly before the animal's London debut, was aware of its provincial performances. He termed pigs "a race unjustly calumniated . . . we do not allow time for his education, we kill him at a year old." In death Johnson was the subject of a rather tasteless ditty which appeared in the *Public Advertiser* of April 6, 1785:

On the LEARNED PIG

> Though Johnson, learned BEAR is gone,
> Let us no longer mourn our loss
> For lo, a *learned* Hog is come,
> And Wisdom grunts at Charing Cross.

> Happy for Johnson—that he died
> Before this *wonder* came to town
> Else it had blasted all his pride
> Another brute should gain renown.

On July 25, the pig, rewarded for his scholarly efforts, made it to the "big time." He moved from No. 55 Charing Cross to Sadler's Wells Theatre as the headline act on a mixed bill of sketches and variety entertainment. He told the time, distinguished colors, cast accounts by "means of typographical cards, in the same manner as a printer composes," and read the thoughts of ladies in the audience.

The Irish problem elucidated by a learned pig, October 31, 1885.

Again, the papers were most complimentary in their assessment of the pig. Not so the other performers. Signor Placide, Mr. Redigé (the Little Devil), Mr. Dupuis, Mr. Meunier, and La Belle Espagnole, accomplished tightrope dancers and acrobats, were outraged at their second billing to a porcine pretender to prophecy. "The performers above mentioned," said Richard Wroughton, the theater manager, "thinking themselves degraded, neglected the business and refused to perform in their usual manner." When Wroughton chided them for their actions, he received the classic ultimatum of the stage: "Either the pig goes or we do." The troupe quickly sought new employment.

This writer is indeed sensitive to the feelings of the tightrope troupe. My own television debut, at the age of seven, on a show called *Time for Pets*, found me underbilled to a larger and more theatrically experienced Saint Bernard. This trend continued with a peculiar CBS special entitled *The Hocus Pocus Gang Live at Sea World*, starring Shamu the Killer Whale (as if being part of the Hocus Pocus Gang wasn't indignity enough). Even in the company of Michael Landon on Doug Henning's NBC magic special, I found myself obscured by Taj the Elephant, who vanished none too soon as far as I was concerned. The sordid experience of sharing the stage with grouse, geese, and gerbils, I do not deem worthy of recollection.

The Little Devil, La Belle Espagnole, and friends, I am happy to report, were granted almost immediate employment at Astley's Circus. In fact, their success probably inspired the letter written to the *Gazetteer* on August 1, 1785. Outlining the reasons for the engagement of Mr. Nicholson and his pig ("who has been the admiration of the nobility and gentry of this kingdom all the winter") and the departure of the acrobats, Mr. Wroughton assumed the role of the injured party. In the throes of jingoistic passion, he pleaded his case: "I submit it to the public consideration, how far it is consistent either with his interest, or with justice and honour, to encourage such a combination of foreigners against an honest Englishman, who had at least an equal right to earn his bread in a British theatre."

Whether this furor hastened the pig's departure from the metropolis is not known, but he soon arrived in Bristol, welcomed by this feeble greeting:

> Haste to the Pig make no delay
> His time is short and does not mean to stay
> Your future he is sure to tell
> Which to everyone is wonderful
> And on the pig you may rely
> For he did never tell a lie.

The "Scientific Pig," as he was now called, having no doubt received his "moniker" in the provinces, returned to London in March of 1786. He could be seen with Mr. Nicholson at the Academy Room in the Lyceum, Strand, performing his usual routine, but with the added refinement that "he never divulges the thoughts of any lady in the company *but by her permission.*"

Competition, as could be expected, was just around the corner: In May "The Amazing Pig of Knowledge" appeared before "all lovers and Admirers of the Docility and Sagacity of the Brute Creation" at the Crown Inn in the Cornmarket. This pig's repertoire was largely the same as his predecessor's, but his proprietor, J. Fawkes, had the cheek to have playing cards selected and later located by his star attraction, while the pig was blindfolded.

The following year a pig, under the direction of Sieur Garman, appeared at Astley's. (Mr. Hughes, Astley's great rival and the proprietor of the Royal Circus, had as early as April of 1785 exhibited an automaton pig of knowledge, as well as a mechanical monkey who did evolutions on the tightrope; both were presented by Signor Spinetti.) The pig at Astley's, said the papers, "articulated, *oui, oui*, with an uncommon fine accent—a proof of his having an early polite education."

This influx of sagacious swine may have once more prompted Mr. Nicholson and his pig to make their way up the countryside, apparently never to return to the city of their greatest triumph. During the following year the pig could be seen in various locations in Yorkshire and Scotland. In November of 1788 the following obituary appeared in the *Gazetteer*:

> We are extremely sorry to inform the public that their old friend and favorite the *Learned Pig* has departed this life. Much learning, he found, was a weariness to the *bones*, for of *flesh*, he has not of late possessed much. We are sorry to add, that of his *writings* and *arithmetical calculations*, there is nothing left by which the world can profit; these having been generally washed away by the Gothic mop of a Gothic chambermaid. Whether Sir John Hawkins [who wrote the first biography of Samuel Johnson] has a *Life* in view, or Mrs. Piozzi [another of Johnson's biographers] any *letters*— we are not informed.

Another obituary claimed the pig made more money "than any other actor or actress within the same compass of time." After mourning the loss of the pig, "so long a favorite of the town," it mentioned that "his master is now confined in a madhouse in Edinburgh. Too much learning we suppose had driven the pig mad, so he bit his master!"

Thus the saga of the original learned pig must end with this dark observation: For the fame and fortune he acquired, he drove both his owners to distraction, delirium, lunacy, and death.

Americans had an opportunity to see a performing porker in New York by September 1797, when an advertisement for a pig who could read, spell, tell the time of day by any person's watch in the audience, and distinguish ladies from gentlemen, appeared in the *Daily Advertiser*. By April 1798 Americans had an opportunity to buy one. "The pig of Knowledge at Major King's Tavern is for sale. A good chance for speculation is offered, as the animal is going for a low rate."

The pig may have belonged to William Frederick Pinchbeck, a transplanted Englishman descended from the famous family of automata makers. Pinchbeck, who exhibited a pig of knowledge in Boston earlier that year, published his methods for training such an animal in

1805. *The Expositor: or Many Mysteries Unravelled* was the first original work on conjuring to be published in America. The frontispiece featured the pig spelling the word "Boston" (the city of the book's printing) and featured lessons in animal training, legerdemain, and ventriloquism, all written in epistolary form.

"Take a pig seven or eight weeks old," it stated, and "let him have free access to the inferior part of your house, until he shall become in some measure domesticated." (This would dissuade all but the most resolute pedagogues.) Eventually, a card is placed in the animal's mouth, which is held shut so he will understand he is not to drop it.

Frontispiece from Pinchbeck's The Expositor: or Many Mysteries Unravelled *(Boston, 1805).*

If he drops the card, he is to be reprimanded in a loud voice (the pig was not beaten or tortured, as Samuel Johnson and many of his contemporaries thought). He was rewarded with a piece of apple or white bread for a task well done. After a few lessons the pig would be placed in a circle of cards and led by a string until the instructor would signal the pig to stop and pick up the card directly under his snout. Eventually, both the string and the signal would be dispensed with. "Even communication is unnecessary. You may relinquish it by degrees; for the animal is so sagacious that he will appear to read your thoughts.

TOBY

THE
SAPIENT PIG,

From the Royal Rooms, Spring Gardens,

The only Scholar of his Race in the World.

THIS MOST EXTRAORDINARY CREATURE

Will Spell and Read, Cast Accounts,

PLAY AT CARDS;

Tell any Person what o'Clock it is to a Minute

BY THEIR OWN WATCH;

ALSO TELL THE AGE OF ANY ONE IN COMPANY,

And what is more Astonishing he will

Discover a Person's Thoughts

A Performance beyond all others the most Incredible.

Mr. HOARE having spent a number of Years in accomplishing this great undertaking, leaves it to a discerning Public, to judge of the laborious task he has had in bringing the above Animal before them, as of all others in Nature, none are so obstinate as his species, and it is only by unremitted assiduity and attention, that he has finally brought to such great perfection what Man never did before.

He is in Colour the most beautiful of his Race, in Symmetry the most Perfect, in Temper the most Docile; his Nature is so far from being offensive, that he is pleasing to all who honor him with their presence.

> The silken rob'd peer, and the delicate *belle*,
> Are unsulled by filth, unoffended by smell;
> Toby turns all disdainful from deeds of offence,
> For what would so blast his pretensions to sense.

He EXHIBITS every day at the
Temple Rooms, Fleet-street,

Near TEMPLE BAR, opposite CHANCERY LANE,

At the Hours of **1** and **3**, precisely,

And again in the Evening at **7** and **9** o'Clock.

ADMITTANCE ONE SHILLING.

Just Published, The Life & Adventures of TOBY the SAPIENT PIG,

With his Opinion on Men and Manners,

May be had at the Exhibition Rooms, Price One Shilling.

Printed by H. LYON, John Street, Edgware Road.

The remarkable Toby: a glimpse of his act, an ad for his book, circa 1817.

WONDERFUL & PLEASING

Exhibition

Mr. HOARE,

THE EXTRAORDINARY CONJURER,

Respectfully informs the Ladies and Gentlemen that he will have the honor of introducing his much admired Performances,

POSITIVELY FOR ONE NIGHT ONLY,

IN MR. PAGE'S

ASSEMBLY ROOMS,

NEXT DOOR TO THE SIGN OF THE HAMPTON COURT PALACE,

FRANCIS STREET,

Opposite Newington Church,

On MONDAY, APRIL 9th, 1838.

Mr. H. ever mindful of the gratitude that is due to a liberal and discerning Public, for its generous and powerful support, most respectfully offers his sincere acknowledgments for the same, and humbly trusts he shall ever be honourably entitled to a continuance, as it has ever been the highest summit of his hopes and wishes to merit and obtain it. Public encouragement is a sure stimulus to Genuine exertion, and imperiously calls forth every species of talent, which Nature in her wonted gifts so powerfully and eventually displays. Long experience has proved, that his Imperial Occult Powers have justly entitled him to the appellation of Grand Arch Master of all Conjurers.

Mr. HOARE, with that eminent confidence that his endeavours to amuse are always sure to be crowned with success, as a complete testimony of the excellence of his Performances, proceeds to add the names of several of the Nobility and Gentry, before whom he has, on several occasions, had the distinguished honor to be sent for to perform at their respective Mansions in the Metropolis and its Vicinity.

Before the Royal Party at Windsor, on the 19th of March, 1818. The Right Honourable the Lord Mayor Venables, and a large party, at the Mansion House on the 13th January, 1826. Her Grace the Duchess of Wellington's, Duke of Argyle's, Earl of Liverpool's, Earl Verulam's, Lady Grantham's, Lady Clark's, Lady Harrowby's, the Hon. Mrs. Kinnaird's, Sir William Clayton's, Sir C. Cockerell's, J. Lawford's, Esq., T. Rhead's, Esq., Captain Dundas's, J. Calvin's, Esq., Lady Fulton's, H. Hoare's, Esq., Grove House, Mitcham; M. Gordon's, Esq., Sydenham; Captain Sullivan's, Langley Hall; H. Thornton's, Esq., Battersea Rise; E. Ellice's, Esq., Wyke House, near Brentford; J. Wooley's, Esq., Denmark Hall, Camberwell; W. Prescott, Esq., Hendon; J. Masterman's, Esq., Whip Cross House, Walthamstow; Sir Edward Paget, Sir George Scovel, and the Gentlemen Cadets, at the Royal Military College, Blackwater; Lord Grantley's, near Guildford; Sir Sandford Graham's; R. W. Hall Dares, Esq., Ilford; Lady Essex, Westbow Hill, Norwood; and a vast number of Ladies' and Gentlemen's Boarding Schools, when on every occasion, the highest encomiums were bestowed on his various and multiplied routine of Performance.

Ladies and Gentlemen who may please to favor Mr. HOARE with their presence, may depend on seeing a most astonishing Performance of truly seeming Impossibilities, Thaumaturgy, Tachygraphy, Metamorphosis, Mechanical, and Mathematical

DEXTERITY

With Birds, Eggs, Cards, Money, Fruit, Handkerchiefs, Boxes, Letters, Medals, Pistols, Rings, Living Animals, Gold, Silver, Caps, Hats, &c.

To things inanimate he will give wings, and to those things apparently immoveable he will give action. With an incalculable succession of variety and most excellent deceptions, that the human eye has witnessed in a peculiar train of superior excellence, the whole so dexterously arranged as to deceive those possessed of the most lively imagination. To particularize the whole of the Performance would almost fill a volume.

The following is an outline of the Pleasing and Curious Experiments which will be presented during the Evening.

He will command Birds and Beasts to appear on the Table in a very extraordinary manner.
He will divide a Living Animal in halves, and make two perfect ones of him in a second.
He will allow Cards to be torn into Pieces and then burned to ashes, and in a moment will make them whole again. And, what is more extraordinary, he will positively command Cards to move themselves from one Person to another, at any distance; in fact, he can make them do any thing but speak.

A very extraordinary Pistol SHOT.

Any person may draw a card and return it into the pack, when he will throw the whole of them up and fire a ball through the one drawn, without touching any of the rest.

SECRET CONCEALERS AND SYMPATHETIC HANDKERCHIEFS.

ART OF SAXIGENUS,

THE BOX OF DIVINATION.

Showing how to make Money pass through the thickest Timber or Stone.

THE IMPENETRABLE SECRET, OR INVISIBLE IMPRESSION.

He will tell the real thoughts of any Person without asking a single Question.

His much admired Deception called the Flight, or Conveyance at the rate of Twenty Miles a Minute!—which no ever attempted but himself.

THE INVISIBLE ARTIST, OR LADIES' FORTUNE-TELLER!!

Surprising Calculation Figure Box.

A piece of Coin borrowed from any Lady or Gentleman, which may be marked; the same will be made to pass imperceptibly away, and afterwards be found locked up in an

ARABIAN TOWER OF BOXES,

He will allow a Gentleman in company to write any word he pleases on a Card, and in an instant he will command the writing to leave the card, and in a second he will put it on again.

A NEW METHOD OF COOKING WITHOUT A FIRE.

HE WILL CONVEY MONEY FROM ONE GENTLEMEN'S HAND TO ANOTHER, HOWEVER FAR APART.

AN ASTONISHING TRICK.—Three or Four Ladies and Gentlemen may each take a Card, and again replace the same; they shall then, as by instinct, leap one by one out of the pack as called for; which makes the Cards have the appearance of Real Life!

THAUMATURGY!

AND UNCOMMON DECEPTIONS.

THE BLACK CAP AND THE FLYING MONEY.

The Enchanted Tinder Box & Burst Card restored.

THE MARVELLOUS METAMORPHOSIS, OR THE DEAD MADE LIVING.

A PACK OF CARDS WILL BE TRANSFORMED INTO LIVING ANIMALS.

A PENNY PIECE CHANGED TO A LIVE BIRD.

AND UPWARDS OF ONE HUNDRED SURPRISING EXPERIMENTS!!

Doors open at half-past 7—begin at 8 o'Clock—and close at 10.
Admittance, Front Seats, 1s—Second ditto, 6d   Good Fires kept.

Mr. Hoare performs sans pig in 1838.

The position you stand in, not meaning any stipulated place, or certain gesture . . . will naturally arise from your anxiety and will determine the card to your pupil." This rather lucid explanation of the phenomenon of "unconscious cuing" would have helped many a puzzled psychic researcher in ensuing years.

Mr. "A. B.," the recipient of Pinchbeck's letters on pig training in *The Expositor*, had such success that, he wrote, "I am thought a man of talents whilst others less informed accuse me of the Black Art, and condemn me as a wizard." Yet in his next letter he wrote: "But the Pig no longer excites admiration," and he lamented that the public was now engrossed in a sensational new attraction.

The frontispiece from Toby's autobiography.

This eagerness to embrace every new amusement (often at the expense of the old) is indicative of the curiosity and fickleness that characterized the age. It very likely accounts for the fact that with the exception of a few brief references to learned pigs (on either continent), they vanish for the next twenty years. In June 1817, however, with the arrival of Toby the Sapient Porker, London was ready to taste its second helping of learned pigs.

Toby could be seen at the Royal Promenade Rooms, Spring Gardens, every afternoon and evening. He would, said the advertisements, "Discover a Person's Thoughts, a Thing never heard of before to be exhibited by an Animal of the SWINE RACE." While we know Toby was not the first to read thoughts, in later advertisements Mr. Hoare, his trainer, added a new feature to the mind reading demonstration:

Any Lady or Gentleman may put Figures in a Box,
and this wonderful Pig will absolutely tell what number
is made before the Box is opened!

Hoare, an experienced conjurer, had applied a mechanical magic principle to enhance his pig's reputation. Occasionally Hoare would "exhibit the Art of Legerdemain in a most superior style" in conjunction with the pig, but generally the animal would hog the limelight. Long after the pig was gone, Hoare could be found touring the countryside with a magic show which, though not original, was representative of the conjurers of the period. He was the publisher of a pamphlet supposedly authored by his star attraction: *The Life and Adventures of Toby the Sapient Pig: With Opinions of Men and Manners.* Written by Himself (London, c. 1817), published and sold by Nicholas Hoare, price one shilling.

Toby's tome, "embellished with an elegant frontispiece descriptive of a literary pig sty with the author in deep study," is a masterpiece of whimsy. Addressed to "the Nobility, Gentry and Public at large . . . who have witnessed my talents and raised me from obscurity to the proud eminence on which I now stand, I dedicate my following maiden essay in literature."

Toby called himself the "first of my race that ever wielded a pen." (In 1786 an earlier literary pig *dictated* his memoirs to a retired Officer of the Royal Navy. *The Story of the Learned Pig* (published by R. Jameson, London) is a Pythagorean romp of 113 duodecimo pages. The pig recounts his disparate former lives: as a dog, a scorpion, a fly, Romulus, Brutus, and, as an acquaintance of Shakespeare's called "Pimping Billy," the *real* author of *Hamlet, Othello, As You Like It, The Tempest,* and *A Midsummer Night's Dream.*) Toby, unlike the dictating porker, took pen in hoof and gave a lively account of his roots. His father, he said, was an "independent gentleman" who roamed the Duke of Bedford's estates; his mother, "a spinster in the service of a local innkeeper." Toby was the result of their "illicit amour." Mr. Hoare happened by the inn on April 1, 1816, just in time to witness the auspicious birth. Hoare purchased the pig, who had never even suckled his mother, and took him from the company of his own race, which he believed would be detrimental to the piglet's education. It was his master's recitation of Hamlet's most famous soliloquy, "To be or not to be . . . ," which was to provide the young pig with his name.

Toby, under Hoare's patient tutelage, learned quickly. At four months he could read "tolerably well," and having no companions other than his master, "took to learning as one would a playfellow." At the age of six months he made his professional debut for a group of workingmen under the nervous eye of his master. "Though before an indifferent tribunal, his hopes and fears were all alive, and never did

*Patronized by Her
Royal Highness
the Princess Augusta,*

*the NOBILITY,
Gentry, &c. &c.*

RE-OPENING OF THE
Extraordinary EXHIBITION
OF THE
INDUSTRIOUS FLEAS.

Performing most astonishing Feats, the whole different from last Season,

At No. 238, REGENT STREET,
Opposite Hanover Street. *May 1: 1833*

L. BERTOLOTTO, sensible of the distinguished Patronage which attended his efforts last Season, and desirous, if possible, to increase it in the present, by the Exhibition of such Objects, (little short of impossibility) and which would not be believed, if his fame, (in training Fleas) was not well established:—the following is the PROGRAMME, which he hopes will meet the approbation of the Public.

The Siege of Antwerp.

Representing the Fort, besieged and defended by Fleas, with Fire Arms, such as Cannons, Obus, Mortars, &c. which they set fire to, and make sufficient report to be audible all over the room, although the Gold Cannons, &c. are not larger than a common Pin. General Chàsse and Mareschal Gerard riding on Fleas, and encouraging their respective Soldier, i. e. the flea, to victory

A Ball Room,

In which two Fleas are dressed as Ladies, and two as Gentlemen, dancing a Waltz; twelve Fleas at the Orchestra, playing different instruments of proportionable size; the Music is audible, and the Room, (1½ inch square,) elegantly fitted up, with a Glass Chandelier.

The Royal Mail Coach,

Drawn by Four Fleas, completely harnessed, the Coachman, and the Guard, (also Fleas) the former holding the reins and whip in hand, belabouring his Four *Chesnuts!* the latter flourishing his horn of office.

An Elephant,

Richly decorated with Oriental Splendor, carrying a Tower filled with Warriors; the whole drawn by a single Flea; and a variety of other objects, including Microscopes, optical illusions, &c. too long to enumerate. Most of the Fleas stand on their hind Legs, and the workmanship of the objects is as superior to that which received general encomium last Season, as the Feats of the little Insects surpass the former. The improvements which L. Bertolotto has been able to adopt, precludes all Charges of cruelty to the Fleas, and the most rigorous Observer of Mr. Martin's Act will not find occasion to exert his humanity.

Open from 10 till Dusk, Admittance, ONE SHILLING. Evening Parties attended; the History of the Flea, by L. B to be had at the Exhibition Room.

NB—L B, has no Connexion whatever with a man who travels about the Country, exhibiting a pretended fac simile of part of his late Exhibition

Perhaps the most famous of all flea trainers, Bertolotto taught his pupils to reenact the Siege of Antwerp, etc., in 1833.

I see a man so agitated as he was during that my first entrance on the boards." Both teacher and student survived the ordeal, in spite of a drunken heckler—who soured our performer forever on the effects of drink. After honing his craft in the country, and enduring the hardships of a provincial player for some eight months, Toby gave his debut in London at the Promenade Rooms. The pig expressed the incredible pressures he faced: "Those who have been in a similar situation, can alone be able to conceive what I must have felt. . . . As the time grew nearer, it was dreadful . . . the day arrived that was to *make* me or *mar* me forever. . . ."

Toby overcame his stage fright and was successful beyond his wildest imagination. In a poetical review, one paper entitled *Toby the Sapient Pig; or the Three Great Actors*, even compared the pig to the great thespians Junius Brutus Booth and Edmund Kean:

> Then which of these rivals, amidst their range of parts
> Who from nature, for a moment never departs;
> Why the *Public* at Large, will with Critics agree,
> That *our Sapient* Pig Toby's the best of the three.

In spite of his critical success, Toby was skeptical of the press. "They twisted me sadly: some of the editors, from what they wrote, I firmly believe had never been there."

The most logical explanation of his literary passion comes from an anecdote the pig is almost embarrassed to mention: His mother, during the early stages of her pregnancy, unwittingly entered a

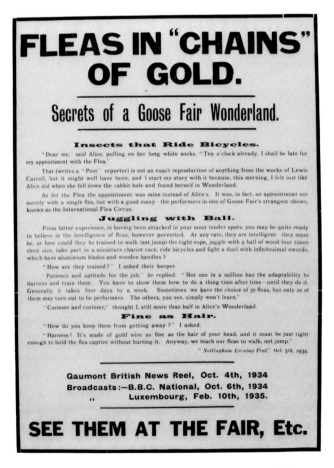

Flea power still harnessed one hundred years later at an English country fair.

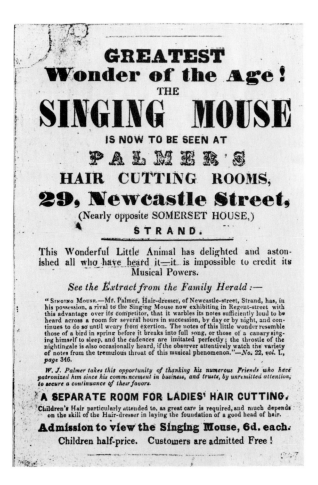

Palmer's Singing Mouse elicited better notices
than did his competitor in 1847.

gentleman's flower garden. From there she meandered into the house and settled in the library, where she cast her eye over numerous volumes. Knocking them over, she "slightly passed over some, while others she minutely perused, nay, absolutely bereaved of their leaves, chewing and swallowing them, so great was her avidity."

Not one to place all his bacon in one rasher, Hoare, in 1829, exhibited "His Incredible and Astonishing Learned Goose," which he claimed was five years in training. "What makes it the truly more remarkable is, that his species have ever been deemed the most silly and stupid. . . ." But even with the goose, Mr. Hoare was not first. Another of the species had been exhibited in London more than forty years earlier at the shop of Mr. Beckett, the trunk maker. The goose, by the way, performed his card tricks while blindfolded. Pinkey, a later "Wonderful, Intelligent Goose" appearing at Pantechnicon Arcade, Belgrave Square, performed the "figures-in-the-box" effect made popular by Toby.

Account of a most Wonderful and Laughable

BATTLE

BETWEEN

Jack Bull and a Company of

ITALIAN

Dancing Dogs, Monkeys, Mice, Rats, Dolls, &c.

WE have just been informed of a most extraordinary and wonderful Battle, which took place some few days ago, at a famous sea-port town, between a sturdy fellow, named Jack Bull, and a company of monkeys, dancing dogs, rats, white mice, snakes, dolls, and turtles.

From the Italian shores the above-named miserable crew arrived in a Green Barge, commanded by Gen. Baboon and Capt. Rabbit. Immediately on their landing, they set up a most dismal yell, and proceeded to the house of Mr Bull, who, had ust sat down to a smoaking sirloin, when the noise began. Johnny started up from the table and ran to the door, and, to his unspeakable surprise beheld the odious party, who, tempted by the delicious scent of Jonhny's beef, made no more to do but rashed bodily into his house, seized upon the meat, and were upon the point of shoving it into a large green bag, when gen. Baboon met with a most unwelcome salute from the gallant capt. Bull-Dog, who, in a few seconds, had both his ears off. The piercing shrieks of the gen, struck consternation and terror into the Italian army. Capt. rabbit and lieut. monkey hid themselves in the green bag, but, were presently pulled out by the brave Bull family, who, determining, not to be insulted by such miserable wretches, committed such havoc among them, that they speedily scouted off to their Green Barge, and set sail, half dead with fright and hard blows, leaving the B ll family to finish their sirloin, and to enjoy a good laugh at their enemies' discomfiture.

Catnach, Printer, 2, Monmouth-court.

The surfeit of trained animals at the beginning of the nineteenth century may have prompted this amusing broadside.

While the many sagacious dogs, cats, and birds who flourished during the period are worthy of public attention, they are not unusual enough to warrant extensive description here. Time and space forbid a longer dissertation on the learned goat (one was in Massachusetts performing card tricks and solving arithmetic problems in 1803) and Chevalier St. Louis' "Extraordinary Stud of Rats" (which frolicked with a cat in 1835, predating the classic twentieth-century vaudeville turn "Swain's Cats and Rats.") Of course, one should mention trained fleas, a perennial favorite, and the singing mouse, or rather, the singing mice, as one was exhibited at 209 Regent Street, and another at 29 Newcastle Street in Palmer's Hair Cutting rooms in 1847. Mr. Palmer's attraction had, said the *Family Herald*, an advantage over its competitors, in that it "warbles its notes sufficiently to be heard across a room for several hours in succession and continues to do so until weary from exertion."

Toby the Sapient Pig inspired, as had earlier pigs of knowledge, poets and competitors. Pinchbeck soon appeared in London, at No. 14 Old Bond Street, with a pig who he claimed was "taught by Souchanguyee, the Chinese philosopher, and shown in Spanish America under the sanction of the Inquisition, at five dollars admittance for each person." Pinchbeck, during his tour of Bath and Gloucester, offered a "One Thousand Guineas Reward to any individual who will produce any quadruped whatever, which will perform the feats of this Pillar of Pythagorus, and the wonder of the present age."

In 1833, the redoubtable James Fawkes exhibited a pig of knowledge at Bartholomew Fair, where James Burchall, taking no chances, appeared with a seeming hybrid of Hoare's and Pinchbeck's whom he called "the Unrivalled Chinese Swinish Philosopher, Toby the Real Learned Pig." Burchall's pig, it should be noted, was exhibited "in conjunction with the proprietor's monstrously fat child."

Toby seems to have become a generic name for any learned pig, and the training process which began with Bisset's sixteen months was reduced, in some cases, to one week, according to Lord George Sanger,

A "canine clock" entertained turn-of-the-century audiences.

The heralded clown and his porcine companion.

the British circus impresario, in his *70 Years a Showman* (London, 1908).

Learned pigs, however, were soon uprooted by their less scholarly and more athletic brethren who, usually in troupes, would go through acrobatic routines, climbing ladders, pushing carriages, rolling hoops, and operating seesaws. Pigs, too, became comic tools as sidekicks of such famous clowns as Dan Rice, Tony Grice, and Billy Hayden. The sensational Russian trainers the Duroffs had great success with pigs (and rats and hippopotami—almost any animal one could imagine).

The Kerslakes provided comic pigs for Hagenbeck-Wallace and Ringling Brothers circuses and Keith and Loew's vaudeville circuits. Rhinelander's pigs became outstanding attractions in vaudeville. The highlight of their act was when the pigs would refuse to do a particular trick and the trainer, dressed as a butcher, would take out a large carving knife and begin to sharpen it; the pigs would pause, look at the knife, and instantly perform their stunt.

Bobby Nelson, perhaps the best of the more recent pig trainers, dispelled myths about the porkers to Bill Ballantine in *Wild Tigers and Tame Fleas* (New York, 1958): They are among the cleanest animals; they have good eyesight and fine hearing. Nelson even used their sense of smell to advantage, hiding three or four pieces of bread in a rolled-up carpet—whereupon the pig would open the carpet to gain his reward.

Pigs, in fact, are intelligent and easily trainable. The biggest problem, however, is their size. At six months of age, many pigs weigh three hundred pounds. Methods to retard their growth have been jealously coveted by trainers, but often the animals just get too big to perform their acts. Such was the case with Fred Leslie, whose "Porcine Circus" worked the Lemen Brothers Show around the turn of the century. When his star pigs grew too large to perform their acrobatics gracefully, he purchased a new group of shoats to take their place. The newcomers watched the old troupers and were trained to do the act. When the youngsters were ready to perform, Leslie sold the fattened veterans to a farmer whose land bordered the circus lot. That evening, as the music for the show began, the old-timers recognized their cue and, using their ladder-scaling prowess, climbed over the farmer's fence and made their way into the circus tent in time for their act to begin. The image of them nudging the rookie pigs out of carts, away from seesaws, and off ladders in an attempt to do their old routine is a testament to the finest traditions of show business.

PIG-FACED LADIES

No matter how cunning, prophetic, or intelligent the animal, for the bulk of the populace the word "pig" was simply descriptive or clearly pejorative. Consequently, the birth in 1618 of a baby girl with a pig's face was greeted with all the wonderment but none of the approbation bestowed upon Toby the Sapient Swine.

According to an anonymous seventeenth-century work, *A certaine Relation of the Hog-faced Gentlewoman called Mistris Tannakin Skinker, who was borne at Wirkham, a Neuter Towne betweene the Emperour and the Hollander, scituate on the river Rhyne. Who was bewitched in her mothers wombe in the yeare 1618 and hath lived ever since unknowne in this kind to any, but her Parents and a few other neighbours. And can never recover her true shape, tell she be married, &c. Also relating the cause, as it is since conceived, how her mother came so bewitched* (London, 1640), the child was normal in every respect save "the nose of a Hog or Swine: which was not only a stain and a blemish, but a deformed ugliness, making all the rest loathsome, contemptible, and odious to all that looked upon her infancy."

As a teenager, Tannakin Skinker grew to pleasing proportions, but unlike baby teeth or snakeskins, her face remained the same. Her parents were wealthy landowners in Wirkham, a neutral town between Holland and the German Empire, situated on the Rhine River. They tried to keep their daughter's deformity a secret: her face was kept covered, even before the servants, and she was tutored only by the elder Skinkers.

The cause of such a prodigy was a subject of much discussion. The generally accepted theory is as follows: While pregnant, the wealthy wife was accosted by an old beggar woman seeking alms. When the beggar was rebuffed, she was heard to mutter the Devil's paternoster as she shuffled away, pronouncing ominously, "As the mother is hoggish, so swinish shall be the child shee goeth withall." It was thought that the old woman was a witch and her pernicious murmurings responsible for the monstrous birth. The old beggar lady was brought to trial (and eventually, the stake), but either by "perverse obstinancy" or "deficiency of power" she was unable to reverse her spell.

These proceedings made the plight of the child public, and the parents, to their dismay, had to contend with curiosity seekers as well as their peculiar offspring. Advice was sought from a man called Vandermast, famous as both a mathematician and astrologer and rumored to be well versed in the Black Arts. After consulting with the child a few hours, the occultist pronounced that "whilst she continued in the estate of a Virgin, there was no hope of her recovery." Further, Vandermast suggested, a marriage should be made, not with "Clowne, Bore, or Pesant, but to a gentleman at least."

Consequently the Skinkers decided to outfit their daughter in the most fashionable and expensive clothing of the day and to encourage suitors to call on her, the encouragement in this case being a dowry of £40,000. "This was a baite sufficient to make every Fish to bite at, for no sooner was this publicly divulged, but there came suitors of all sorts. . . ." The proceedings resembled a lottery, "every one hoping to carry away the great prize of forty thousand pound; for it was not the person, but the prize at which they aimed."

Those arriving to stake their claim found that the subject of their intentions was able to respond to "sweet nothings" only by grunting bilingually, the French *"owee, owee,"* or the Dutch *"hough, hough."* To one intrepid fortune hunter even this deficiency translated into an

FAIRBURN (SENIOR'S) PORTRAIT

OF THE

PIG-FACED LADY,

OF

Manchester-Square.

DRAWN FROM THE INFORMATION OF A FEMALE WHO ATTENDED ON HER.

SECOND EDITION, WITH ADDITIONS.

DESCRIPTION.

THIS most extraordinary Female is about Twenty Years of Age, she was born in Ireland, and is of high family and fortune ; on her life and issue by marriage a very large property depends.

Her body and limbs are of the most perfect and beautiful shape, but her head and face resembles that of a *Pig*. She eats her victuals out of a *Silver Trough*, in the same manner as *Pigs* do ; and, when spoken to by any of her relatives or her companion, she can only answer by a *Grunt*.

The female who attends on her and sleeps with her is paid at the rate of One Thousand Pounds per Annum for her attendance ; but, although the salary is so great, her late companion has quitted her situation, having been terribly frightened by her.

The following Advertisement, from a young Female to attend on her and be her companion, appeared in the *Times* of Thursday, February 9, 1815:

" A young gentlewoman having heard of an advertisement for a person to undertake the care of a lady who is heavily afflicted in the face, whose friends have offered a handsome income yearly, and a premium for residing with her seven years, would do all in her power to render her life most comfortable : an undeniable character can be obtained from a respectable circle of friends : an answer to this advertisement is requested, as the advertiser will keep herself disengaged. Address, post paid, to X. Y. at Mr. Ford's, Baker, 12, Judd-street, Brunswick-square."

Also the following Advertisement, from a young gentleman of respectability, declaring his sentiments respecting a final settlement (matrimony) with this most Wonderful Female, and stating his intentions to be sincere, honourable, and firmly resolved, appeared in the Morning Herald, of Thursday, February 16, 1815: " Secrecy.—A single gentleman, aged thirty-one, of a respectable family, and in whom the utmost confidence may be reposed, is desirous of explaining his mind to the friends of a person who has a misfortune in her face, but is prevented for want of an introduction. Being perfectly aware of the principal particulars, and understanding that a final settlement would be preferred to a temporary one, presumes he would be found to answer the full extent of their wishes. His intentions are sincere, honourable, and firmly resolved. References of great respectability can be given. Address to M. D. at Mr. Spencer's, 22, Great Ormond-street, Queen-square."

Another advertisement, from a *Fortune-Hunter*, was sent to the *Times* for insertion, offering to *marry her*, however deformed, but which was refused insertion, (although accompanied with a One Pound Note !!) for reasons best known to the editor of that paper.

This prodigy of nature is the general topic of conversation in the metropolis. In almost every company you join the *pig-faced Lady* is introduced,—and her existence is firmly believed in by thousands, particularly by those who reside at the west end of the town.

Miss Atkinson, by the well-known artist George Morland.

asset, "That if she cannot speake, she cannot chide." Another may be responsible for originating the concept which survives as a bad joke to this day: "Put her head in a blacke bagge, and what difference betwixt her and another woman?" Learning that "she doth feede in a silver trough, or bole; which is always carried with her," a would-be spouse assumed her diet of swill would mean little expenditure on comestibles. From France, Italy, Ireland, Scotland, and England they came, some of lower station spending what little money they had on expensive clothing to pass as gentlemen, and hence to secure their fortune. But no matter what the suitors' elaborate schemes or rationalizations, the moment their intended lifted her veil, each ran away in horror.

To avoid the crowds which she inevitably attracted, she lived out her days in solitude. "And," said the anonymous author, as if anticipating the stories which would follow for hundreds of years, "whosoever shall in Pamphlet, or Ballad write or sing otherwise than is discoursed in this small tract, they erre from truth: for what is here discovered, is according to the best, and most approved intelligence."

In spite of impassioned claims of truth and honesty in journalism, the modern reader might be wise to accept the story in the same way he would a contemporary campaign promise. Accounts of monstrous births and deformities had long been recorded by the time this pamphlet was published: Lion-, goose-, or elephant-faced men, and even a man's head on a pig's body, were pictured in Liceti's well-known work on the subject in 1634. In fact, the baby Skinker would be considered a blessing compared to the offspring of Miss Sarah Smith, who according to an eighteenth-century chapbook gave birth to a strange monster with the body of a fish, no legs but a great pair of claws, talons like a lion's, and six heads. One head was a man's, another a camel's; there was a calf's head, an eagle's, and two dragons'. Early accounts of monstrous births relied heavily on fantasy and superstitions; sensationalists elaborated on simple deformities, using artistic license in representing freaks that may actually have shown some resemblance to animals.

These strange births, when not attributed to witchcraft or God's wrath, were thought to be the result of the mother having been frightened by the specific animal whose shape her baby would then assume during pregnancy. No matter the improbable existence or evolution of such creatures, none captured the public's attention more than the finely figured girl with the pig's face—her story was the basis of legends, broadsides, waxworks, and exhibitions for the next three hundred years.

A ferocious representation of a pig-faced lady appears on a German broadside of 1717. The copy accompanying the portrait characterizes the subject as a woman of high gentry and considerable fortune. She sits in her castle awaiting a husband, who will receive an enormous dowry (in Dutch guilders). Though many suitors arrive, when they see the monstrous girl, they run away.

In the early eighteenth century James Paris du Plessis recorded a drawing of "A Woman with a Hog's Face." She was, he tells us, a woman of noble family and fortune. She was very tall and well proportioned with very fair skin and contrasting dark hair and eyebrows. Her face, which was hairless, resembled that of a sow or cow. When she traveled, her head was covered by a large black velvet mask. Unlike other accounts, that of Paris says she spoke distinctly, although with a disagreeably grunting tone. She lived in London at St. Andrews Parish, Holborn. Significantly, Paris does not claim to have actually seen the woman, although he gives eyewitness accounts of many other anomalies.

A preponderance of pig-faced portraits was published nearly one hundred years later, in 1815. This sudden surfeit of swine-skinned satires came from artists such as George Morland and George Cruikshank. The only attempt known to analyze the sudden rash of interest comes from the unidentified editors (save the initials "P. P." and "G. H.") of the 1869 edition of Wilson and Caulfield's *The Book of Wonderful Characters*. They speculate that the satirical prints were the result of a "magnificently dressed female with a pig's head," sighted in a carriage at various London locations. They also propose a more reasonable theory: "Many persons said that it was someone wearing a theatrical mask, even some of the newspapers mention his name, and we may conclude that it was one of the hoaxes so commonly played off in those days."

Morland was a marvelously eccentric painter of low taste, lush libations, and considerable talent. He had a predilection for pigs. Early in his career, while doing portraits of upper-class patrons, he was often found wallowing with the lower elements at the then-popular pig races. Later in his career this man, called by Hassel "the very extreme of foppish puppeyism," was well known for his paintings of pigs. In 1815 Palmer published a colored print from a drawing by Morland, "The Wonderful Miss Atkinson," a pig-faced lady born in Ireland with a fortune of £20,000 and fed out of a silver trough. The drawing was in the possession of Morland's nephew, but as the artist died in 1804, his inspiration for the caricature is unclear.

An Irish caricature of the pig-faced lady, circa 1815.

The *PIG-FACED LADY, or Manchester-Square. Drawn by an attendant.*

At least eight (not counting different states and editions) other prints picturing the pig-faced lady were rapidly published. John Fairburn's portrait provided this basic story: The subject is about twenty years old and a native of Ireland, although now residing in Manchester Square. Save for her hoggish face she is perfectly formed; she cannot speak but grunts; she eats from a silver trough; she is of high station and considerable fortune. The woman who previously attended her, though paid the enormous sum of £1,000 per year, has left the lady's employ, having been terribly frightened by the woman. "This prodigy of nature," it concluded, "is the general topic of conversation in the metropolis. In almost every company you join, the *pig-faced Lady* is introduced—and her existence is firmly believed by thousands, particularly those who reside in the west end of the town."

Her existence was certainly believed by at least one woman, who on February 9, 1815, advertised in the *Times* for the position of the attendant, noting she "would do all in her power to render her Life most Comfortable."

Even more remarkable was the following item, which appeared in the *Morning Herald* of February 15:

> Secrecy. A single gentleman, aged thirty-one, of a respectable family, and in whom the utmost confidence may be reposed, is desirous of explaining his mind to the friends of a person who has misfortune in her face, but is prevented for want of an introduction. Being perfectly aware of the principal particulars and understanding that a final settlement would be preferable to a temporary one, presumes he would be found to answer the full extent of their wishes. His intentions are sincere, honorable, and firmly resolved. References of great respectability can be given. Address to M. D. at Mr. Spencer's, 22 Great Ormond Street, Queen Square.

Another proposal of marriage was sent to the *Times*, and though it was accompanied by a one-pound note, the editors, for reasons that have not been disclosed, refused to publish it.

These fortune hunters most likely inspired a caricature by George Cruikshank, published by J. Harrison on March 22, 1815, entitled "Suitors to the Pig-Faced Lady." Various tradesmen proffer their attentions to the lady, who rejects them all, saying, "If you think to *gammon* me, you'll find you've got the wrong sow by the ear—I'm *meat* for your masters, so go along, I'll not be plagued by any of you." Cruikshank also did a political satire called "The Pig-Faced Lady of Manchester Square and the Spanish Mule of Madrid."

Another broadside published the same month by William Holland was entitled "Waltzing in Courtship." It pictures a short, deformed

The ambidextrous Irish pig-faced lady.

man (perhaps the often-caricatured Lord Kircudbright) dancing with a pig-faced lady with plunging décolletage and prettily plumed hat.

A very similar drawing (of the lady and her hat and a more modest neckline) entitled "The Pig-Faced Lady of Manchester Square" was published by McCleary. It seems to be taken, in title and copy, from the Fairburn print. The same title graces yet another broadside, this one sold at 98 Cheapside and 50 Piccadilly for one shilling. It pictures the lady slumping from her silver trough with an attendant holding a second serving in readiness. It announces that the lady has occasionally appeared at masquerade balls, where "her movements have drawn to her the attention and unbounded applauses of the first *coteries* of fashion." Remarkably, it continues: "In taste and stile of execution on the pianoforte she is as much a prodigy as in personal appearance, the most difficult pieces of Handel producing to her no apparent labour or difficulty."

The story even made its way to France, where a wonderfully crude portrait, "D'une Dame Irlandaise," was published by the firm of Rabier-Boulard. The text, supposedly provided from a "Journaux Anglais," emended the now-familiar tale with material not found in the other broadsides: a birthday (the girl was born in Ireland on February 6, 1794); a new employee, in addition to the usual attendant (a wet nurse who suckled the pig-faced baby for the extraordinary salary of four thousand French livres); and a new skill (the prodigy was able to write with either hand).

In Ireland especially, the supposed birthplace of the phenomenon, her existence was believed in by many people well past the middle of the nineteenth century. Steevens Hospital in Dublin was thought to be the home of the pig-faced lady, who was sister to the doctor who founded the establishment. Miss Steevens' portrait and silver trough were thought to be kept there long after the girl's death. A similar story claimed that the girl's unfortunate parents, being unable to marry off their daughter in spite of an enormous dowry, founded a hospital with the stipulation that it care for the unfortunate child as long as she lived.

A tale of earlier origin explained that during the Commonwealth, a time of religious unrest and alternative sects, a confused Christian gave up his former beliefs and embraced Judaism. His first child born after the conversion was a pig-faced girl. "Years passed, and the girl grew to womanhood without ever receiving an embrace or a kiss from her wretched father, for how could a Jew touch the head of an unclean beast." Much later, explaining his plight to a Dutch monk, the man was told that the girl was a divine punishment for his embracing the Jewish faith. The man reconverted to Christianity and had his pig-faced daughter baptized. Miraculously, as the girl emerged from the water, her "beastly features were transformed into a divine human face."

The showmen of early nineteenth-century England were no less eager than their print-selling brothers to take advantage of society's piggish preoccupations. Consequently, pig-faced women were soon exhibited throughout the country. In 1828, long after the initial craze had subsided, a pig-faced lady was able to gross £150 at Bartholomew Fair (which, while far less than the take of the leading attraction, Wombwell's menagerie, was in excess of the monies garnered by magicians, jugglers, fat children, fire-eaters, Scotch giants, or the exhibited head of William Corder, who had been hanged for murder).

If the preceding pages are simply a compendium of mass misconceptions—a confusing jumble of mythology, gossip, jest, and hoax—what, you must question, did you see when you paid your shilling and entered the showman's booth? In the early twentieth century you were likely to witness the effigy of a pig-faced lady like Norah Welsh, who was shown in London with Mr. Steward's collection of waxwork freaks.

The nineteenth-century entrepreneurs, however, advertised real flesh and blood. But what flesh and blood! According to Lord George Sanger, who saw what he believed to be the last exhibition of a *live* pig-faced lady at the Great Hyde Park Fair in 1837, the pig was really a fine brown bear. The paws and face were kept closely shaved and the white skin under the fur resembled that of a human being. Over the paws were fitted white gloves, with well-stuffed fingers, so that the pig-faced lady seemed to have nice plump white arms above them.

The bear was now bedizened with a stylish dress, shawl, wig, and a bonnet complete with artificial flowers. She was propped upright and fastened in a large chair in front of which was a draped table. As the showman asked questions, a young boy concealed under the table would prod the bear. The ensuing grunt would be taken for the answer: "You were born in Preston, in Lancashire?" (Prod, grunt.) "You enjoy good health and are very happy?" (Prod, grunt.) "You are inclined, as other ladies, to be led by some gentleman into the holy bonds of matrimony?" Here the boy would give an extra prod, causing the bear to grunt angrily. "What, no! Well, well, don't be cross because I asked you."

The passing of a plate followed the bear's replies, to secure "small comforts and luxuries" for the unfortunate lady. As the crowd left the tent, the exhibitor would run to the front of the booth and shout to potential ticket buyers, "Hear what they say! Hear what they all say about Madame Stevens, the wonderful pig-faced lady."

"This show," said Sanger, "and some others of its class were stopped by the authorities at the following Camberwell Fair, and the pig-faced lady became only a memory; lots of people to their dying day believing such a person really existed."

ATTENUATION AS ART:
Willard,
the Man Who Grows

An advertisement from the National Vaudeville Artists' Annual, 1925.

In the heyday of variety entertainment, on bills with escapologists, cannonball jugglers, quick-change artists, human frogs, and Orville Stamm, "the strongest boy in the world" (who played the violin with a huge bulldog suspended from his bowing arm), Clarence Willard was reviewed as "one of the most distinct and unique vaudeville novelties extant."

A volunteer from the audience stood next to Willard, who, without dislocating his body or using any trick paraphernalia, would begin to grow. The volunteer, who was taller than the performer when he walked onstage, now looked up to Willard, who had extended his height from 5′10″ to 6′4″.

Willard's twelve-minute act consisted of stretching his arms and legs while delivering a pseudo-scientific monologue on his peculiar physiology. This was made even more entertaining by the addition of comic anecdotes. He was fond, for instance, of telling the story of dancing with a Russian countess. Before concluding their schottische, he had grown five inches taller and she had fainted dead away.

"In Madrid in 1912," he said, "I was watching a parade. As King Alfonso approached, I stretched a few inches to get a better look. A woman saw me and screamed. The crowd stared and left me standing all alone."

One could imagine a tailor's consternation as Willard had a suit altered. Imagining Willard's visit to a tailor prompts a brief look at an old show-business tradition. Contortionists or posture-masters have been popular since at least the fourteenth century. In the seventeenth century one of London's most famous eccentrics was Joseph Clark. Though of normal appearance, he was capable of exhibiting almost every kind of deformity and would, according to contemporary accounts, "tease his tailors almost to madness; for when they came to measure him he would have an immoderate rising in one of his shoulders; and when his clothes were tried on, the deformity was moved to the other shoulder." When the tailor apologized and remade the outfit, Clark would return "as straight as any man could be."

Daniel Cureton, a ladies' shoemaker who entertained Londoners with his curious skills in the last half of the eighteenth century, was considerably larger than most posture-masters on record, being 5′6″ tall and weighing more than two hundred and fifty pounds. Cureton's crowning party stunt consisted of his borrowing the coat of the largest man at a gathering and expanding his chest to such a size that the coat could not fit him, but then, moments later, he would reduce himself and comfortably don the jacket of a small boy of fourteen.

Willard, whose technique was unlike that of the old posture-masters, was born in Painesville, Ohio, on July 9, 1882. The left side of his body was paralyzed, and as a small child, he could take only a few steps unaided. He overcame his early illness to become a remarkably robust and healthy man whose youthful appearance often belied his age. As a boy, he claimed to have been with Barnum & Bailey's Circus and an assistant to the great conjurer Alexander Herrmann.

For years he did a magic act—at one point heading a large illusion show—but he soon realized that to capture the limelight he would need to stretch and elongate his talents.

A series of photographs illustrating Willard's technique.

While in England he met Carlton, "the human hairpin," a very popular comedy-magic entertainer of the music halls. Carlton learned to do Willard's act "mainly by stretching the muscles of the knees, hips, chest, and throat and other parts of the body, maintaining them rigidly in that position by what is more or less an exercise of will power." This, Carlton added in his memoirs, *Twenty Years of Spoof and Bluff*, was both painful and exceedingly difficult.

Doctors tested Willard and were amazed to see the vast differences in X rays of his normal and extended bodies. Willard occasionally lectured on "stretching for health" and was known to address police departments on how certain phases of Bertillion measurements (a system for classifying criminal physiognomies) could be altered. He also presided over the Clarence E. Willard Foundation for Autorelaxation. His system, he claimed, would relieve muscle spasm or occupational tension.

After a long and successful career studded with a number of Royal Command performances and a stint at the 1939 World's Fair,

Carlton, the "human hairpin," as he usually appeared on stage.

NORMAL HEIGHT   THREE INCHES TALLER   SIX INCHES TALLER

CARLTON AS A "HUMAN TELESCOPE"

Carlton's "growth" seemed less subtle than Willard's.

Willard retired to Oakland, California, where he managed business properties and was the proprietor of a restaurant in nearby Alameda. He died on July 31, 1962.

Orville Stamm, who never lived in Oakland, ended his act by lying face up on the stage and arching his back into the wrestler's "bridge" position. A small upright piano was placed on his stomach. A pianist stood on Orville's thighs and provided the accompaniment as Orville sang "Ireland Must Be Heaven 'Cause My Mother Came from There."

MORE THAN THE SUM OF THEIR PARTS:
Matthew Buchinger,
Sarah Biffin, and
Other Anomalies
of Nature...

Zeichnet mit der Feder. Spilt mit Wierflen. Allhier schreibt er. Schnäd eine Feder.

Präsentirt an Stuck mit Geld. Spilet auf einem Hack-Brett

Steckt ein Faden in ein Nadel. Ladet ein Gewehr.

Mischet Karten. Barbiert sich selber.

Spilt aus der Taschen. Schiebt Kegell. Schnäd curiose Sachen v. Holtz

In the early eighteenth century Matthew Buchinger (sometimes Buckinger) was one of the best-known performers in the world. He played more than a half dozen musical instruments, some of his own invention, and danced the hornpipe. He amazed audiences with his skills at conjuring. He was a marksman with the pistol and demonstrated trick shots at nine pins. He was a fine penman; he drew portraits, landscapes, and coats of arms, and displayed remarkable calligraphic skills.

Surely he could be considered one of the most versatile of all entertainers. His accomplishments seem even more impressive when we realize he never grew taller than twenty-nine inches.

That he displayed these (and many additional) skills, though lacking feet, thighs, or arms, surely makes him one of the most remarkable men who ever lived.

Buchinger was, according to Caulfield's *Portraits, Memoirs and Characters of Remarkable Persons*, "little more than the trunk of a man saving two fin-like excrescences growing from his shoulder blades, resembling more the fins of a fish than the arms of a man." He could, however, combine his fins to grasp the objects which he so ably manipulated.

That he possessed one fully operative appendage is verified by a prodigious supply of offspring. Buchinger proudly listed, in the short autobiographical sketches that often accompanied his artworks, four wives, who bore respectively one, three, six, and one children. Although Caulfield listed the year of Buchinger's death as 1722, he survived until 1739, and fathered three additional children, bringing the total to fourteen.

Born Matthias (he used the name Matthew in Great Britain) on June 2 or 3, 1674 (original drawings in his own hand give both dates), in Germany at Anspach, near Nuremberg, he was the last of nine children. Proud that as a youngster he was not exhibited as an attraction, Buchinger was allowed instead to enjoy the benefits of an education and the time necessary to practice his unusual skills. When his parents died he began his career as a performer. The first accounts of his shows were recorded in 1709 in Nuremberg, Augsburg, Stuttgart, and Zurich. A calligraphic document requesting permission to obtain a booth at the Nuremberg New Year's Festival was drawn by Buchinger on December 19, 1708.

A contemporary account of "The Wonderful Little Man of Nuremberg" can be found in a fascinating manuscript: *A Short History of Human Prodigies and Monstrous Births, of Dwarfs, Sleepers, Giants, Strong*

Beck's engraving of Buchinger demonstrating his great versatility.
With an original inscription drawn forward, backward, and in mirror writing, 1712.

Men, Hermaphrodites, Numerous Births and Extreme Old Age, Etc. Its author was James Paris du Plessis, a servant of Samuel Pepys.

For many years Paris witnessed, described, and sketched the peculiar characters he encountered. The result was a book of more than three hundred pages, which included fifty-four hand-colored drawings of strong men, giants, dwarfs, fire-eaters, Siamese twins, frog-faced children, and horned women. Particularly fascinating was a two-part, before and after, series of sketches of a hermaphrodite which detailed the showperson's method of exhibition via a trapdoor in its clothing, which lifted to allow viewers scrutiny.

The Paris manuscript was apparently the source of an oft-quoted story about Buchinger:

> He got a great deal of mony but his last wife [Paris lists but two] was a very perverse woman who would spend all his mony very prodigally and luxuriously in eating, drinking, and clothes and would not permit him to eat nor drink as she did and did Beat him Cruelly, which he had born patiently but one day, she having beat him before company, that so provoked him, that he flew at her with such force that he threw her down and getting upon her belly and Brest and did so beat her with his stumps that he almost killed her, threatening to beat her in the same manner if she ever did so any more—and she became after a very dutiful and loving wife.

Paris drew Buchinger in a gaudy raiment with a fashionable wig ("which he combed, oilyd and powdered . . . very well") and a plumed hat of the kind we are accustomed to see on pirate captains.

This unique manuscript was sold by the author, then destitute in old age, to Sir Hans Sloane, doctor, collector, and founder of the British Museum for one guinea.

Also in Sloane's collections at the museum is a handbill for a performance of Buchinger's at "The Corner House of Great Suffolk Street near Charing Cross." There the "Little Man" exhibited his skills at five and seven o'clock for the fees of one shilling for the "fore-seats" and sixpence in the back.

In 1723 Buchinger showed at a room "next door to the Two Blackamoor's Heads in Holburn, near Southampton, exactly at the hours of 10, 12, 2, 4, 6, and 8, which will be punctually observed, that no person may lose any time." This schedule was too exhausting for

The famous engraved self-portrait of Buchinger, published in 1724.

LONDON, April the 29. 1724. This is the Effigies of Mr. Matthew Buchinger, being
Drawn and Written by Himself He is the wonderful Little Man of but 29. Inches high, born without
Hands, Feet, or Thighs, Iune the 2. 1674. in Germany, in the Marquisate of Brandenburgh, near to Nuren-
burgh, He being the last of nine Children, by one Father and Mother. Viz: Eight Sons, and one Daughter The same little Man has been married four times, and has had Issue eleven Children. Viz: one by his first Wife, three
by his second, six by his third, and one by his present Wife.
This little Man performs such Wonders as have never been done by any, but Himself. He plays on various Sorts of Music to Admiration, as the Hautboy, Strange Flute in Consort with the Bagpipe, Dulcimer and Trumpet; and designs to make Machines to play on almost all Sorts of Music. He is no less eminent for Writing, Drawing of Coats of Arms, and
Pictures to the Life, with a Pen: He also plays at Cards and Dice. performs Tricks with Cups and
Balls, Corn and live Birds; and plays at Skittles or Nine-Pins to a great Nicety, with several other
Performances, to the general Satisfaction of all Spectators.

*A detail of the engraving, showing the Psalms and
the Lord's Prayer in the curls of his hair.*

even so remarkable a fellow, who never seems to have exhibited with
such alarming frequency again.

Buchinger pleased the royalty and nobility. An end-of-year ad-
vertisement in the *Daily Post* announced appearances "before three
emperors and most of the Kings and Princesses of Europe (including
Leopold I, Joseph I, and Karl VI)." He was particularly proud to have
obtained the favor of King George I of England on several occasions.
Robert Harley, the Earl of Oxford, was also a patron and a number of
Buchinger's pieces are preserved in the Harleian Collection at the
British Library.

According to *A Biographical Dictionary of Actors, Actresses, Musicians,
Dancers, Managers & Other Stage Personnel in London, 1660–1800*, Edward
Godfrey observed Buchinger finishing a self-portrait six by four inches
in which "instead of shades for the curls of his hair are psalms written
in different characters which at some distance look like shades done
with a hair pencil."

A similar drawing was acquired by Mr. Herbert of Chestnut, who edited *Ames's History of Printing*, and who collected many samples of the Little Man's work. This self-portrait was "exquisitely done in vellum." Herbert's son, a bookseller, had this portrait engraved by Mr. Harding at a cost of fifty guineas.

The copy here illustrated reveals the 121st, 127th, 128th, 130th, 140th, 149th, and 150th psalms—and the Lord's Prayer, each completely and minutely inscribed in the Little Man's wig.

The size as well as the style and execution of Buchinger's work are worthy of approbation. In many examples the text cannot be read even by those of keenest eyesight without scientific aid. One such drawing, now in the author's collection, done in brown ink on vellum at Bath in 1717, is probably the same piece mentioned by Edward

An original Buchinger drawing done in ink on vellum,
reproduced in its actual size.

Wood in *Giants and Dwarfs* (London, 1868): "In Mr. Fillinham's collection was a beautiful specimen of Buchinger's calligraphy . . . being the Lord's Prayer, the Ten Commandments, Creed and other things in very minute writing, within an architectural design."

The survival of such ephemeral sheets over nearly three hundred years is further testimony to Buchinger's prowess. Samples exist in many museums and private collections in England, Scotland, Germany, and the United States.

Examples of minute writing have long been recorded: Cicero claims to have seen the Iliad in a nutshell, and Peter Beales, a celebrated Elizabethan calligrapher, lettered the entire Bible "in a walnut shell no bigger than a hen's egg." These scribes, of course, had the benefit of conventional digits, hands, and arms with which to produce their Lilliputian work.

Although Buchinger for a time supported his family comfortably via his exhibitions and sale of his wide variety of artworks—he produced ornate fans, coats of arms, and perhaps one of the earliest known valentines (as a gift for one of his daughters)—he was later to face financial troubles.

The problems for Buchinger were the same as for many contemporary showmen. In petitioning for money, he explained: "his wonderful arts no longer a novelty—having shewed them through all the kingdom. But your petitioner's expenses and great charges in traveling and keeping servants who must support the entertainment with music and other employments, eats out, washes, and consumes much the greater part of the profit; so that now your petitioner despairs of getting any more."

Perhaps hoping to attract new audiences, Buchinger constantly varied his repertoire. His act consisted of playing musical instruments, "not in the manner of general amateurs, but," said Caulfield, "in the style of a finished master." He performed on a Bavarian folk instrument called the hackebret, the dulcimer, trumpet, bagpipe, guitar, oboe, drum, kettledrum, flute, and strange flute (thought to be the German transverse flute)—which he tried to combine mechanically with the violin as a separate instrument. He shaved himself, threaded a needle, ground corn into flour, and carved figures in wood. Paris witnessed the "Little Man cut paper in severall curious shapes, forms and figures . . . load and discharge a pistol and never did fail of hitting the mark, he darted a sword at a mark at a great distance."

Buchinger was also an expert gamesman and was proficient at shuffleboard and roly-poly. "Nor could the most experienced gamester or juggler obtain the least advantage of any tricks or games with cards or dice." It was at "skittles" or "nine pins," a popular precursor to bowling, that we have the most complete account of his exhibition.

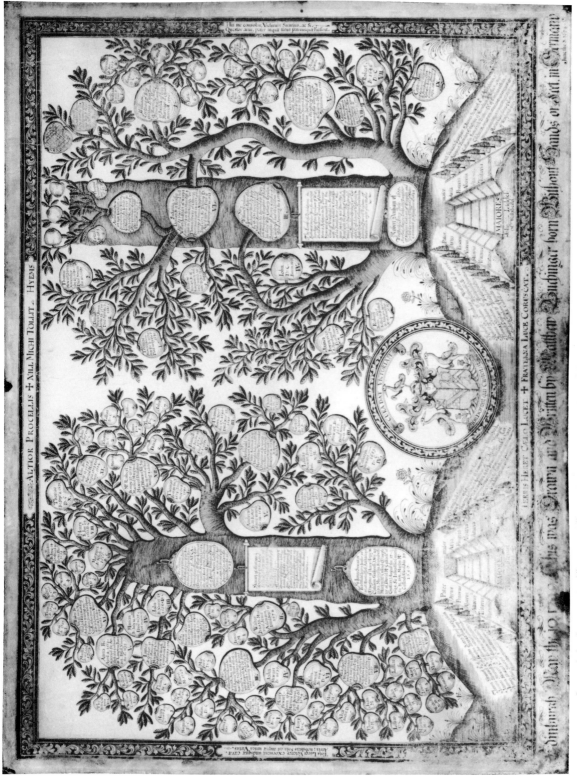

One of the largest (16″ × 12½″) and most spectacular of Buchinger's original drawings. This marriage picture uniting the two family trees was done by him on May 10, 1739, and is the last known sample of his work to be located by the author.

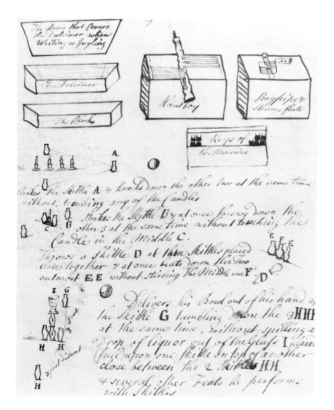

Remarkable series of contemporary drawings of Buchinger at work.

On February 20, 1730, the artist Peter Tillemans sent an account of Buchinger's performance to the Reverend Cox Macro:

Sir,

In obedience to your commands I went last night in Company with my friend Mr. Ram, to see the wonderful little Man, and inclosed I send you a specimen of his performance, and the Pen he wrote with, while we were there.

He plays on a Guitar and hautBoy, both of his own working, as well as invention, sounds the Trumpet and would have danced but for a violent cold. He gave us a touch of Cup & Balls, and Tip'd Nine pins all sorts of ways. He has a Piece of Writing that contains the Decalogue, about 8 inches long & 4 broad, with a Glass & Frame which I think very curious. The purchase is but half a Guinea and I am sure you will be very much pleased with the surprising neatness of it. If you approve of it I will send it down.

Tillemans made sketches during the exhibition. These showed the settings for the Little Man's instruments, the way he held the pen for writing, and diagrams of his trick skittle shots. Long thought lost, these drawings are in the manuscript collections of the British Library. Four skittle shots were sketched and described: hitting specific pins while avoiding others; striking designated pins while passing the ball through a maze of lit candles (two variations); and knocking down pins on which a glass of liquor was balanced, without spilling a drop. Buchinger's own rather modest assessment of these accomplishments was that he "plays skittles or nine pins to a great nicety."

Another important manuscript which gives insight into how Buchinger moved physically, played his strange flute, and sold his calligraphic pieces was affixed to a sample of his handwriting from Dublin, 1720. It was written by Lewis Nicola, a Philadelphia public official and curator of the American Philosophical Society, who moved to the United States from Ireland about 1766.

Of the Dublin specimen, a typical example of Buchinger's forward, backward, and mirror writing, Nicola said:

The above I found among my mothers papers, which, by the date appears to have been wrote about two years before my birth, but when in my thirteenth or fourteenth year, I saw him write a similar piece, which was his constant practice, when company came to see him exhibit his extraordinary performances, at the price of one shilling, & anyone might take the piece on paying another shil[ling].

This extraordinary person was a german, & little more than the trunk of a man, a body with only a Head and upper Arms, having an excrescence at one Elbow bearing some resemblance to a Thumb; the lower part of his Body was cased in strong Leather, & he twisted himself about the Floor with considerable agility, raising one side a little & turning on the other as on a Pivot. His performances, besides writing, holding the Pen between his stump arms, were drawing, also with a Pen. One of his pieces was a Head of king Charles, with a bushy wig, in the curls of which was wrote a part of the Bible, if I recollect right the Book of Psalms, not legible by the naked Eye, but distinct with the aid of a glass, & the letters made formed—a Picture of a Tree with circles pending from the Branches, in some of which were the names & dates of his Children, the number I do not recollect; under the Root were ovals for the names of his wives, three filled— He played on a common Flute, fixed in a Box with stops to cover the holes & Keys outside, which he struck with his stumps, while he blew with his mouth.— He coged the Dice from a

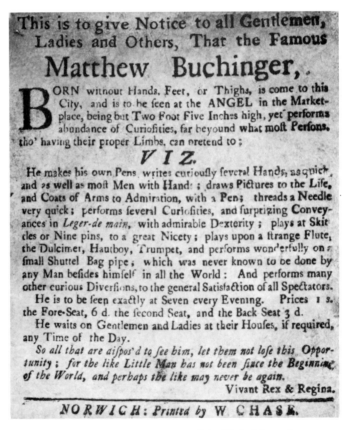

Playbill advertising the appearance of the Little Man, circa 1733.

*One of the earliest known engravings of Buchinger with a gun, signed
with his customary flourishes, Stuttgart, 1709.*

common Box,—set a Card—played at Scittles, picking out
any particular pin with a Bowl, at about ten feet distance;
or, if so situated that it could not be hit singly, he would
strike others so as to through that one down.

Perhaps even more impressive were his attainments as a conjurer.
In all his skills, practice and dedication were important. In magic he
was required not only to learn the techniques of sleight of hand, but
to master the physical and psychological principles of deception. His
handicap would seem to make this impossible. For example, the skill
necessary to make small cork balls appear, vanish, and multiply under
various cups is considerable. As Buchinger needed both of his small
appendages to move each cup, he could hardly misdirect the attention
of the audience to one cup while surreptitiously introducing a ball
under another. Consequently he was forced to invent techniques which
would accomplish his goals. *The Whole Art of Legerdemain . . . To which
are added, Several Tricks of Cups and Balls, &c., As performed by the little
Man without Hands or Feet . . .*, a rare pamphlet most likely first published
in the 1730's, described Buchinger's method: an ingenious mechanical
device which enabled him to produce or vanish balls without the use
of digital manipulation. Additionally, by switching the three cups used
in the routine for three others kept in his bag, Buchinger managed to

produce a startling finale: the appearance of ears of corn, a large orange, and even a live bird from the supposedly empty cups.

Buchinger's impact on the conjuring world was so considerable that even years after his death his methods were still explained in conjuring books. Buchinger's skill at cups and balls is mentioned in the long satirical "Elegy on the much lamented death of Matthew Buckinger," published in the *Drapier Miscellany* (Dublin, 1733). Although some of the *Miscellany* was written by Jonathan Swift, the Buchinger piece is not attributed to him.

Ironically, Buchinger survives even today in one of the strangest terms ever recorded in a slang dictionary. In Richard Spear's *Slang and Euphemism* (New York, 1981) appears the entry: "Buckinger's Boot: The female genitals. From a tale about a man named 'Matthew Buckinger.' [British 1700's–1800's]." The first appearance of this peculiar phrase seems to be the second edition of Frederick Grose's *Classical Dictionary of the Vulgar Tongue* (London, 1788), which reads:

> Buckinger's Boot: The monosyllable. Mathew Buckinger was born without hands and legs; notwithstanding which he drew coats of arms very neatly, and could write the Lords Prayer within the compass of a shilling: he was married to a tall handsome woman, and traversed the countryside, shewing himself for money.

"Monosyllable" he elsewhere defines, rather politely and delicately, as "a woman's commodity."

In researching this book, there were many surprising discoveries, revelations, and unearthings. Perhaps none was as satisfying as solving the riddle of the origin of "Buckinger's Boot," a riddle which has puzzled the foremost linguists and etymologists.

How did Matthew Buchinger become forever linked with that certain part of the female anatomy? As he had no arms and legs, the only appendage on which he could put a boot was his . . . appendage.

Not willing to leave this marvelous "Little Man" on such a concupiscent note, I feel duty-bound to say farewell by reproducing a wonderful broadside from 1726 (p. 57).

There are several accounts of performances attributed to, but not in fact by, Buchinger. He was the most famous, but only one of *many* accomplished performers who exhibited without the use of legs or arms. Three "High German Artists" are often confused with our Little Man. One was a woman who exhibited with no arms or legs, another a magician who performed at Bartholomew Fair. The most interesting of the three performed at the Talbot Inn, near the Maypole in the Strand. He was capable of writing with his mouth or either foot. He groomed and dressed himself but, according to a contemporary cutting,

A
POEM

ON

MATHEW  BUCKINGER,

The greateſt GERMAN living.

SEE Gallants, wonder and behold
This German, of imperfect Mold,
No Feet, no Leggs, no Thighs, no Hands,
Yet all that Art can do commands.
Firſt Thing he does, he makes a Pen,
Is that a Wonder! Well what then ?
Why then he writes, and ſtrikes a Letter,
No *Elziverian* Type is better.
Fix'd in his Stumps, directs the Quill
With wondrous Gravity and Skill ;
Upward, downward, backward, forward,
Eaſtward, Weſtward, Southward, Northward.
In Short to every Compaſs point,
Tho' ſhortned at the Elbow Joint.
The Foliage round it he diſplays
Does more our Admoration raiſe,
For Hair Stroaks to the Eye they paſs,
And yet they're Letters thro' a Glaſs.
Thus he with double Art can write,
At once to pleaſe and cheat the Sight.
When with his Wife at Cards he plays,
The Trumps already play'd conveys
Into his Stumps ; the Standers by
Confeſs them quicker then their Eye :
His Wife exclaims, but all in vain,
He plays them o'er and o'er again,
Nay what is more when all is done
They own the Game is fairly won.
He throws the Dice as careleſs down
As any Gameſter in the Town.
And tho' the Number caſt be three
Two Sixes you ſhall ever ſee :
Thus raffling with his Wife he wins,
And every pleas'd Spectator grins ;
All croſs Legg'd whilſt he is at play,
A Compliment he can't repay.
His Dulcimer he next attacks
With nimble and melodious Thwacks ;
The Strings, like Birds with warbling Throats,
Send forth ten Thouſand blended Notes,
Though great the Numbers, all agree

In well concerted Harmony:
No Sound can pleaſe the Ear ſo much,
No Hand can have ſo ſweet a Touch ;
And yet you'd think 'twou'd more beceme
His Stumps to thump a Kettle Drum.
The Tricks he plays at Cups and Balls,
'Tis wrong in any Man, who calls
Them Slight ot Hand, as he gives out,
Their Slight of Stumps, and are no Doubt.
The Nine-Pins quite ſurpaſs my Muſe,
In vain his Art ſhe there purſues,
The wond'rous Wiſdom of his Bow,
For ſurely it muſt have a Soul,
When one Direction makes it go
To this, to that, and too and fro,
Trips up theſe Pins, and lets thoſe ſtand,
Obſerving *BUCKINGERS* Command.
Thus *Homer* made his Jav'lins fly,
And choſe the Men that were to die.
Great Sir, ot three Foot high to raiſe
To thee a Monement of Praiſe,
Requires a lofty *German* Strain,
A noble and exalted Vein.
No, ſhe's not worthy, my poor Muſe,
I cannot ſay to wipe your Shooes ;
But had you Shooes to wipe, I Swear
It ſhou'd be thine great *BUCKINGER*.
Great Trunk of Man be not aſham'd,
That Nature has thy Body maim'd,
In thee juſt Emblem, ſhe wou'd try
The mighty Force of Induſtry ;
What Gifts are to thy Mind deny'd,
By Art and Care may be ſupply'd.
Obſerve the Moon, the Stars, the Sun,
How conſtant thro' their Work they run ;
Among them all we cannot ſpy
A Hand, or Foot, a Leg, or Thigh.
The Oak could not the Thropy bear
Till that the Branches cropped were,
Nor wou'd thy Fame have been ſo great,
Had Nature form'd thee quite compleat.

Printed in the Year 1726.

A seventeenth-century engraving of Thomas Schweicker.

considered "Jumping and Vaulting his masterpieces, and what he does, no Body can do the like, he also has several Inventions with glasses, it is impossible to express it all."

Johannes Grigg was probably born in Hungary in 1690 with no legs or thighs, only peculiar rounded stumps. Although his right hand was normal, his left hand, with the wrist twisted permanently into a crablike configuration, had just two fingers and a thumb. In spite of this severe deformity, Grigg enjoyed popularity as a multi-talented entertainer: equilibrist, musician, and magician. His performances, no doubt, were aided by his ability to speak eight languages.

In the war-ridden, superstitious Hungary of the seventeenth century, his unusual physical form was attributed to his mother's witnessing mutilated corpses on the battlefield near the military camp at Papa, where the child was born.

Unlike Buchinger, Grigg was forced to perform at an early age to support his mother. One story claims he was actually sold outright to an itinerant showman who traveled with a fair circuit throughout Europe, carrying Grigg in a box "2 elbows" high. An early English notice gives a general description of his act:

> This young Man was Born in Hungary, and is about 18 years
> of Age, a Foot and a Half High: In the places where the
> Thighs, or Legs should be; hath Two Breasts in all points
> like a Woman's on which He Walks. The Natural parts are

of the Male kind; Climes, or gets from the Ground upon a
Table, and sits on a Corner of it, but 3 Quarters of an Inch
broad, and shews more Artful Tricks, to the General Diver-
sion, Satisfaction, and Admiration of all Spectators, and
speaks several Languages. Vivat Regina.

Grigg's career as a performer was a long and often difficult one
and he never attained the fame of his contemporary Buchinger. Grigg
was taken advantage of by unscrupulous promoters and exploited by
his own family. In some cities it was recommended that he not perform
lest pregnant women view his show and produce similar progeny of
their own. In spite of his setbacks, he was considered intelligent, moral,
and apparently not bitter about his misfortunes. Contemporary medical
accounts, particularly concerned with his deformities and subsequent
behavior, found his demeanor all the more remarkable because of
his association with unsavory characters. Through examination, doctors determined that Grigg was capable of consummating a marriage
but, unlike Buchinger, he expressed no interest in the matrimonial
state.

Grigg used his hands *as* feet and was capable of revolving around
on them at great speed, apparently sometimes thus frightening his

Engraving of Johanna Sophia Liebschern.

This is the shape of that which is instead
of a hand to mee and the manner of
holding the Pen to Write, it is only one
Thumb and one Finger which issues out
but one span from my Shoulder on the
right side and on the left there's no impress
of any yet by own industry I have invented a
Glove and with the help of that Glove, I hold the
Pen to Write and the Pen-Knife to make Pens
Which I doe for a Livelihood.

*A facsimile of the writing of John Cox, showing
the odd configuration of his appendage.*

audience. He could balance on either his head or hands and perform
various acrobatic stunts.

A famous print of Grigg shows him in two poses: the foreground
features the strange breast-like configuration of his thighs, while in the
background he sits behind a conjurer's table holding a magic wand,
with familiar props in front of him: the ball vase, cups and balls, and
even a live bird, which he probably produced from under one of the
cups. In the caption to one version of this print, Grigg explains that
what had been deprived him by birth was repaid to him by other
presents, principally speed of hand, which, according to Grigg, is the
very "soul of a conjurer."

As early as the sixteenth century there are detailed accounts and
illustrative material on many fascinating handicapped characters. A
German woman in Frankfurt am Main in 1556, and Thomas Schweicker,
born in 1580, showed the ability to clean and feed themselves, and
exhibited considerable writing skills with their feet. Schweicker (sometimes Schweickart), the darling of the scientific and artistic crowd,
became the subject of many epigrams and portrait paintings and a
commemorative medallion.

Pietro Stadelman, an armless seventeenth-century Italian, played
the dulcimer with picks attached to his feet. Somewhat later, Johanna
Sophia Liebschern won fame writing, spinning cloth, and firing pistols
using only her pedal extremities.

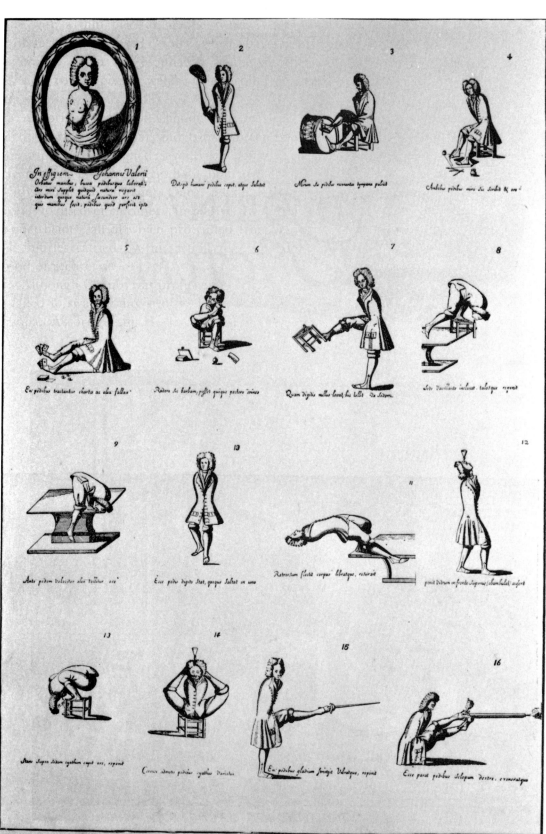

1. Portrait of John Valerié, born without arms. 2. Putting on his hat. 3. Playing a drum. 4. Writing. 5. Playing cards. 6. Shaving. 7. Lifting articles with his toes. 8. Balancing on a stool and taking up a dice with his teeth. 9. Taking up a dice from between his toes. 10. Dancing on one toe. 11. Bending backwards and rising again. 12. Walking with wine-glass on his forehead. 13. Lifting wine-glass with his teeth while on a stool. 14. Placing wine-glass on his head. 15. Fencing. 16. Loading and firing a gun.

Wynistorff tips his hat with his feet and additionally pleases viewers in 1745.

John Cox was born in Hereford, England, in 1684, without arms or hands save for a short stump with one thumb and finger growing from his right shoulder. He eventually taught himself to write and earned a livelihood drawing and cutting pens.

Johannes Valerius was well known for a variety of accomplishments at the beginning of the eighteenth century. Without arms he exhibited the usual wide range of skills—grooming, playing at dice, etc.—and was illustrated and described in Caulfield's *Remarkable Persons*.

Johannes Wynistorff, an armless prodigy, exhibited many of the stunts of Valerius and was the subject of a fine engraving by Thomas Back, circa 1745. Thomas Inglefeld had neither legs nor arms and produced fine drawings and calligraphy by guiding his pen with the muscles of his cheek and arms. Inglefeld's deformity was attributed to a "fright" suffered by his mother during pregnancy.

Miss Biffin, lithographic portrait, 1823.

Perhaps the most well-known nineteenth-century fairground performer was Sarah Biffin (sometimes Beffen). Born without hands, feet, or legs, Miss Biffin supported herself by her artistic talent. She painted landscapes, portraits, and miniatures, some done on fine china.

Her success was largely instigated by the Earl of Morton, who sat for his likeness with her. At the end of each session, he took the canvas away with him to ensure against chicanery. He wanted to be satisfied that the work was done only by Miss Biffin (who placed the brush in her mouth and supported it with her shoulder), and not by another person. Convinced of her remarkable talents, he hired Mr. Craig, a

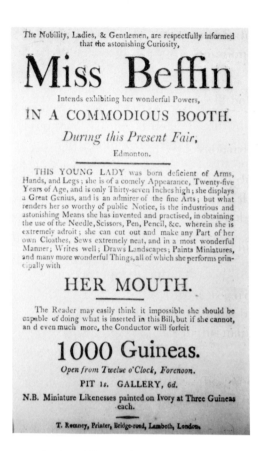

The Nobility, Ladies, & Gentlemen, are respectfully informed
that the astonishing Curiosity,

Miss Beffin

Intends exhibiting her wonderful Powers,

IN A COMMODIOUS BOOTH.

During this Present Fair,

Edmonton.

THIS YOUNG LADY was born deficient of Arms, Hands, and Legs; she is of a comely Appearance, Twenty-five Years of Age, and is only Thirty-seven Inches high; she displays a Great Genius, and is an admirer of the fine Arts; but what renders her so worthy of public Notice, is the industrious and astonishing Means she has invented and practised, in obtaining the use of the Needle, Scissors, Pen, Pencil, &c. wherein she is extremely adroit; she can cut out and make any Part of her own Cloathes, Sews extremely neat, and in a most wonderful Manner; Writes well; Draws Landscapes; Paints Miniatures, and many more wonderful Things, all of which she performs principally with

HER MOUTH.

The Reader may easily think it impossible she should be capable of doing what is inserted in this Bill, but if she cannot, and even much more, the Conductor will forfeit

1000 Guineas.

Open from Twelve o'Clock, Forenoon.

PIT 1s.   GALLERY, 6d.

N.B. Miniature Likenesses painted on Ivory at Three Guineas each.

T. Remney, Printer, Bridge-road, Lambeth, London.

Skeptics prompted Miss Biffin to offer a reward. It was never claimed.

master of miniature painting, to give her additional instruction. He also provided an impressive client list. Kings George III and IV, William IV, the Queen Dowager, the Duke of York, the King of Hanover, the Duke of Sussex, and the Princess Augusta all patronized her.

When George IV saw one of Miss Biffin's paintings and was informed that the artist had neither hands nor arms, he said to Sir William Knighton, "Well, Sir William, we cannot reward this lady for her *handy-work*, I will not give her *alms*, but I request she be paid for her industry." He rewarded Miss Biffin with a draft of twenty-five guineas.

In 1821 Miss Biffin received, from the Society of Arts and Commerce Promoted, a medal and endorsement signed by the Duke of Sussex. In 1822 she was appointed miniature painter to his Royal Highness, the Prince of Orange.

At Kilton in Somersetshire on September 6, 1824, Miss Biffin married Stephen Wright, "a gentleman who had been long attached to her." During the ceremony, the Reverend Mr. Hole suggested the ring might be held against the bride's shoulder. Afterwards, it was placed

The Greatest Wonder in the World.
During the Fair.

PATRONISED  BY THE

Royal Family.

THE CELEBRATED

Miss BEFFIN

Miniature Painter.

WHO WAS BORN

Wtihout Hands & Arms,

IS NOW EXHIBITING

DURING THE FAIR.

Whose Wonderful Improvement since she last had the honor of appearing here, must be seen to convey an adequate idea of her astonishing Powers, and this being the last opportunity the Public will have, being her farewell Visit to the Fair.

Miss BEFFIN Writes well, Works at her Needle, Cuts out and makes all her own Dresses, uses the Scissars with perfect ease, Draws Landscapes, Flowers, Feathers, &c. all of which she does principally with her Mouth, and in the Presence of the Company.

EACH VISITOR
Will be Entitled to a Specimen of her Writing.

And in addition to Miss B's. other Accomplishments, she has lately acquired a perfect knowledge of that much admired and elegant Art, China Painting.

Correct Miniature Likenesses taken on Ivory,
From 3 to 10 Guineas Each.

Admission, Ladies & Gentlemen 1s.   Children & Servants 6d.

T. ROMNEY, PRINTER, Bridge-road, Lambeth.

*An enormous playbill (29½" x 19½") printed in red and black advertised
her appearance "Wtihout Hands" at Bartholomew Fair in 1811.*

on a gold chain which she wore around her neck, placed in her bosom.

Mr. Wright first captured Miss Biffin's favor by the composition of the following lines:

> *Sweet Biffin*, though admired your charms,
> Your lover sighs not for your *arms*,
> He took a nobler part;
> And while your happiness he plann'd,
> Aware you could not *give your hand*,
> Aspired but to your heart.

Through the encouragement of her husband and the Earl of Morton, the new Mrs. Wright began to live a private rather than a public life. After both men died, she came out of a fourteen-year retirement and once again exhibited her skills.

In a letter of September 1, 1841, Mrs. Wright requested information for a proposed visit to America, but "as the voyage would entail considerable expense upon me I am most anxious to obtain the opinion of someone who has visited those shores." She promised to exchange some of her drawings for the proffered advice. There is no record of her having made the journey.

Mrs. Wright spent her last years in Liverpool in reduced circumstances. A compassionate testimonial advertisement for her appeared

MISS BIFFIN.

*An unusual look at three states (proof with pencil corrections, proof without letters, and final copy)
of a lithograph by R. J. Stothard, taken from the original gouache self-portrait done by Miss Biffin
(see color plate 2). It is interesting that the states are progressively less flattering but
more realistic. One imagines Miss Biffin requesting a more honest interpretation.*

on February 13, 1843: "On the verge of sixty, her sight, consequent
upon close application and necessary proximity of the eye to her work,
is failing, and this gone, all that remains for Miss Biffin and the needful
attendant on her wants is an annuity of £12 from his late Majesty. To
anticipate the distressing results consequent upon such a meritorious
female, left without limbs, without friends, without money will perhaps
be sufficient to enlist the benevolent in her cause. To those who have
at any time whiled away their half hour in her studio, listened to her
anecdotes, joined in her cheerful laughs, or been impressed with
admiration at her persevering talents, this appeal is especially made,
that by their contributions an annuity may be purchased for the support
of her few remaining years." Due largely to the efforts of Richard
Rathbone, a small annuity was purchased for her.

Sarah Biffin Wright died in Liverpool in October 1850.

Madame Hanakawa, an extremely talented Japanese woman without
arms, was able to shoot a bow and arrow, and do origami paper folding

Friedlander lithograph of Unthan the marksman.

with her toes. Her calligraphic skills were used to paint the sign for her own exhibition, as featured on the woodcut illustration in the color photo section.

Jean de Henau, from the south of France, did rapid paintings with his toes in a heralded stage act. He also gave mandolin concerts with his wife and sister. He is most likely the same artist described by the Great Roland in Houdini's *Conjurer's Magazine* in 1907. Roland saw him do the popular and difficult illusion the multiplying billiard balls, using only his toes!

According to Signor Saltarino's *Fahrend Volk* (Leipzig, 1895), Henau was the only legitimate stage rival of Carl Herman Unthan, one of the most famous handicapped performers of the late nineteenth and early twentieth centuries. Unthan was born without arms on April 5, 1848, at Sommerfeld, East Prussia. Encouraged by understanding parents, the youngster learned to take care of himself and grow independent. He could wash, dress, sharpen pencils, and manipulate a knife and fork with his feet. At the age of twelve he tied a violin to a stool, picked up the bow with his feet, and attempted to play. Later he would dazzle the vaudeville world as "Unthan, the Pedal Paganini." He had a long and successful career playing in concerts, music halls, and the circus. Franz Liszt saw him play, and he once performed on Paganini's own Stradivarius.

Unthan's autobiography, *The Armless Fiddler: A Pedescript*, first published in Germany in 1925 and then translated into English and published after his death in 1935, abounds with tales of cruelty and joy. He did not escape the machinations of unscrupulous managers and agents, who attend to all branches of show business. The book was a sometimes maudlin, but sensitive and passionate account of his life.

In 1893 he wrote a letter to Koster and Bial, who had just hired him to perform in the United States, which exhibits both his charm and sense of humor. Complimenting the men on their "enterprising pluck" in hiring him where so many other American managers had been afraid to do so, he thought, "for fear of feet, so that I had come to the conclusion those useful lower members must have been rather neglected by the U.S. Public, to cause such animosity. Well, I shall

Unthan in London, a versatile performance.

Johnny Eck's unique one-hand balance.

come and see myself, and I trust I'll do like Caesar; vene, vidi, vici. I wish and hope that the New York Public will reward your courage and flock in by thousands to see my act; you fully deserve it."

Unthan appeared in the United States on a number of occasions. "The longer I travelled," he said, "the more America appeared to me as a battlefield on which all men were struggling desperately to get ahead."

Unthan was skilled on the typewriter, and fired the rifle, according to Saltarino, with enough skill and accuracy to be compared with the great trick shot artists Ira Paine and Doc Carver. He also appeared in comic skits in which he played the elegant host, serving food and wine and tending to his guests. He was happily married to a Czechoslovakian woman, and, after a long and fruitful life, he died in 1929.

For hundreds of years anomalies of nature have evoked paradoxical feelings of fear and fascination. Writers, scientists, and medical men have explored the psychologies and physiologies of these prodigies; they and the public alike are intrigued by the relationship between the horrific and miraculous. That relationship is explored in the following story, perhaps the most bizarre tale in the annals of conjuring:

During the performance of a stage illusion show, a magician requested the help of a volunteer from the audience. An unassuming fellow stood up and climbed onstage. The man was placed in a wooden box and the familiar sawing-in-half illusion commenced. The box was severed and each half separated to the delight of the audience. The halves were then pushed together and the volunteer restored. The volunteer walked back to his seat amidst resounding applause. Suddenly, in full view of the audience, he toppled over and split apart at the waist. His legs walked off to the left, and his torso crawled to the right. Gasps and screams were heard in the audience. Many people fainted. Others fled the theater. The disturbance it created was so disruptive, they dared not repeat the effect for another season.

The illusion was based on a devious switch of the original volunteer for two men. One was well known, Johnny Eck, who without thighs or legs was a star of the Tod Browning film *Freaks*. The other was a midget who was covered from the top of his head to the tips of his toes in a pair of trousers. Eck mounted the shoulders of his midget friend and "fell off" at the appropriate moment. But the crowning touch, the element that gave the proceedings such credibility, was that the "volunteer" from the audience was Johnny Eck's full-size, perfectly normal, twin brother!

BLIND TOM

Lithograph by the Ledger Job Company of Philadelphia.

In 1853, four-year-old Tom Bethune was brought to a music store in Columbus, Georgia. There the youngster heard a local professor of music play an original but unpublished composition. The child immediately sat down at the piano and exactly duplicated the piece. On April 6, 1866, Tom was reminded of the story. He remembered the incident. He sat down and perfectly reproduced the composition he had not heard once in the intervening thirteen years.

Tom was born totally blind (he later gained partial eyesight) and, save his remarkable musical ability, was probably an imbecile. He spoke only in disjointed monosyllables. While there have been numerous instances of musical prodigies, Tom was one of the most memorable of a very unusual group of people who possess a single astonishing skill but who are unable to perform the simplest functions outside their specialty. They are often called "idiot savants."

Tom was born to slave parents on May 25, 1849, and as a baby was brought with his mother to the plantation of his owner, General Bethune in Muscogee County, Georgia. As a child he would inflict pain on his brothers and sisters, not, as first thought, with sadistic intent, but because cries and screams provided him unbounded pleasure. By the age of two he was able to sing songs that he had learned from the general's daughters; his pitch was perfect, and he was able to improvise accompanying harmony. When the family purchased a piano shortly before Tom's fourth birthday, his talent was clearly manifested.

He immediately used both hands on the keyboard to duplicate the songs he had heard. He was promoted locally and declared a prodigy. At a young age he began a professional career. In Louisiana he met Robert Heller, considered by some critics the greatest magician of the nineteenth century. A splendid humorist and accomplished piano player and composer, Heller was in a strong position to guide the boy's career. He worked with Tom on his presentation and helped expand his repertoire. Years later, Harry Houdini, too, wrote about Tom, implying that people could confuse his remarkable musical memory with psychic ability.

By the age of ten, he elicited reviews like the following from the Baltimore *Sun*:

> We enjoyed an opportunity last night to hear the performances of the blind negro boy "Tom," at Carol Hall, and though prepared for something uncommon, all expectation was surpassed by the reality. Nay, more, all preconceived ideas of music as a science, an art or an acquisition were thoroughly baffled, and a new question thrust upon us as to what music really is in the economy of nature. Accustomed to regard it as a gift, improved and perfected by cultivation and practice, we here find it perfectly developed

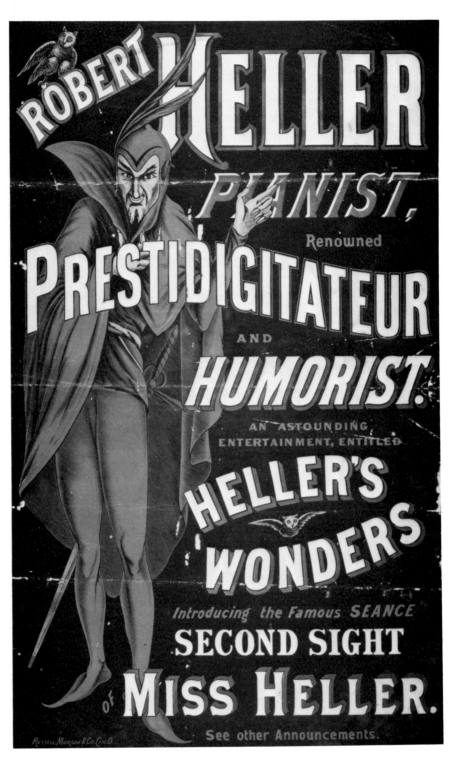

*Robert Heller's talents as a musician and magician
helped him guide the career of Blind Tom.*

*Heller's versatility further expanded by the manipulations
of Punch and Judy figures.*

in a blind negro boy, and constituting a part of his nature,
as much so as the color of his skin.

We have our reminiscences of Thalberg and other great
masters but with these some idea of development, growth
and all the advantages of education, sight, society, experience
and years of professional exercise—Yet here is a being in
the lowliest scale of humanity, destitute of all adventitious
aid, scarcely sensible of his own wonderful nature, a master,
a very phenomenon in the musical world—thrusting all our
conceptions of science to the wall and informing us that there
is a "musical world" of which we know nothing. That there
is in nature a spontaneous musical condition which invites
the subtliest investigation of Philosophy. Our citizens may
enjoy and puzzle themselves with this problem at Carol Hall,
but we question if anyone can give us a solution of it.

Blind Tom became one of the leading attractions of his day. With
the exception of a brief engagement at Hope Chapel in New York in
January of 1861, Tom appeared only in the South until after the Civil

War. In October of 1865, he received great notices in Philadelphia and New York and went on to perform in the principal capitals of Europe. His programs carried endorsements from leading musicians like Moscheles (the teacher of Thalberg and Mendelssohn), who was particularly amazed by Tom's ability to identify every individual note of many keys played at random in flagrant discord. Moscheles also worked with Tom to improve his technique.

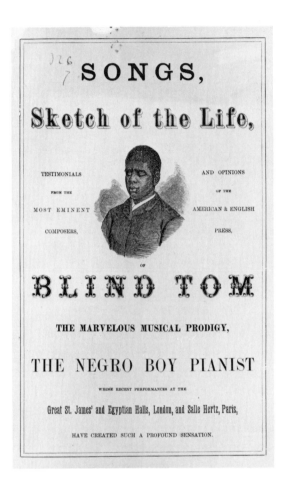

Tom was a splendid mimic and his shows included recitations (none of which he could understand) in German, French, Greek, and Latin; he also did vocal imitations of the bagpipe, hurdy-gurdy, and fiddle. In Washington, D.C., he visited Congress and thereafter performed the speeches of the politicians with such accurate vocal inflections as to amuse and delight his audiences.

Perhaps more remarkable yet was his ability to compose original music, which he did throughout his career. The inspiration for his novel work was often the wind, the trees, or the rain, which he thought "spoke to him," and he responded with improvisations on the piano.

In one piece, "Sewing Song" (New York, 1888), he imitated the sound made by a sewing machine on his piano. Another famous piece of Tom's was his rendition of the Civil War "Battle of Manassas." It was published (Cleveland, 1866) with the following explanation:

> The director of Blind Tom's concerts was at first accustomed himself to announce the pieces to be played; connecting with them such incidents or facts with regard to this wonderful being as would be of interest. Noticing however that Tom often repeated to himself what had been said, after they returned to their apartments from the performances, it occurred to him that it would be interesting to the audience to have Tom announce himself, which is now done; and he speaks of "This boy Tom" "This singular being" &c; with as much gravity and earnestness as if he were speaking of another person. The following are the exact words with which Tom announces his Battle of Manassas. (Remember that it was the director who was laid up by the accident.)

> Tom will now play for you his Battle of Manassas. This is a piece of his own conception of a battle.

> The circumstances under which he produced it were these: Soon after the battle occurred, I happened to a very serious accident which kept me in Nashville for several months, Tom was often in my room. Every little paragraph about the battle was discussed in various forms for a week or more. He heard this thing read of and talked of, and after hearing it for ten days he took his seat at the Piano and produced what he will now play for you; and when asked what that was, he was playing, his reply was, that it was his battle of Manassas.

> In the first place he will represent the Southern Army leaving home to their favorite tune of "The Girl I left behind me" which you will hear in the distance, growing louder and louder as they approach Manassas, (the imitation of the drum and fife). He will represent the Grand Union Army leaving Washington city to the tune of Dixie. You will all recollect that their papers, and our papers, and their prisoners, spoke of the fact that when the Grand Union Army left Washington, not only their bands were playing Dixie, but their men were also singing it.

> He will represent the eve of battle by a very soft sweet melody, then the clatter of arms and accoutrements, the war trumpet of Beauregard, which you will hear distinctly; and then Mc Dowell's in the distance, like an echo of the first. He will represent the firing of cannon to Yankee Doodle, Marseillaise Hymn, Star Spangled Banner, Dixie, and the arrival of the train of cars containing Gen.

Kirby Smith's reinforcements; which you will all recollect was very valuable to Gen. Beauregard upon that occasion after the arrival of which, the fighting will grow more severe, and then the retreat.

Although Tom received great acclaim as a performer, he was exploited by his owners. Even though he was granted freedom, as were all blacks by the Emancipation Proclamation of 1863, General Bethune and his son John retained, by various "legal" means, virtual ownership of Tom until 1887. Historian Arthur LaBrew has speculated that Tom's idiocy was less severe than imagined and that his blindness might have been cured surgically. However, Tom was purposely not helped in order to increase both his dependency on the Bethunes and his earning power. In addition, Tom never owned the copyrights to his own compositions until after the 1887 court battle in which Elsie Bethune, acting on behalf of Tom's mother, Charity, became the guardian of the pianist. Remarkably, Tom may have been undaunted by the controversy which surrounded him. Even after Tom's death, legal battles over the disposition of his earnings continued.

An interesting contemporary account of his later career is provided by Amalie Tutein. The story of her meeting Tom dispelled the generally accepted belief that he was able to play *any* piece perfectly after hearing it only once. Urged to the stage at Tom's Philadelphia concert, Mme. Tutein responded by playing Beethoven's very difficult Concerto No. 3, which the boy was unable to reproduce accurately. She was consequently engaged by the family to expand Tom's skills. "The proposition," she said, "was extremely distasteful to me, as Tom was very repulsive in many ways. He was a great gormandizer and ate prodigiously and was by then enormously fat." He hated to bathe and as he was very strong and largely uncontrollable by others, he rarely did. "When not engaged in playing or listening or eating, his favorite pastime was drawing circles with his hands on the floor while standing on one foot. Time and time again he would draw circle after circle in a manner which was pathetic. He was, indeed," continued Mme. Tutein, "removed only a few degrees from an animal." Nevertheless, she thought him a fine piano player, "better than many contemporary pianists who made great pretensions and who took years to learn what Tom could learn in a few hours." She added, "His original compositions were astonishingly interesting and often very beautiful." And if it did take Tom repeated listenings to master really difficult compositions, he possessed talents which were utterly incomprehensible. After learning the aforementioned Beethoven "Third," he turned his back to the keyboard and played the entire concerto in standing position. "In other words," said his startled teacher, "his right hand played the left-hand part and his left hand played the right-hand part."

After a long career, Tom Bethune died in 1908.

THE EIGHTH WONDER

OF THE WORLD.

THE GREAT MUSICAL PRODIGY OF THE AGE.

THE MOST MARVELLOUS GENIUS LIVING!

EMANCIPATION COMPLETE

The Last Slave Set Free by order of the Supreme Court of the United States.
Come and hear him play for himself and for your entertainment.
The Genuine, Original and Only

BLIND TOM

The son of ordinary Southern field hands, untutored and sightless from birth, is presented to a critically discriminating public as surpassing anything ever known to the world as a MUSICAL PHENOMENON. There is no art about him. Unlike the great masters, whose manipulations result from deep and unwearied study, his instructions come from a higher power, and this philosophers are pleased to term GENIUS, which enables him without a knowledge of either language to SING IN GERMAN, FRENCH and ENGLISH, without understanding a single rudiment of written music, to compose artistic gems,

Evincing Rare Natural Ability

and to perform the most difficult CLASSICAL COMPOSITIONS with all the correctness, purity of expression, skill and excellence of the most distinguished artists. He can execute

THREE AIRS SIMULTANEOUSLY,

each in a different key, and perform music correctly with HIS BACK TO THE INSTRUMENT. He will play SECOND or BASS to any piece of music that can be produced by any performer from the audience, and will afterwards change seats and play the PRIMO. His wonderful memory and remarkable faculty for analyzing and locating sounds enable him to imitate upon the piano-forte almost every known musical instrument, and to repeat, without understanding their meaning, the speeches of our greatest orators (to which he has listened at different times) with most faithful accuracy, and to reproduce upon the piano any piece played in his presence after once hearing it. This Great

NATURAL MUSICAL CURIOSITY

was born in Georgia, blind from his birth, and with his mind clouded from infancy, possesses musical ability such as has never been acquired by any individual but after years of laborious study. But when the veil of darkness was drawn over his eyes, as if to make amends for the affliction upon the POOR NEGRO BOY, a flood of light was poured into his brain, and his mind became an OPERA OF BEAUTY, written by the hand of God in syllables of music for the delight of the world.

For Particulars See Newspapers and Other Advertisements.

JACOB DUX & CO. Steam Printers, 350 West 42d Street, N. Y.

A two-color playbill of Blind Tom, declaring him
the last slave set free by the Supreme Court.

MAX MALINI:
The Last
of the Mountebanks

Lithograph used to advertise Malini's appearance at King's Theatre in New York.

MAX
MALINI:
THE
LAST
OF THE
MOUNTEBANKS

Feigning familiarity, Max Malini approached an impeccably attired gentleman he had never met. With practiced panache he swooped in front of the startled stranger, bit at his suit coat, and emerged triumphantly with a button between his teeth. In a flash, before the stranger could lodge a protest, Malini magically reaffixed the button and secured a lucrative engagement in the process.

Malini was rarely featured on music hall or theater stages, even though he performed in the heyday of the great illusionists. Yet far more than Malini's contemporaries, the famous conjurers Herrmann, Kellar, Thurston, and Houdini, Malini was the embodiment of what a magician should be—not a performer who requires a fully equipped stage, elaborate apparatus, elephants, or handcuffs to accomplish his mysteries, but one who can stand a few inches from you and with a borrowed coin, a lemon, a knife, a tumbler, or a pack of cards convince you he performs miracles.

Stories about Malini are still told, with a true sense of awe, by some of the world's greatest magicians. His history is part of the great oral tradition of magic. It is primarily anecdotal, but augmented and corroborated by numerous articles in newspapers around the world. Malini, even without an agent, garnered remarkable fees and generated publicity that would have had Hollywood public relations men demanding raises and bonuses.

He probably worked for more heads of state and wealthy families than any other performer of his day. He lunched with President Warren Harding and spent weeks in the company of the Prince of Wales. He sang with Enrico Caruso and accompanied General Pershing on a four-day drinking spree. He defied protocol and got front-page headlines performing for royalty. He entertained the Baron de Rothschild, John Jacob Astor, John D. Rockefeller, and Al Capone. The King of Siam gave him a jade bracelet with the name "Malini" spelled out in diamonds. He was asked to do his magic for Chiang Kai-shek and Sun Yat-sen. Presidents Machado of Cuba and Ibanez of Chile were befuddled by him. In Japan he worked for the Mikado and the House of Peers. George V of England admired his skill, as did Presidents McKinley and Coolidge. Teddy Roosevelt, who, as president, saw him perform, remembered watching Malini years earlier when he was police commissioner of New York and the magician was a poor, busking bar performer.

Malini came to his royal patronage by passing the hat in some of New York's toughest saloons. The data surrounding his birth are unclear, but most likely he was born Max Katz or Max Katz-Breit in Ostrov, on the Polish-Austrian border in 1873. He came to the United States with his parents at an early age. As a youngster he was taken with acrobatics, but at the age of twelve he began his tutelage with Professor Seiden, an old-time professional trickster who had retired to run a bar in the Bowery. Practicing for a crowd not known for its gentility, Max soon learned to sharpen his skills. By his early twenties he had far surpassed his teacher and had acquired an ability to master the most difficult performing situations (a fringe benefit of his on-the-job training).

He adopted the name "Malini," and in spite of his most unaristocratic appearance (he was short, had tiny hands, and very short arms; he spoke with a gruff voice and a very thick eastern European accent), he turned his seeming disadvantages into a marvelous presentation.

Malini performs cups and balls as a youngster.

He dressed impeccably, often sporting a fur-lined top-coat and a gold cane. "He was a real dude," said his son, Oziar. He became a character who was soon in demand at the most fashionable gatherings.

Malini received national prominence as the result of a trip to Washington early in 1902. While strolling through the halls of Congress, the magician approached the influential Mark Hanna. He grasped the senator by the lapel button and engaged him in conversation. Hanna, startled by Malini's approach, backed away, but as he did so there was a ripping sound and Hanna's jacket button came off. Magically, Malini instantly restored the button to its proper place, and the amazed senator hired Malini for an engagement that was to launch a ten-week stint of entertaining for the most influential people in the nation's capital.

As a master of both human psychology and the ability to "think on his feet," Malini was a hit in the quick-paced world of Washington. At one gathering Senator Hale tossed Malini an orange, admonishing, "Here, change that into a lemon." It was done almost before the senator finished the sentence. A ten-dollar bill borrowed from Hale vanished and reappeared inside the lemon. (This now-classic magician's effect was worked out by Malini and Emil Jarrow—later to be one of the great magic-comedy stars of vaudeville—when they were both broke and busking in the Bowery. They theorized that if the borrowed bill was soggy with lemon juice they would be asked to keep it as a tip.) The way the press reported the story, the senator impulsively tore off a corner of the bill before handing it to Malini. When the money was produced from the lemon the missing corner matched perfectly.

At a dinner given by Alexander Graham Bell, Malini asked Mr. Wu, the Chinese minister, to tear up a card and retain one little piece.

MAX
MALINI:
THE
LAST
OF THE
MOUNTEBANKS

87

Seiden playbill.

The other pieces magically vanished. Malini asked Senator Fairbanks to walk into the library and bring out the dictionary. "Open it to page 856," he said. Inside was the torn-up card, now restored; the corner that Mr. Wu held completed the jigsaw puzzle. In another variation of this effect, the selected card wound up in a second-story flowerpot.

At a party given by Henry Hay, Malini baffled the Russian ambassador, Count Casini, who selected a card and returned it to the pack. Borrowing the count's watch, Malini asked if he ever talked to the timepiece. The puzzled ambassador looked on as the magician explained that one could ask the watch a question which it would answer by ringing out once for a yes and twice for a no. Cassini explained that the watch was not a repeating chimer. Nevertheless, it rang out the suit and number of the ambassador's selected card.

Congressman Sulzer, after watching in amazement, started to leave the room. Malini stopped him. "Excuse me, but there's something in your hat." "No, there's not," said the puzzled representative. Malini took the derby and from it produced a hefty brick covered with dry mortar.

The furor he created led to a performance for President Roosevelt and coverage in newspapers around the country—not just notices, but headlines and multiple photographs. "An unknown little wizard appears in Washington and mystifies the entire Congress with his new tricks," declared the Philadelphia *North American*. "Today it may be said," reported the New York *World* on April 13, 1902, "that he is the most talked-of person in a city of talked-of personages and stories of his queer doings with diplomats, cabinet members, senators, representatives, and other great men who go to make up life at the nation's capital are daily rehearsed over the tea cups of the fashionable."

Although initially frustrated in his attempts to perform for British society, Malini was able to turn the tide by visiting the American ambassador, Joseph Choate. Presenting the official with a letter of recommendation from President Roosevelt, Malini convinced Choate to give a party for Prime Minister Balfour with Malini to entertain. The event was so successful that a second party was given with the Prince and Princess of Wales as guests of honor. "Mrs. Wales, take a leetle peek at a card, please," he said to the startled princess. The company apparently found his peculiar protocol and his astounding magic equally pleasing, and Malini was soon rewarded with a command performance for Edward VII and Queen Alexandra at Welbeck Abbey. For this performance Malini was briefed by a group of show-business and sporting swells who gathered around Romano's restaurant. The magician was told to kneel, address the royal highness in flowery language, and only walk backward. Malini ignored their leg-pulling advice and the next day told them the story of his success: "Ah, you tink me von big fool, eh? I know ver well how to speak wit kings. He

The Malinis posed before a teahouse in Yokohama, 1913.

jus come to me after I have perform and say: 'Ver goot, Meestaire Malini, ver goot, indeed,' and I answer: 'Much obliged to you, Royal Meestaire!' "

"Then the King he laff an' say, 'Haf a schmoke,' and I take a cigar an' say, 'You bet—I keep zis wit' my other keengs' cigars vot I haf gollect' and he laff again and say, 'Vell, here's annuder, and don't keep zat.' " So the king and Malini enjoyed a smoke together.

Not only the British papers, but the American press, too, wrote about "The New Yorker Who Fooled The King."

For the next thirty-five years Malini was to travel the world and to enjoy a series of adventures unprecedented in magic. "I doubt if there is anyone in the magic profession," said well-known conjurer S. Leo Horowitz, "who made and lost more fortunes than Malini, but his misfortunes never fazed him." Malini did seem to have remarkable resiliency and incredible faith in his own ability to bounce back from any hardship. Once, when he was broke and running up an enormous bill at the elegant St. Francis Hotel in San Francisco, he asked the manager for a loan to get passage for his wife and son, Ozzie, to an upcoming engagement in the Orient. The manager somewhat reluctantly agreed. Malini found a dice game on board the ship and had a streak of "good fortune." The manager was repaid (along with the hotel bill) before the boat ever docked in the Far East.

*Of the many celebrity photographs autographed to Malini, none was as
surprising as this one by a Maori chieftain whose people still worship the
rock produced by Malini in a performance in 1918.*

This same manager reluctantly loaned Malini a very expensive
antique table for one of his performances. A featured effect of the
magician's was to have ten or more people select cards and return
them to the deck. The cards were scattered on the table and Malini,
who was blindfolded and had a coat over his head, would stab each of
the selections, in order, with a borrowed penknife. The hotel manager
was horrified to see Malini had used his priceless table for the card-
stabbing effect. "Max, you've ruined the table—what will I tell people?"

"Tell them," said the magician, "tell them Malini did it!"

Malini became friendly with Morris "Two-Gun" Cohen, the legendary East End Londoner who became a general in the Chinese army.
On one of his trips to the Orient, Malini sat in the general's office.
While talking to Cohen, Malini idly picked up a pencil from the desk
and, in the heat of conversation, broke it in two. A second pencil was
snapped in the same way. Without saying anything, Cohen subtly

moved the pencil jar away from Malini. Max noticed the gesture, and the general apologized, "I'm sorry, but these are impossible to get in China. They're Koh-i-noor pencils—I have them shipped in specially . . ."

"You really hurt me!" Malini said. "Vat do you take me for?"

He picked up the four parts, ran them through his hands, and dropped two perfectly restored pencils on the general's desk.

Malini had a well-deserved reputation as a promoter and a remarkable ability to secure performing space (often with elaborate floral decorations), fashionable living quarters, and priceless gifts from his wealthy acquaintances. When friends, delighted by his impromptu miracles, asked what they could do to repay him, Malini had the chutzpah to tell them. Consequently, his portrait was painted by one of South America's most famous artists, and he received exquisite antique carvings and jewelry. Said Dai Vernon, "He certainly wasn't bashful about asking for things," but Malini had the knack of asking in a way that made people like him.

Much of his success was based on his wonderful storytelling ability. He was fond of relating the stunt he supposedly performed for a well-known English duke. Invited to an elegant dinner party, Max managed to sneak into the kitchen with a live chicken which had had all its

MAX
MALINI:
THE
LAST
OF THE
MOUNTEBANKS

91

THE WHITE HOUSE
WASHINGTON

January 22, 1923

I am writing this note to tell you how much Mrs. Harding and myself, as well as various of our friends, have enjoyed the occasions when you have performed for us. Of course, I still feel a little uncertain whether you did all the things that you seemed to do, or merely exercised some mysterious influence which compelled us to assume that you had performed them. However, the entertainment was in no way marred by reason of such uncertainties.

Sincerely yours,

Mr. M. Malini,
The Waldorf Astoria,
New York City.

President Harding canceled appointments in order to spend hours in the company of the great magician.

feathers plucked. Rocking the fowl under his arm, he hypnotized it, laid it on a platter, and covered it with a paste that made it appear roasted. He also garnished the plate with potatoes, vegetables, and fruit. He then returned to the table and waited for the bird to be served.

Just before the duke was to carve the chicken Malini said, "Meestaire Duke, I show you a leetle trick." He gestured mysteriously at the chicken just as the duke poked the bird with his fork. The chicken woke up, jumped off the plate, and ran squawking down the table. That this story, under the title "The Droll Trick of a Cambridge Scholar," had appeared in many eighteenth-century conjuring books did not bother Malini. He had the raconteur's ability to make everything seem as though it had just happened for the first time. And knowing Malini, his audience was ready to believe he just might have performed it himself.

The host of stories by and about Malini are so entertaining that they seem to obscure his abilities as a sleight-of-hand performer. This is a great mistake. He was an exceptional and even revolutionary magician. He is largely responsible for modernizing *the* classic feat of

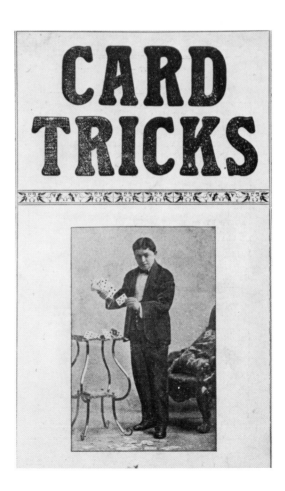

*Malini graced
this anonymous
book of card tricks
early in his career.*

MALINI

The Magician.

ROYAL PAVILION
MUSIC ROOM.

Commencing JULY 31st
to AUGUST 5th, 1922
Each Night at 8.30

Caricature of Malini by his buddy, the great tenor Enrico Caruso.

legerdemain, the "cups and balls," performing it not behind draped tables as it was done in his day but in impromptu fashion. He used borrowed glasses wrapped in newspaper and balls made by cutting a wine cork. He was an acknowledged master of misdirection, the technique of getting an audience to look where the performer wants them to look, and away from any covert manipulation. He was the inventor of numerous techniques and "touches" which play a large part in contemporary card magic. Most important, he *fooled* people. Laymen and magicians alike were absolutely befuddled by his effects. Dai Vernon and Charles Miller, probably the two greatest living exponents of sleight of hand, still speak reverentially about his skill.

An early photo of Leipzig manipulating billiard balls.

One of the most famous of the Malini stories involves a dinner given by Bert Morey, a wealthy friend of Dai Vernon's who was well acquainted with Malini's magic. Morey told Vernon about an amazing trick of Malini's which had fooled him numerous times, and asked Vernon specifically to watch for it to learn the method. After the dinner, during which Malini never once left the table, he asked to see the hat of one of the women present. Admiring it, and recognizing it as a Parisian chapeau, he was about to return it when he said, "Vait a minute; I show you a leetle trick." He spun a half dollar on the table and covered it with the hat, asking whether the woman thought the coin showed heads or tails ("Lady or eagle?" he would say). The woman called it correctly. Repeating the effect, he again lifted the hat—the coin had vanished and a great block of ice was revealed.

To this day, Vernon, who knew what was to take place, swears he had no idea how Malini got the ice. Malini had not left the table during the long dinner and conversation. "That little guy fooled the hell out of me," said Vernon. "I don't know what he did."

Not just this once, but many times he completely baffled both Vernon and Miller—no mean accomplishment.

Of course, the ice production amazed everyone, but even more remarkable to a well-schooled magician was that Malini could completely fool you by making a single half dollar vanish. Max would toss a coin

The *Incomparable*

MALINI

THE MOST MARVELOUS
OF MASTER
PRESTIDIGITATEURS

In Every Civilized
Country of the World
MALINI has

ASTOUNDED and STARTLED

Emperors—Kings—Presidents and Public Men,
The High—The Low—All alike are Amazed
At His Feats of Ledgerdemain.

*Malini program
signed by Max
and his son, Oziar.*

from hand to hand, saying, "Look—a lady, an eagle . . . a lady, an eagle." Suddenly he would lift his hands and the coin would be gone. It just wasn't there.

Nate Leipzig, Malini's contemporary and the greatest vaudeville sleight-of-hand performer of his time, was a master exponent of pure magic technique. "I would give up everything I know in magic," he said, "just to get the reaction Malini does from vanishing a single coin."

Malini was called the "Last of the Mountebanks," a combination of street hustler and masterful artist who appeared with his "medicine" to enrich your life and then vanished in a flash. He was fond of the slogan "You'll wonder when I'm coming, you'll wonder more when I'm gone."

He was also a remarkably compassionate and generous individual who did countless shows for underprivileged children and hospital patients. In his last years while living in Hawaii he spent much time entertaining American servicemen. According to his obituary in the Honolulu *Advertiser*:

> Max had not been well for months but everywhere there was a clamor of Army, Navy, Marines and Civilian defense workers for entertainment.
>
> Time and again Max Malini left his couch to dress slowly, but always with dignity and, often performing his magic from a chair set near the front of the stage, he continued to fulfill engagements when those who knew and loved him said he should be in bed.

He died on October 3, 1942.

DATAS:
The Man Who Knew
Too Much

Datas, the Memory Man.

DATAS:
THE MAN
WHO
KNEW
TOO
MUCH

"When were top hats invented? When did the Glasgow bank suspend payment? When was the first cannon cast in England? What is the current price of strawberries? When was an observatory built on top of St. Paul's Cathedral?"

These questions, extemporaneously posed by members of a music hall audience, were correctly answered by Datas, "The Memory Man." When asked, "Where is the Large Black Pig Society?" he responded, "At 12 Hanover Square, West, and it was founded in 1899. Am I right, sir?" He was.

Born W. J. M. Bottle on July 20, 1875, he was a rather poor student—"backward" was how he described himself—and quite unremarkable. "He has little more education than the average labourer, is scarcely more articulate, writes in no better style; he is by no means well read or in any degree cultured," said Leonard Crocombe in a magazine interview. Even though he left school at the age of eleven he had already developed the habit of "committing things to memory for the occupation of being able to repeat them afterwards at leisure."

One day, June 16, 1901, Mr. Bottle went to work as usual, stoking the furnace at the Crystal Palace Gas Works, and that evening, without so much as a thought of embracing show business, he walked onto the stage of the Standard Music Hall, Victoria. He was a legitimate overnight sensation. Earlier that day he had overheard two men discussing the case of Arthur Orton, the claimant to the Tichborne fortune and the principal in one of the most famous Victorian legal battles. Bottle corrected some misinformation in the conversation and provided many little-known facts about the case. A third observer asked if Bottle was as knowledgeable on other subjects. His affirmative answer was borne out by testing. The man took Bottle in a hansom cab—his first cab ride—to the theater, where he was questioned by the manager, who frantically sought to verify his answers in an almanac. Greatly impressed, the manager put Bottle on the stage that night to answer questions as he had done privately.

Datas, as he was soon to be called, answered about fifty questions during each performance. As he learned to entertain rather than simply astound audiences with his memory, he began to relate material which augmented the original answer. Such was the case with President Teddy Roosevelt, who asked, "Who was the only president to be elected by the whole of the people?"

"George Washington," Datas replied, "who was elected president in 1789. He was again elected . . . thus serving two terms of four years each. He was born on 11 February 1732, according to the old-style calendar, and on 22 February, according to the new style. There were eleven days put onto the calendar in 1752 to make it come in line with the old Gregorian calendar of 1582, and Russia is the only country in

PICTORIAL SOUVENIR

OF THE

GREAT TICHBORNE CASE.

BEING A READABLE NARRATIVE OF THE REMARKABLE LIVES OF

ROGER TICHBORNE & THE CLAIMANT,

WITH A CLEAR AND SUCCINCT ACCOUNT OF THE TWO GREAT TRIALS FROM FIRST TO LAST.

Illustrated by Portraits of Roger Tichborne, the Claimant, the late Lady Tichborne, the Orton Family, Mr. Hawkins, Dr. Kenealy, Jean Luie, and others; Sketches in Court, General Views of the Courts of Common Pleas and Queen's Bench, Examination of Lady Radcliffe, Pictures of Tichborne House and Park, and the "Claimant" in Prison.

PUBLISHED AT THE OFFICE OF THE PENNY ILLUSTRATED PAPER.

10, MILFORD-LANE, STRAND, LONDON.

The case that launched a career.

existence which has not adopted the new style of calendar today. Am I right, sir?"

Although distinctly not a humorist, Datas was able to provide comic relief with answers to questions like, "When was beef the highest?" "When the cow jumped over the moon." "Why did it take four days to win the Chester Cup?" "It took five. The owner, trainer, and jockey were all named Day, the horse was Peep-O'-Day, and the *day* on which it was run was May 28, 1848."

When asked to name the age of the great music hall star Marie Lloyd, he replied, "I am glad to say, sir, that is not yet a matter of history." There is reason to assume that at least on some occasions a confederate in the audience was used to spice up the performance by asking questions which allowed amusing answers. Occasionally his act suffered when the questions were so simple (as Charles Waller mentions describing a show in Australia in 1910) that the answers might have been supplied by any well-advanced schoolchild.

Datas had a peculiar penchant for morbid trivia and his passions, both private and public, were murders, hangings, and disasters. When he traveled to new towns on his music hall tours, he would start each day at the police station to learn of crimes and accidents, and then spend a few hours at churches, museums, etc., which was all the preparation he needed to make his act topical.

Doctors were puzzled by the methods he used. On his first trip to America in 1904, he was tested by four physicians who pronounced his 69-ounce brain the heaviest they had ever examined. These men bought the rights to his head for two thousand pounds cash, paid on the spot. Years later he took delight in telling that he never had to "pay off," as he outlived all four doctors.

Datas apparently used no mnemonic system to commit his material to memory, but rather spoke of creating "mind pictures" which could be recalled later. He authored a system of memory training and an autobiography, but is probably best remembered as the inspiration for the character "Mr. Memory" in Alfred Hitchcock's film *The 39 Steps*. He died at the age of 82 on August 31, 1956.

EQUINE
AMUSEMENTS

A well-known engraving of Banks and Marocco, 1785.

Sagacious seals, prancing ponies, and charming chimps have not been dealt with kindly by history. They have lost their identities and blended into society's collective grouping of ephemeral entertainments. Notable are the exceptions, and rarely has an exception been more notable than Marocco, the learned horse.

Shakespeare, Ben Jonson, and scores of their contemporaries thought enough of Marocco and his trainer, William Banks, to make them *the* most mentioned entertainers of Elizabethan times. The recipient of such acclaim must boast an impressive repertoire, and by every account, Marocco surely did. Although contemporaries could not agree on the horse's breed, size, or color, they described the following feats:

- He fetched objects thrown by the audience and returned them to their rightful owners.

- He identified spectators wearing spectacles and other distinguishing articles.

- He knelt, lay down, or played dead on request.

- He drank a great quantity of water and divested himself of it on command.

- By tapping his foreleg, he totaled figures on dice, counted coins in a gentleman's purse, and identified cards selected from a shuffled pack even though his trainer was blindfolded.

- He imitated how he would walk if carrying: a lady (with poise and gentility); a valet (in an impatient trot); or a riding master (executing airs, bows, and passades with impeccable precision). Scholars contend Marocco's dancing act was the origin of the modern "haute école" or high school riding act.

The horse was the subject of numerous stories and it is difficult to separate fact from fiction. Marocco's most remembered stunt, however unlikely, was climbing to the top of St. Paul's Cathedral, an imposing edifice more than five hundred feet high and containing perhaps one thousand narrow spiral steps.

In another anecdote, when Banks and Marocco were accused of sorcery, the trainer asked the horse to seek out a man with a crucifix and kneel down in front of him. The horse was then asked to rise and kiss the cross, thus acquitting himself and his trainer.

A story is told of Tarleton, the famous jester, asking the horse to choose the "verriest fool in the company." Marocco immediately put his mouth on Tarleton's collar and dragged the clown forward. Next, he asked the horse to produce the "verriest whoremaster in the

The educated-horse lithograph by Heinrich Lang, from
Voltigeurs, Jongleurs, et Saltimbanques, *1881.*

company," and again Tarleton was brought forth, to the delight of the
crowd.

Marocco's apparent mind reading abilities inspired contemporary
exposures as well as a school of believers that continues to the present
day.

In 1929, Dr. J. B. Rhine, the famous parapsychologist, was amazed
by the horse Lady Wonder and her owner, Claudia Fonda, near
Richmond, Virginia. As late as 1956 Lady Wonder made headlines
spelling out words on a special typewriter operated by nudges from
the horse's nose.

In 1904, a horse called Clever Hans inspired an extensive psychological investigation. The horse was capable of performing marvelous
stunts including arithmetic-problem solving and the answering of
questions (by pushing letter blocks forward) on a variety of subjects.
When Hans' trainer, Wilhelm von Ostend, died, the horse was left to
a wealthy German businessman named Karl Krall. In Elberfield, where
Krall lived, he trained other horses to produce similar startling effects.
His prize student was a beautiful Arabian stallion called Muhamed.
This horse mastered in two weeks what it had taken Hans three years
to learn. Muhamed, along with Zarif and Mustapa, a pair of clever
stable mates, performed stunts in what one reviewer called "the most

A nineteenth-century children's game featured the antics of a learned mule.

Thurston's first publicity picture, signed to John Mulholland.

sensational event which has ever appeared in the field of animal psychology, perhaps even the whole realm of psychology."

Ironically, the basic explanation for the seemingly psychic powers exhibited by these horses was described three hundred years earlier.

The first book in the English language to deal exclusively with conjuring (and the third to explain the methods of a learned horse) was Sa. Rid's *The Art of Juggling or Legerdermaine* (London, 1612). Rid, in one perceptive sentence, gives the key to all such entertainments: ". . . nothing can be done [by the horse] but his master must first know, and then by his master knowing, the horse is ruled by signes. This, if you mark at any time, you shall plainly see."

Actually, these signs are often missed by the untrained eye. They may require one well trained in deception, like Milbourne Christopher, who exposed magician's tricks in the cuing of Lady Wonder. Psychologist Oskar Pfungst determined that von Ostend and even impartial spectators subconsciously imparted information to Clever Hans by subtle changes in their body language which would let the horse know he had successfully completed his task.

Horses have played a role in more traditional conjuring performances. Lafayette, Thurston, Dante, and Blackstone (among the most famous twentieth-century magicians) all reaped important publicity from equine helpers.

In 1925, when Howard Thurston was the pre-eminent magician in America, he introduced what was then the largest illusion in the world: the disappearance of "Beauty," the Arabian steed. Beauty and his robed rider were hauled high above the stage on a swinging platform. The platform was covered for an instant and the horse and rider seemed to vanish in midair. A variation of the stunt was done the following season: A small open cage was raised above the stage; when Beauty vanished, the cage crashed dramatically to the floor.

The illusion was advertised as costing $50,000 (the actual figure was closer to $5,000) and required a special baggage car for its transportation. In 1928 Thurston sold the effect to Dante, who was then touring South America. Although Dante's posters continued to announce the disappearance of Beauty, another Arabian was used. Beauty was retired by Thurston to a farm in Pennsylvania.

Dante's only trouble with the illusion came in Montevideo, Uruguay. He wrote to Thurston in frustration explaining that local officials demanded a payment of forty cents for every poster hung in the city (usually thousands of lithographs like the ones illustrating this book would herald the show in each new town). In addition, he reported, the fee for parading a horse through the city streets was eighty dollars. Dante thus relied only on "word of mouth" to promote his show.

Harry Blackstone also did the illusion featuring the "Phantom Stallion" in his "Oriental Nights" sequence. Doug Henning featured it in his Broadway musical, *Merlin*, and Siegfried and Roy vanish a horse in their spectacular Las Vegas show.

The Great Lafayette featured an Arabian stallion, an African lion, and his dog Beauty (a gift from his friend Houdini) in an elaborate show at the turn of the century. Lafayette was an eccentric in a field resplendent with peculiar performers. His personal checks bore pictures of Beauty and sacks of gold with the inscription: "My two best friends." His dog traveled in a separate railroad compartment, complete with pint-sized plush couch and tiny porcelain bathtub. Lafayette's house

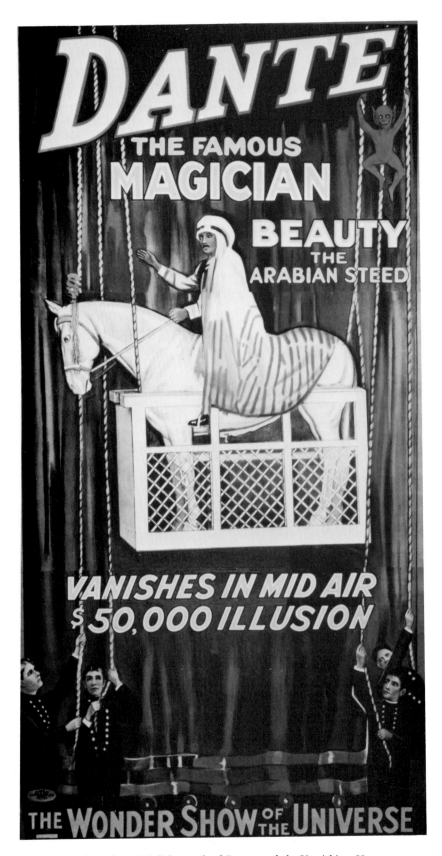

A three-sheet Otis lithograph of Dante and the Vanishing Horse.

was painted in multi-colored stripes; above the entrance archway was the inscription: "The more I see of men, the more I love my dog."

It was this love of animals that cost him his life when a fire broke out on the stage of the Empire Music Hall in Edinburgh on May 9, 1911. Lafayette reached the street safely, but still distraught over the death of Beauty a week earlier, he returned to the blaze to rescue the other animals. Apparently the lion, its mane in flames, blocked the exit door and prevented his escape. Sadly Lafayette, ten members of the cast, and all the animals perished.

Some magicians performed magic on, rather than with, their horses. In the early years of the nineteenth century, an English equestrian named James West performed sleight-of-hand effects while he rode around the circus ring. West brought his own show to the States in 1816. He traveled with his troupe instead of setting up the customary permanent amphitheater and consequently became the first truly successful circus entrepreneur in America.

Over a hundred years later, a German circus featured an equestrian escape artist. He was, according to historian A. H. Kober, "placed on his horse with both arms and legs securely fettered, and after a couple of circuits around the ring was able to cast off the last of his bonds." (See color illustration of Fred Rithlow) One evening the would-be Houdini galloped out of the ring before effecting his release, his face bearing a particularly pained expression. It seems that a practical joker had filled his pre-performance cocktail with a strong aperient from which there was but one escape.

*Blackstone
photographed in profile
with the shadow
of the devil.*

Lafayette and his dog Beauty: "An early morning call."

By the middle of the eighteenth century equestrian exhibitions had become the rage in England. The wedding of the horse and circus took place on an open field in Lambeth in 1768. There Philip Astley, a discharged cavalryman, combined for the first time the skills of trick riders, performing animals, jugglers, and acrobats into the modern circus. The horse was the key element, the other acts being brought in to accompany the performance of mount and rider.

Astley featured Billy, "the Little Military Learned Horse, three feet high from the deserts of Arabia." The miniature horse displayed many of the feats shown by Banks and Marocco, and like Banks, Astley was brought up on charges of witchcraft that were soon dismissed.

The fate of Billy is the stuff of which heartrending novels used to be made. William Davis took care of the horse after Astley's death, and in an act of kindness loaned him to Abraham Saunders, a talented but unfortunate trick rider and entrepreneur. Shortly thereafter Saunders' show was lost through debt and the little horse mistakenly auctioned with the rest of his stud. Billy was bought by a tradesman, who, though he called the horse "Mountebank" because of his odd prancing, was ignorant of Billy's higher education. For three years the horse pulled the tradesman's cart until he was spotted by one of Astley's riders.

Thinking the horse might be Billy, the rider clicked his fingernails, the cue for the horse to tap his foreleg in a counting exhibition. When the horse perked up and began to count, he was purchased and taken home. "Even in his old age he would ungirt his own saddle, wash his feet in a pail of water, fetch and carry a complete tea equipage, take a kettle of boiling water off the fire, and act like a waiter at a tea garden."

Eventually losing his teeth and unable to eat corn, Billy was fed on soaked bread at considerable expense. Late in life he was still called upon to give an occasional performance. When he died at the age of forty-two his hide was fashioned into a special-effects thunderdrum used for many years in the amphitheater: a curious but laudatory gesture.

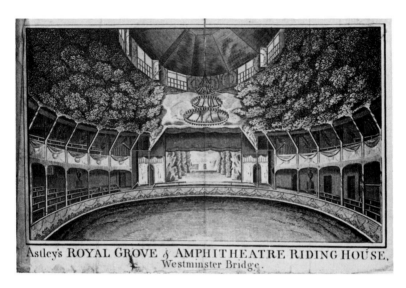

Astley's ROYAL GROVE & AMPHITHEATRE RIDING HOUSE, Westminster Bridge.

As the popularity of the circus grew, so did the accomplishments of its performers. Much like professional athletes, horsemen competed for glory by introducing ever more novel effects. These are some of the performers one might have witnessed in the eighteenth century:

- Thomas Johnson, the Irish Tartar (who may have been the first trick rider to perform in London), stood up while riding three horses simultaneously.

- Sampson played the flute while standing on two horses without using reins; his wife is considered the first female trick rider. Thomas Price, also astride two horses, jumped over a three-foot bar. Perhaps the first equestrian juggler, Price also rode while spinning plates on tops of canes in each hand.

- Charles Hughes, the founder of the Royal Circus and Astley's great rival, vaulted forward and backward over three horses

An equestrian image from an early nineteenth-century fan.

and encored by jumping over a single horse forty times without stopping. In an attempt to stay abreast of Astley, he exhibited a "Horse of Knowledge" that fired a pistol and a cannon.

- In Paris, in 1774, Hyamm (called the "English Hero") galloped around the ring with a child standing on his head. His partner, Miss Masson, rode standing with one foot on the saddle, holding her other foot aloft between her hands.

- Jacob Bates, who charmed Europe and America with his comedy trick-riding, straddled four moving horses. He also picked up a pistol from the ground at full gallop, and while hanging upside down fired the gun under the belly of the horse.

- Peter Mayhew, Thomas Pool, Mr. Cayetano (Cayetano Maviotini), and John Bill Ricketts were all early jugglers on horseback. Ricketts founded the circus in America. In the early 1790's he tossed marbles into bottles and caught oranges on forks while speeding around the ring. Ricketts placed a wine glass in a hoop and spun the hoop rapidly around without spilling a drop. He then drank to the health of the assembled company, all the while galloping around the ring without bridle or reins. So impressive was Ricketts that George and Martha Washington were among his admirers.

- In France, Astley founded a circus that was eventually taken over by the Franconi family. Laurent Franconi charmed Paris performing trick-riding and a splendid school routine (on a wonderful mare called Blanche). He introduced novelties like Coco, the trained stag who jumped over four horses, and the first aeronaut horse, who ascended in a balloon piloted by Testu-Brissy at Franconi's Cirque Olympique.

• Perhaps the most unusual of all these early acts was Daniel Wildman, who exhibited on "all but wet evenings" in 1772 at the Royal Tea Gardens. A horseman and apiarist, Wildman combined his skills and rode through the ring standing on his horse while a swarm of trained bees covered his face. Upon his firing a pistol, half the bees returned to the hive while the others marched over a nearby table. A respected and popular figure of his day, Wildman inspired the following verse:

> He with uncommon art and matchless skill
> Commands those insects, who obey his will;
> With bees others cruel means employ,
> They take their honey and bees destroy;
> Wildman, humanely with ingenious ease
> He takes the honey but preserves the bees.

In the 1760's and 1770's, Wildman exhibited at numerous locations in England and even before the French Academy of Sciences in Paris.

JOHNSON, Standing on One, Two & Three Horses in full Speed.

Johnson, the Irish Tartar.

One of the oldest of all circus families, the Chiarinis, gave equestrian per-
formances as early as the sixteenth century. This woodblock engraving is
most likely from the late eighteenth century.

(In Germany an imposter using the same name tried to capitalize on
the popularity of the original.) Wildman was able to control as many
as three separate swarms of bees simultaneously. This he accomplished
by a method called "caging the queen." The leader bee was confined
by a hair or very fine thread tied around her thorax by which her
movements could be controlled. The other bees would follow the lead
of their queen and consequently move from place to place as Wildman
directed.

Perhaps assuming his act was not novel or entertaining enough
to stand on its own, Wildman occasionally added "a grand display of
Dexterity and Deceptions" to his repertoire. This consisted of exhibits
of machinery, a pair of oriental caskets, and tricks with watches.
According to the 1803 *Dictionary of the Wonders of Nature*, Wildman was
able to control "whatever swarm was offered to him, and even wasps
and other flies, and . . . could tame the most mischievous in the space
of five minutes without being stung."

A law which prohibited non-musical theatrical performances with
spoken words gave birth to Equestrian Drama. To bypass the edict

A representative view of early nineteenth-century acts is found in this 1818 bill of the Olympic Circus. Note the sagacious little pony which performed part of the repertoire of Astley's "Little Military Learned Horse."

Remarkable early nineteenth-century etching of Baptiste Loisset,
the founder of a dynasty of great haute école riders.

(which protected existing legitimate theaters such as Covent Garden
and Drury Lane), horses became featured entertainers. They rode
around the ring while riders displayed banners detailing essential
elements of the drama, a precursor to the film subtitle.

The key figure to emerge from this peculiar amalgamation was
Andrew Ducrow, said by many to be the greatest horseman of all time.
Exhibited at age four as the "Infant Hercules" by a talented but cruel
father, Ducrow learned to combine strength with acrobatic, balancing,
and equestrian skills that were to set him apart from his competition.

He was the romantic hero on horseback of dozens of melodramas
like *St. George and the Dragon*, *Rob Roy*, and *Timour the Tartar*. He was a
man of ungovernable temper, called "indelicate, even revolting," but
imbued with great talent and panache.

Among his innovations were classic postures of strength and grace
called "poses plastiques," which he performed while standing on a

cantering horse. A protean act (lightning changes of costume) done while moving around the ring at breakneck speed, highlighted another routine. He was a master of mime and caricature as well as horsemanship.

Ducrow produced *Mazeppa and the Wild Horse of Tartary*, the most famous of all equestrian dramas. Based loosely on the Byron poem, it dealt with a young man who falls in love with a woman of ostensibly higher social standing. The irate father of the girl, in a gesture modern

In Raphael's Dream, Ducrow's most famous spectacle of tableaux vivants, *he performed his poses on a revolving pedestal rather than on the back of a horse.*

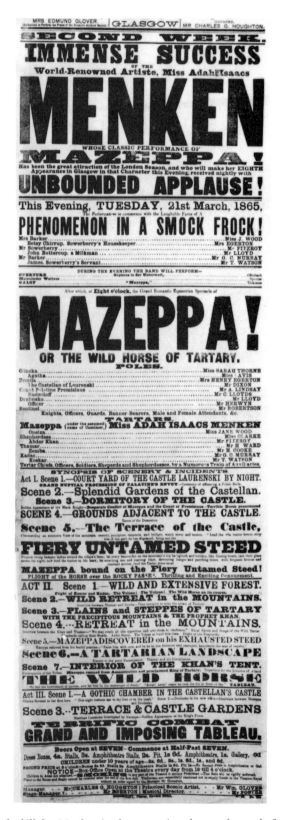

A playbill for Menken in the equestrian drama she made famous.

viewers might find excessive, has the man strapped naked to the back of the horse and sent galloping off into the Polish countryside (a fate worse than death). Sparing the reader the thrilling resolution of the play is an exercise in journalistic prudence. Suffice it to say that *Mazeppa* survived thousands of performances, substantially added to Ducrow's pocketbook, and much later, effected the stardom of a most unlikely woman.

Adah Isaacs Menken, an undistinguished rider, actress, and dancer, was catapulted to stardom as England's first female Mazeppa in 1864. A striking woman, scantily clad in pink silk fleshlings, she refused a stunt double and rode to fame bound to the back of a fiery steed.

Scandal rather than skill promoted her, but she was an extraordinary woman. People came to gape rather than admire, but they came. Her shows were sellouts. When Charles Dickens was unable to buy a ticket to see her she wrote him letters and dedicated a book of verse to him. All London talked of her romantic conquests, and so did she. In Paris she was toasted by royalty and shared more intimate pleasures with the elderly Alexandre Dumas.

Back in London she focused on literary luminaries like Algernon Swinburne and Dante Gabriel Rossetti. She had a much-publicized affair with Swinburne at the height of his fame. (Whether it was consummated is still a subject for debate.) In America she fascinated Bret Harte, Walt Whitman, and Mark Twain. Adah was the subject of innumerable stories (many self-perpetuated) and interminable debate. When she died at the age of 33 she had published and inspired controversial poetry, ridden semi-clad through most of the world tied to a horse, and gone through four husbands (one of whom was a famous demonstrator of psychic phenomena, another a contender for the heavyweight championship of the world).

In the words of one biographer, "While she lived no woman was more eagerly discussed and after her death more mercilessly slandered."

Even in more recent times, the spectacular accomplishments of horses, trainers, and riders have left us breathless. Lucio Cristiani somersaulted backward from one horse, past a second, and onto a third, landing in a standing position as the horses trotted around the ring.

Margot Edwards consistently juggled five balls on horseback in her act, and practiced doing seven, a feat supposedly performed by Hubert Cooke, perhaps the greatest of all bareback jockey riders. The Russian Nikolai Olchowikow juggled five knives and also seven balls on horseback. Emile Aquinoff was credited with a seven-ball equestrian juggle. In another routine, also on horseback, he juggled three burning torches which he threw high into the air. Then he somersaulted, caught the torches, and continued juggling.

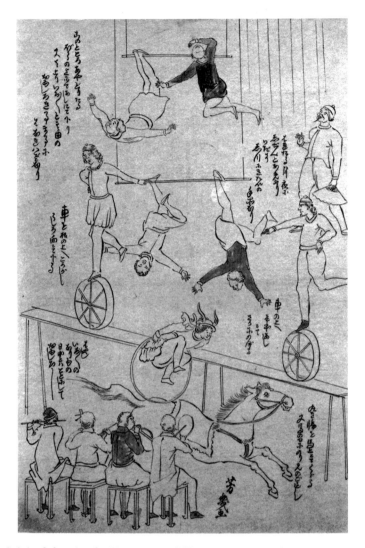

*Original drawing by Utagawa Yoshiiku (1833–1904) for a panel from
an apparently unpublished triptych of a foreign circus visiting Japan.*

Poodles Hanneford was a great circus clown, a master of equestrian tumbling and vaulting; his act was played for comedy. The Fredianis successfully performed the "three-man-high" on horseback, each brother standing upon the shoulders of the next as the horse circled the ring.

May Wirth, a dainty Australian girl, was the world's greatest equestrienne. A "performer's performer," she delighted in doing stunts that would impress other riders. She jumped from the ground onto the back of a galloping horse with baskets on her feet; she also threw backward, twisting, and forward somersaults. In 1912 she was the first woman to throw a somersault from one moving horse onto another.

The Loyal-Repensky Troupe created a pyramid of seven people— four on bottom and three on top while balanced on five moving horses.

In 1885 Signor Corrandini presented the "Blondin Horse," named after the first person to walk over Niagara Falls on a tightrope. At the Theatre Royal, Covent Garden, the horse climbed a flight of stairs and walked across a nine-inch-thick rope at an elevation of twenty feet. Cottrell exhibited a Blondin mule who walked across a row of bottles balanced on the tightrope. (See color illustration.)

Doc Carver, Buffalo Bill's first partner in the Wild West Show, exhibited horses which dived from a forty-foot platform into a twelve-foot tank of water. Posters of Freyer's Pony Circus pictured horses, somewhat unbelievably, walking on stilts.

As early as 1607 Gervase Markham, in *Cavelarice, or The English Horseman*, questioned the training of horses to lie down, kick, dance, and count as being inconsistent with the natural dignity of the animals. He nevertheless explained the stunts, concluding that in these tricks are revealed some worthy and extraordinary equine qualities.

No matter what the reader's views, the pitfalls of equine education have never been so clearly exposed as in the following story, related by Aristotle: In the ancient city of Sybaris lived a hedonistic and effeminate people (from whom we derive the word "sybarite"). Having

*The Forepaugh & Sells Brothers show featured
a variety of equestrian entertainments.*

A beautiful May Wirth lithograph, notable for the unusual spelling of her name and the length of her hair.

the free time essential to a voluptuary existence, they taught their horses to dance to the music of the pipe. When the Sybarites were engaged in a war with the neighboring Crotonians, their enemies, knowing of the terpsichorean predilections of the opposing steeds, brought a large number of pipers to the battlefield. The pipers began to play and the Sybarian horses began to dance. The riders, unable to control their shimmying steeds, were "thrown into confusion," and summarily slaughtered.

GENIUS
OR CHARLATAN?:
Walford Bodie, M.D.

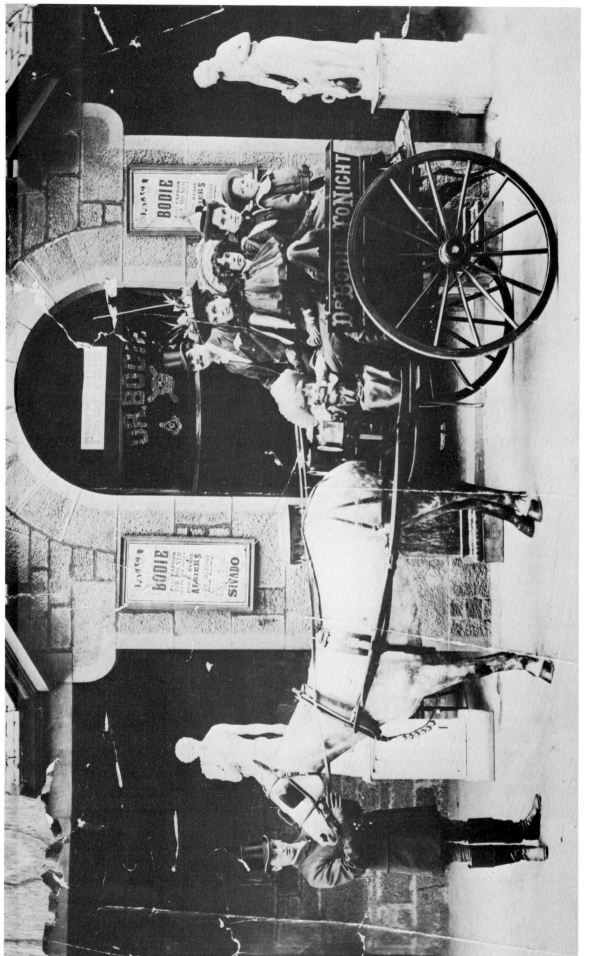

An early photo of the doctor and his retinue in front of the People's Palace Theatre.

Walford Bodie, M.D., was billed as: "The British Barnum / The Rage of London / The Money Magnet / The Record Breaker / The Pride of the North / The Idol of Scotland / The Electric Wizard / The British Edison / The Sensation of the Age / The King Laugh Maker of the World / The Modern Miracle Worker / The Greatest Novelty Act on Earth and / The Protector of Suffering Humanity."

But it was his use of the word "Doctor" which led to court battles, theater riots, and the eventual destruction of his career.

From a modest beginning in rural Scotland, Bodie became one of the most famous and controversial performers of the British music hall. He did magic, ventriloquism, and hypnotism. He performed remarkable experiments with electricity, and as a "Faith Healer" cured people on the vaudeville stage.

He was born Samuel Murphy Brodie in Aberdeen, Scotland, on June 11, 1869. His parents wanted him to study medicine or prepare for the Presbyterian ministry. An early interest in electronics, however, led to employment with the Scottish National Telephone Company. The telephone, especially in rural Scotland, was in its infancy, and this job provided Bodie with a practical education in electricity that he would later use to advantage on the stage.

As a child Bodie (the name he decided to use) taught himself the rudiments of magic and ventriloquism. At the Stonehaven Town Hall, a few miles from his home, local residents were encouraged to lecture and perform, and it was here that Bodie made his debut. One weekend he would demonstrate conjuring effects and the next give a talk on the sights of South Africa, a place he'd never visited.

When his sister married H. Werner Walford in 1897, Bodie's career began to take shape. Walford was the manager of the Connaught Theatre of Varieties in Norwich. Bodie worked with his brother-in-law in the management of the theater, and within a year became the proprietor of another theater in nearby Macclesfield. He soon realized, however, that his talents belonged *on*, rather than behind, the stage.

He adopted his brother-in-law's surname, promoted himself to "Doctor Walford Bodie, M.D.," and his career quickly prospered. He formed his own variety company and advertised: "Absolutely the most Wonderful, Weird, and Sensational Demonstration in the World, Introducing his Gorgeous Fit-Up at a cost of £2,000."

Bodie's stage was set with awesome-looking devices. Strange whirring noises were heard and sparks flew across the proscenium as a young girl stepped forward to assist him. As he touched her hand, every hair on her head stood straight up.

Volunteers from the audience were then asked to examine equipment which consisted of a large induction coil, spark dischargers, a Leyden jar, and other imposing accoutrements. Bodie showed them how thousands of volts of electricity could pass through his body without causing harm. Grasping two wooden handles connected by wire to the large coil, Bodie withstood the electrical current and invited the volunteers to do the same. Each was given the handles to hold and as the current was applied they began to shake and writhe, providing, according to contemporary accounts, much humor: "As the current increases, each person will be more or less grotesque, and most laughable to behold."

A playbill
of the doctor and his
company, 1914.

Next, a man and a woman, each holding a handle, were told to kiss. As their lips approached, sparks flew, preventing the consummation, to the delight of the crowd.

Other volunteers were invited to remove a coin from an electrified bucket. The hapless subjects were unable to do more than dip their fingertips in the water.

According to a review of the show in the Leicester *Daily Post*, Bodie contrasted his own power with that of the audience by passing "4,000 to 6,000 volts through his body." He apparently did this by grasping two electrodes from an immense induction coil. With the resulting current, he lit sixteen incandescent lamps and two arc lamps, holding them in his bare hands. By 1922, Bodie claimed to withstand a current of 240,000,000 volts of electricity. Practice, practice, practice!

The first court-sentenced electrocution, that of convicted murderer William Kemmler at Sing Sing Prison in 1890, had instigated a public outrage at what was thought to be an inhumane death. Bodie, always one to capitalize on topical and controversial issues, introduced a mock electrocution in his act and garnered substantial publicity from this stunt.

A volunteer from the audience was brought onstage, hypnotized so he would feel no pain, and placed in a replica of the chair used at Sing Sing. (Later, in 1920, Bodie obtained and exhibited the *actual* chair used in the first electrocution. It was a gift from his friend, the great American mystifier and publicity hound Harry Houdini.) The

The back cover of Bodie's pamphlet How to Become a Hypnotist *looks like a still from the movie* Frankenstein.

subject was strapped and wired into the chair. When the current was turned on, according to the Aberdeen *Journal*, "the awfulness of execution was borne to the audience which remained spellbound. Dr. Bodie watched closely and when the [subject's] face became black the current was switched off. After vigorous slapping, the subject was restored to consciousness."

"I suppose it was a morbid taste I was gratifying," said Bodie. "I suppose that when my audience saw every muscle in my subject's body quiver and watch his face grow blacker and blacker, they for the moment imagined they were witnessing the execution of some criminal."

Bodie was able to accomplish this stunt by his method of wiring the subject and rigging the stage. The subject was placed in a chair that was insulated where it touched the floor. The copper cap was connected by a wire to a large condenser, and the current passed through the condenser, wire, and cap to the subject. Insulation was also placed under various portions of the stage. When Bodie stood on the insulation and touched the subject nothing would happen, but when he lifted one foot off the insulation, electricity would pass through the subject but cause no harm. The electricity was not "current" or "dynamic" electricity as used in a real execution, but rather "static" electricity, which is not painful. This accounted for many of the stunts which he performed. For instance, a cigarette, gas burner, or electric light could all be lit merely by bringing them close to an exposed part of the subject's body.

Bodie's success, of course, inspired many imitators, but of all his stunts none was ever more widely copied than the electric chair, which, in considerably toned-down form, may still be seen in current carnival sideshows. In fact, not too many years ago, at an age when one is apt to trade scholarly lucubrations in the groves of academe for real experience, I was offered the opportunity of journeying to Singapore as a cabin boy aboard a tramp steamer or becoming a magician and pitchman at a small carnival sideshow. No "old salt," I chose the latter and quickly departed the ivy-laden halls for the earthy reality of rural America.

Part of my ordeal was to bind a strange girl/woman, of indeterminate age and unelevated social position, in an electric chair. As she would plaintively extend her extremities the short distance the straps would allow, I would touch her exposed arms and legs with a light bulb, which would, on contact with the bare skin, begin to glow. The ensuing illumination elicited gasps from even the most jaded observers.

Approaching my labors with the passion of a sociology field researcher, I adopted the cant and mannerisms of my peers. During the physical procedures just described (and before my arrest by the Canandaigua Sheriff's Department), I recited the following spiel:

"See the magician; the fire 'manipulator'; the girl with the yellow e-e-elastic tissue. See Adam and Eve, boy and girl, brother and sister, all in one, one of the world's three living 'morphrodites. And the e-e-electrode lady. . . . Yes, you see Tinavelma, the electrode lady. The e-e-electrode lady. At the age of seven she and her sister were struck by lightning. The sister died, but she lived to tell the tale. Twenty thousand volts of e-e-electricity through the little girl's body. The doctors say she lived 'cause she is immune to the shock of e-e-electricity. Show time, circus time, let's go, be goin'."

It is doubtful whether any performer got as much out of the electric chair stunt as Bodie, who carried on his war against the injustice of the American system of capital punishment. Once while Bodie was pleading for the humanity of the English gallows, he got support from a gentleman in the front of the hall. The man turned out to be Billington, the famous public hangman of the period. Bodie invited him onstage to demonstrate the chair. Billington was fascinated but refused to sit in the device even when the doctor announced he would only use a mild current.

"I'll make you an offer, Doctor," Billington said. "I'll sit in that chair of yours for a couple of minutes if you'll agree to hang on my ropes for another couple. Well, I'll be just as fair to you, I'll give *you* a short drop."

A friend asked Bodie why he featured the electric chair. "Why do you pander to the taste for the morbid and horrible? . . . Why don't you edify your audiences instead of shocking and terrifying them?"

Bodie replied with candor. "Because," he said, "I've got a living to make, to put it plainly; there is more money in 'shocking and terrifying' than there is in 'edifying.'"

Bodie also understood the power of laughter. His hypnotic vignettes provided one of the most amusing aspects of his show. In fact, the doctor often ended his performance by having a number of volunteers from the audience enact comic scenes onstage at his command. The scenario included the spectacle of hypnotically controlled men and women cackling about the stage as barnyard fowl, giving stump speeches as would-be politicians, and delivering heartrending arias from *Madame Butterfly*.

Though Bodie was not the first stage hypnotist, many comic interludes which form the basis for today's hypnotic shows were originated by him. Even though Bodie was accused of using paid confederates and stooges for these demonstrations, there is little doubt that he was a serious and knowledgeable student of hypnotic technique.

The good doctor wrote much on hypnotism and was careful to point out the dangers of its misuse. He was fond of relating the incident of a man named Dowling, who was accidentally killed by Aberdeen medical students in a mock execution. Dowling was blindfolded and told that his throat would be cut by a sharp knife. A wet towel was then drawn across his throat and Dowling died instantly, according to Bodie, from the power of suggestion.

Bodie also wrote fiction. He created "Harley the Hypnotist," a detective who solved crimes by use of his hypnotic power. In *Novel Magazine* and later in book form, Harley was popular enough to be called "a serious rival to Sherlock Holmes" by the London *Express*.

Bodie's own experiences, however, may be more amazing than his fictional creations. He became friendly with a regimental colonel. The colonel's wife was skeptical of Bodie's powers as a hypnotist and issued him a challenge. Bodie noticed a magnificent single-stone diamond ring on her hand and decided to use it to induce a trance. He had the woman stare at the ring until she was under his control, then performed several hypnotic experiments, which, according to the colonel and his wife, were quite successful.

A few days later the distressed colonel told Bodie that his wife felt the diamond ring had some mysterious control over her. The frightened woman corroborated the story. "Yes," she told Bodie, "you hypnotized the ring as well as me." Bodie again put the woman in a trance and under hypnosis told her the ring no longer had power.

Soon thereafter Bodie received a letter of thanks from the colonel saying his wife had never felt better. Enclosed was the ring. The colonel confessed he had tried to dissuade his wife from sending it to Bodie, since it was expensive and a family heirloom, but the wife felt compelled to present it.

Bodie admired the ring but gradually became uneasy. "I felt that this diamond was an eye challenging mine, and that behind it there was a will setting itself up against my will."

Accordingly, Bodie summoned up all his powers and challenged the ring. "A faintness came over me and I realized what it was like to be the subject and not the hypnotist." Staring at the ring relentlessly, he evoked inner power, and soon sensed victory. "The diamond seemed less bright and clear. . . . And then suddenly," he continued, "an extraordinary thing happened. There was a faint noise and the fall of some dust in the palm of my hand. The eye that had challenged me, and the will that had set itself up against me, had gone. This I knew at once. But it was not for some moments that I knew something else had gone. The diamond itself! That noise had been the noise of its bursting, and the dust was its dust. In my hand lay a plain gold circle with an empty socket where the diamond had once shone. If in truth any hypnotic power had ever been in the ring, that power had died when the diamond died."

Having worked his power on people and rings, Bodie next turned his attention to the animal world. In one of his books the doctor gave his technique for mesmerizing rabbits, toads, dogs, and even a glass of water. Although he confessed difficulty with some birds, parrots responded to his power.

> Take a bright object and move it to and fro before a pigeon or a parrot, and in a few minutes it will begin to show signs of losing its balance and in the end will fall from its perch hypnotized. Parrots are easily put off their balance by any circular motion. The Australian blacks discovered the trick of this long ago. Selecting a tree with a number of parrots sitting in the branches, a black will set out to walk round and round it at a distance of ten or fifteen yards from the trunk, and will keep this up monotonously for a long time. The birds look down and follow him with inquisitive eyes. Presently they grow dizzy and fall one after another to the ground, where they are easily captured by the wily hypnotist.

Armed with this information, I set out for the home of my good friends Chuck and Hilda Fayne, who own a hardy and talkative specimen of the Colombian Red lored parrot, called George.

Much to the dismay of my friends, I proceeded to wave a multicolored bauble in front of George in a wide circular pattern. Although I was asked to stop, each time they left the room I felt a strange compulsion to repeat the motions. Once or twice the bird did sway his head in time with my hands, but he steadfastly resisted my attempts to hypnotize him.

The next day I received a call from my friends. They had noticed nothing unusual in George's behavior that evening, but the following afternoon they returned home from the picture framer with a large poster of me. As they walked past George's cage his eyes followed my likeness on the poster. Suddenly the bird fell off his perch and thumped to the ground. Though temporarily dazed, George has completely recovered and I have turned my gaze to small diamonds.

The most unusual and controversial part of Bodie's performance was the cure of afflicted persons from the theater audience. These sick and crippled unfortunates, waiting for salvation, were forced to witness the spectacle of Dr. Bodie's minstrel ventriloquism routine and the comic evolutions of eccentric jugglers, gentleman equilibrists, and cavorting simians.

"A strange combination, I hear someone say," explains Bodie in *Stage Stories*. "By that he means, I suppose, the association of the healing arts with performances that are frankly intended simply to amuse. Not so strange after all. For to amuse people is to cure them of the worries, the anxieties, and the fits of despondency caused by untoward incidents in the daily struggle for existence."

The psychology of the faith-healing performance was a wonder in itself. Every detail was carefully planned to increase the odds of success. The theater lobby was posted with letters and testimonials of cured patients. Discarded crutches, iron boots, and braces were prominently displayed. Posters of the impressive and imposing doctor with lightning bolts emanating from his fingers, and "before-and-after" photographs of cured patients, lined the walls.

The level of anticipation, particularly among those hoping to be helped, was incredibly high. Of course, at a pre-show interview in the afternoon only those patients who were likely to be cured were asked to come back for the evening performance. The others were dismissed, usually with instructions to purchase Electric Liniment. The liniment, described on the label as "the most powerful embrocation in the world," was manufactured by the Bodie Electric Drug Company (which also made Electric Life Pills, "the greatest discovery of the age, renews health and vigor," and Hypnotic Discs, to aid amateur hypnotists in trance induction).

At the performance a volunteer (the most effective was a crippled child) was carried down to the center of the stage. The lights were turned down and the subject hypnotized. While the orchestra played, Bodie examined the affected extremity and fussed over the child with a lavish display of concern and attention. With his powerful hands he broke down any adhesions that may have formed under the skin. Next, Bodie connected himself to an electrical condenser and applied the current to the subject by touching him with his hand or boot. Flying sparks added to the mystery. After the application of the current the child was told to move the limb and walk across the stage. The audience shook the hall with their approval.

"I can explain my system generally by saying that I try to combine the natural gift," says the doctor in *The Bodie Book*, "with a knowledge of first anatomy, physiology, and psychology; secondly of electricity (animal and vegetable); and last of the magnetic polarity of the human body."

In addition the doctor introduced an electrical "extra" he called Bodic Force:

"Bodic Force is my peculiar discovery. Franklin tamed the lightning; Morse taught it the English language; I have instructed it in anatomy and physiology, and endowed it with intelligent sympathy."

The cover of the "Karlyn" exposé, 1912.

He combined his Bodic Force with his skills at breaking down adhesions. "There is no occultism in bloodless surgery," he said, "but there is an art, and it is difficult to master. I rely on for success first a knowledge of the exact articulation of the bones, secondly a very acute 'muscular sense,' and last upon strength of the hand and particularly the thumb to cure the patient."

In an insightful paragraph on the nature of faith-healing, Bodie explains that bloodless surgery is important but not essential to the cure of a patient. "Suggestion, and hypnotic suggestion, however, ARE essential. The stage itself, the music, the subdued light, the electrical apparatus—are all suggestions which tend to induce in the patient the mental attitude of belief, without which I should struggle with the disease in vain. . . . In short, my method of cure may be summed up

The doctor (left) and his impersonator, Charlie Chaplin.

as this: I employ electricity to awake my patients' vital forces; hypnotism to allay their pain; but it is by mental suggestion that I direct nature to the cure."

In 1912, Karlyn (a pseudonym of J. F. Burrows) wrote *Secrets of Stage Hypnotism, Stage Electricity and Bloodless Surgery*. A thinly veiled exposure of Bodie's act, Karlyn's slightly more succinct instructions for curing a patient are as follows:

> If the reader should decide to go in for bloodless surgery, he should first:
> Cultivate a very convincing manner, etc.
> Train himself to believe without hesitation that he can really effect the cures.
> Decide whether or not he will break down adhesions or rely upon massage.
> Then study a few good medical books to get a fair knowledge of the cause and effect of the various ailments he will endeavor to cure.
> Practice first on a few patients who are only slightly affected.

Bodie was a firm believer in the aphorism "All publicity is good publicity." He was probably not troubled, therefore, by the many imitators calling themselves "Professors" of Electricity and Bloodless Surgery, or the many parodies he inspired.

In 1906 the doctor was impersonated onstage by an unknown seventeen-year-old comedian. His name was Charlie Chaplin. In his parody of Bodie, Chaplin developed some of the antics that would later be so associated with his tramp image. He appeared onstage with a false mustache, a top hat (stuffed with paper to fit correctly), and carrying a gold-tipped walking stick. According to one biographer, "In a dignified entrance perfectly aping his model, he hung his cane on his arm by the wrong end and it clattered to the stage. Startled, he stopped to pick it up and his hat bounced off. Its paper wadding dropped out, and when he put it back on, it settled over his ears. Pushing his hat back, he then spoke his lines. This bit brought bursts of laughter."

Other parodists of Bodie were not noted for their restraint. In 1909 the Empire Theatre, Glasgow, ran the following act as listed in the program:

THE BURLESQUE OF THE CENTURY

BY ONE WHO KNOWS

DR. AWFUL BOGIE

M......D....!!!

Who has been all over the world and up the Magnetic Pole (in his dreams) will indulge on this visit his "showman's privilege" to the utmost and present an act full of Electric Blunders, Hypnotic Humbug, and Mirthful Magnetism, introducing

THE HUMAN JAM JAR

and

CAGE OF CODOLOGY

"Dr." Awful Bogie will pass £130,000 to his private banking account (if he gets the chance) without the slightest injury to himself or the orchestra.

Bodie inspired militant as well as comic attacks. In November of 1909, medical students, angered by Bodie's use of the title they worked so hard to obtain, rioted at the doctor's performance in the Glasgow Colosseum. Bodie was pelleted with a "fusillage of missiles of all descriptions (eggs, oranges, flour, red herrings, etc.) and forced to retire with his outer garment a coat of many colors." The students then rushed the stage and tangled with theater employees and police, who were powerless to stop them. Bodie reappeared but was once again driven off the stage with the students chanting, "Bodie, Bodie, Quack, Quack, Quack."

Riots, court battles, and parodies all served the doctor by keeping his name in print. Even World War I offered opportunities for publicity.

In 1915 he offered the government, "asking no monetary reward," the Bodie Shell, a device to be fired at an enemy regiment. When it hit the ground, fumes would arise, and although totally harmless, would leave the enemy "hors de combat long enough for the allies to make a dash and take them prisoner." If dropped within ten yards of the enemy, each shell was powerful enough to overcome five hundred men.

Bodie also claimed to have invented a mine destroyer and a submarine searchlight. Though newspapers carried stories about them, and Bodie boasted letters of thanks from the war office, there is no record of any actual use of the devices. He offered the British government "MacDuff," his enormous estate in Scotland, for use as an emergency hospital (complete, no doubt, with facilities for bloodless surgery) during the course of the war.

Even cartoonists capitalized on the doctor's misfortune.

In 1916 Bodie and his company were aboard the *Arabia* returning from India to London when the ship was attacked by German submarines. Although Bodie lost his entire show in the disaster, his heroic conduct garnered him considerable newspaper coverage.

Ironically Bodie's publicity began to backfire and his popularity began to wane. A series of letters from Bodie to Houdini reveals a sadness the doctor rarely displayed in public. Bodie clearly suffered, personally and professionally, from the notoriety of court cases and medical student protests in 1909. Even though Bodie's name was before the public, the better music halls and leading theatrical managers no longer offered engagements.

As early as 1913, the doctor and his son Albert had been denied admission to the London-based Magicians Club. Bodie wrote to its president, Houdini, to rectify the situation. Houdini, who had no knowledge of the rejection, went to Bodie's aid. In a thank-you letter dated May 7, Bodie wrote, "I have been inundated with offers and hope before long to be again on the top despite all that has been said against my good name." In a letter dated April 8, 1920, Bodie wrote, "Sorry I did not get up to the Ladies Night at the Magicians Club but not being a member I felt a bit 'shy.'" In the same letter he said, "You will be pleased to know I am still going strong but can't get on the big time houses again. I don't know why, my show bigger & greater than ever." On April 22 he reiterated, "I am delighted to tell you that I have been doing very well lately playing to very big houses but I should like a farewell run of the big time houses. Could you put in a word for me to Mr. Day [Harry Day, a leading theatrical booker]. I am sure he could fix me up with a run. I have not got an agent. I should like to play the 'Gulliver Circuit,' 'Moss Empires' one run round & then I think I would retire from the stage." Later he queried, "How would I do in America?"

On April 30, Bodie again asked Houdini to speak to Harry Day about a major tour, stating, "My show bigger and greater than ever." Early in 1921 he wrote, "I wish you could get a run for me in America. I am sure I would do well. . . . I am still holding my own against all Comers and Imitators. Like your good self there is only one Houdini & only one Bodie. . . ." And once again, sadly, "I know Harry Day is a big pal of yours. I wish you would give me a note and ask him to book me in London on the big time houses. . . ."

Perhaps the wonders of electricity were no longer astounding to the sophisticates of the 1920's, and the medical cures less easily accepted by a more enlightened public.

By 1930, in an attempt to keep up with the times, he billed himself as the "Talkies' Only Rival," but he no longer drew crowds. Personally

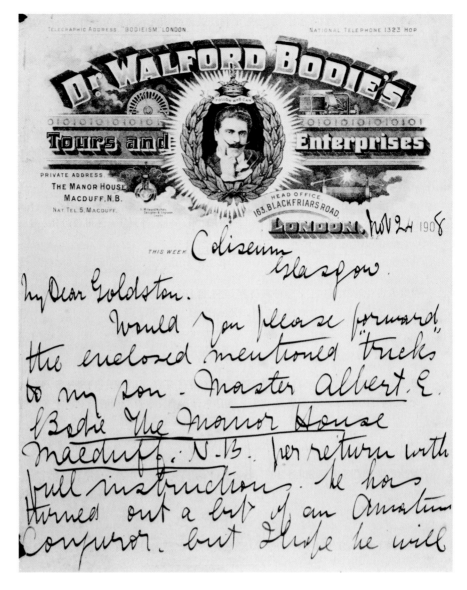

A letter to magic dealer Will Goldston on Bodie's elaborate stationery.

and professionally there were many problems. The early deaths of his assistants and family members, Mystic Marie and La Belle Electra, as well as the death of his son Albert, were devastating. In 1931 his wife, "Princess Rubie," died and soon thereafter Bodie, in his sixties, married Florrie Robertshaw, a twenty-two-year-old dancer in his show. He continued to spend money extravagantly, but the former headliner was reduced to playing the small time. He was appearing in the Blackpool Sands just a few weeks before his death in 1939.

The ironies of his life and career remain. GENIUS OR CHARLATAN? his posters asked. He was probably both. His sense of humor is evidenced in his writings, and he was not the least bit embarrassed to admit using the "powers of the press" or "artistic license" to further his career. But there is no doubt that many people were cured by him, whatever the method.

Perhaps the most significant insight to his character and methods of operation is revealed in the examination of his most famous trial.

In 1909 Charles Irving, a former assistant of Bodie, sued to recover damages for alleged misrepresentation by which Mr. Irving had paid £1,000 to the doctor. Irving paid the money, he claimed, to learn the sciences of hypnotism, mesmerism, bloodless surgery, and medical electricity from Bodie, whom he believed to be a qualified doctor.

Bodie was involved in many court actions over the years, but this case is particularly revealing in the discussion of the fraudulent methods sometimes used in the doctor's performance. In addition, the presiding judge, Justice Darling, exhibited a quick wit and an amusing manner.

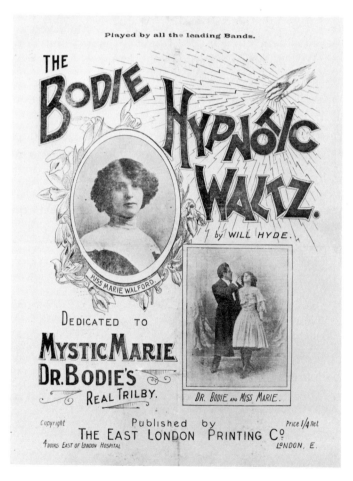

The doctor and Mystic Marie immortalized in song.

The case received much attention in the London press.

When questioned as to whether Bodie taught Irving hypnotism, mesmerism, and surgery, Irving replied, "No. He only showed me how the tricks were done. The patients," Irving claimed, "were tested in the afternoon before the show and if unable to move their afflicted limbs were told to go home."

When describing the electric chair stunt, Irving said the subject was John Legg, a paid assistant to Bodie. He said both the electric chair and the "cage of death" (a large solenoid used in Bodie's show for the application of electrical current) were harmless. A medical supply company representative, Dr. E. Greville, corroborated the statement and explained that while it was not generally known, high-frequency (also called static) current is not at all dangerous.

Irving next explained that the "magic circle," a stunt where men from the audience came onstage to join hands with Bodie as the current ran through him, were also paid assistants who contorted themselves on cue. Hypnotic subjects were also purported by Irving to be paid confederates.

Justice Darling pointed out that Mr. Irving was to be taught hypnotism, which is a real science, and not "stage tricks." Looking through Bodie's book, the judge sarcastically noted that a toad was mesmerized. Bodie's attorney said that Bodie always introduced a little amusement before he commenced the serious business.

Justice Darling: "Whenever I have been to see a doctor I have missed the preliminary amusement."

George Dyas, a laborer and long-time victim of mild paralysis, testified he had seen Bodie one afternoon and was told to return to the theater that night.

Dyas: "I went in that evening and waited my turn with the others behind the scenes. I was not allowed to walk on, though I could have done so. I was forced into a chair. I never had [used] crutches, but some were produced and flung across the stage."

Counsel: "Did he hypnotize you?"

Dyas: "He tried to, but he didn't."

Counsel: "Do you know what hypnotism is?"

Dyas: "I don't know exactly."

Justice Darling: "Tell us what you do know."

Dyas: "It's when somebody has got a 'fluence' over another person and tries to put him asleep."

Justice Darling: "There are lots of counsel who have that influence on judges."

Mr. Dyas said Bodie ran a current through him and told him to use Electric Liniment but he was not helped by this treatment.

John Bowden of Whiston Street was called. He explained that he had gone onstage with two sticks, which he needed to walk. Bodie

One of Bodie's many imitators, circa 1910.

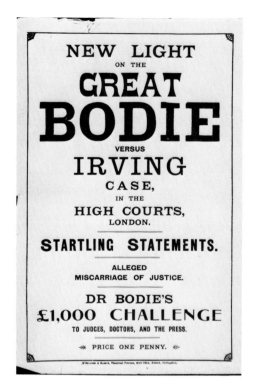

*The cover of a four-page paper
which presented Bodie's view of the case.*

broke them over his knee, telling the audience Bowden would be cured and would no longer need the sticks. He told the audience how Bowden had been turned away as incurable by the hospital, which was not true. Then electricity was put through his legs.

Bowden: "I felt a terrible pain. If not for the orchestra playing a lively tune the audience would have heard me yelling."

Counsel: "Did he hypnotize you?"

Bowden: "No, I was very much awake."

After the show Bowden waited for Bodie and asked how he was to get home without his sticks. He was given a shilling and told to take a cab.

Counsel: "Did you feel better from his treatment?"

Bowden: "No."

Bowden returned to the theater on a second occasion.

Bowden: "Doctor Bodie prompted me to say that he had done me more good in a few minutes than all the hospitals had in eighteen years. He had previously promised me a pair of boots because he said it was my boots that prevented me from walking home on the first occasion."

Counsel: "Did you get the boots?"

Bowden: "No."

*A bizarre combination of a photograph and hand-drawn background
showing the doctor in his laboratory.*

Justice Darling: "Why did you not say to the audience he had done
you no good?"

Bowden: "The boots would not have been forthcoming then."

A number of other witnesses, including a man who for years was
paid by Bodie to pretend he was hypnotized at each performance, gave
similar testimony.

Bodie's counsel then provided witnesses to testify that they had
really been helped by the doctor's curative powers.

Bodie himself took the stand.

Counsel: "Where did you graduate in medicine?"

Bodie: "I have not graduated." (Earlier, Bodie's counsel had
admitted that "Dr. Bodie is not a registered medical practitioner in any
country" and that Bodie had previously been enjoined against using
the letters "M.D." after his name.)

Counsel (reading from *The Bodie Book*): " 'In the U.S. I took my
degree of doctor of dental surgery.' Is that a lie?"

Bodie: "Oh, it's a showman's privilege."

Counsel (reading): " 'And then I went to China, Japan, and other
countries in the Far East to study these sciences which are called
occult.' "

Bodie: "I have admitted that's not true. Showman's privilege."

Counsel: "You have continually represented yourself as an M.D., have you not?"

Bodie: "No, only on one occasion. It means Merry Devil. Theatrical managers call me that."

There was a burst of laughter in the courtroom.

In Justice Darling's summation he raised the following points: "It would be strange, if after attending thousands of cases Dr. Bodie has not been able to bring forward a number of persons to say they had been cured. One would like to know more definitely what had been wrong with these individuals before they saw Dr. Bodie. One would like to be certain they were not merely cases of hysteria which a strong will might cure."

The jury awarded £1,000 damages to Mr. Irving.

How did this affect Bodie? A short time after the trial a theatrical journal carried a New Year's greeting from Bodie. Under his picture were the following credits: Freeman of the City of London; Doctor of Medicine and Master of Surgery, Barrett College (Diploma); Doctor of Science, Arts, Letters, and Literature, London (Diploma); Doctor of Electro Therapeutics, Chicago College of Medicine and Surgery (Diploma); Hon. Snr. Lieut., Briston City Marine Ambulance Corps.; Fellow of the Royal Spectacle Makers; etc., etc., etc.

In addition, he commissioned a striking full-color lithograph showing scenes of the trial and bearing the following copy:

The GREAT *and* ONLY DR. WALFORD BODIE—
A GREAT VICTORY *in the* HIGH COURTS *of* LONDON.
*An expert electrician appointed by Mr. Justice Darling swore on
his oath in the witness box that* DR. WALFORD BODIE *who coupled
himself up to a 16-inch spark induction coil had passed 30,000
volts through his body—a feat never before attempted or duplicated
by any living electrician. This stupendous and daring feat was
accomplished by* DR. BODIE *before a British jury of 12 Honest
Men.*

BORN TO A DRIER DEATH THAN DIVING:
Samuel Gilbert Scott and Other Daredevils

1840

SCOTT'S RE-APPEARANCE

BRIGHTON
SUSPENSION PIER

The Public are respectfully informed that

SCOTT,

THE CELEBRATED

AMERICAN DIVER

Has arranged to repeat his exhibition at the Pier Head, of

HIS EXTRAORDINARY AND SURPASSING
POWERS IN THE ART OF
LEAPING & DIVING,

At the undermentioned times ONLY:—

ON

Monday, 3d Aug., at 5 in the Afternoon,
Wednesday, 5th Aug., at 7 in the Evening,
Thursday, 6th Aug., at 7 in the Evening,

AND ON

Friday, 7th Aug., at 7 in the Evening.

This unrivalled Diver will on these occasions

PRECIPITATE HIMSELF FROM AN EMINENCE

OF UPWARDS OF

140 FEET.

No extra charge for admission to the Pier will be made, SCOTT being wholly dependent upon Voluntary Contributions for Remuneration.
A CANNON SIGNAL will announce the commencement of the Performance.

Printed by Edward Hill Cressy, of North Street, and John Baker, of York Place, Brighton, Printers, at their Printing Office, in Church Street, Brighton.

The subject of this chapter is a daredevil performer who was an expert at holding his breath, who accepted challenges to jump into rivers, who exhibited incredible muscular control, and who died as the result of a freak accident. He was not Harry Houdini.

BORN
TO A
DRIER
DEATH
THAN
DIVING

He was Samuel Gilbert Scott, an American diver who made his living and reputation plunging into water from the tops of buildings, shipmasts, and bridges in the 1830's and 1840's.

Born and raised in Philadelphia, Scott first distinguished himself in the U.S. Navy by plummeting off the yardarms and topmasts of government vessels. His dives brought him notoriety and he left the service to perform his stunts publicly. He made successful descents in New York, Philadelphia, and the St. Lawrence River, earning considerable fame and—by passing the hat for contributions—if not a fortune, enough to live on.

It was a leap from a precipice just below Niagara Falls that was his most formidable accomplishment. Although newspaper accounts varied in reporting the distance of his headfirst dive, some giving figures as unlikely as 593 feet, all agreed he completed his stunt with no ill effects. Some years later a daredevil named Samuel Patch was killed at Niagara in a similar stunt.

Scott arrived in England early in 1840 and distinguished himself with dives of 100 feet at Manchester and 167 feet at Liverpool. He dived from a 140-foot scaffold at Brighton Pier, from a 200-foot topmast on the battleship *St. Joseph* at Devonport, and from a 240-foot cliff at Cornwall into only eight feet of water.

Scott received payment for these stunts by subscription or wager. He frequently challenged other divers to duplicate his feats. He also demonstrated breath control and accomplishments of muscular strength and agility on the diving platform before entering the water. Exhibiting even greater versatility, he would, a playbill for a Southwark Bridge jump proudly claimed in 1840, "talk as he is descending!"

His dress on these occasions was checkered shirt, canvas trousers, and a handkerchief tied around his head. He wore no shoes, socks, or protective equipment.

While engaged in pre-dive entertainment on the mast of an American ship at Deptford, Scott had a serious accident. As usual, he demonstrated his acrobatic ability, alternately swinging from his feet and neck on the ship's rigging. While he was maneuvering in his noose, the rope slipped from its fixed position and tightened around his neck, nearly strangling him.

The spectators, thinking this dangling was part of his act, cheered wildly. An attentive sailor, realizing that Scott's face had turned black (to at least one mariner a sign of trouble), leaped to his aid. Scott had, at that moment, thrown his feet aloft in a final effort to extricate

Scott in a characteristic dive, 1841.

himself. The sailor caught his feet and supported his body as Scott loosened the rope around his neck.

The crowd, now greatly concerned for the diver's well-being, asked for assurances that Scott was not injured. "Not at all," he rasped with bravado heartily applauded. "The hemp that's to hang me is not grown yet."

The money taken in on this occasion was almost double that received on previous engagements—a madly portentous example of filthy lucre hastening a worthy's demise.

On January 11, 1841, Scott "challenged the world for 100 guineas." He would run, he said, from Harry Godfrey's White Lion Pub in Drury Lane to Waterloo Bridge, jump forty feet into the river, and return to Godfrey's, all between the hours of 1:00 and 2:00 P.M.

On the appointed day Scott easily completed the run and climbed the scaffold for his plunge. Attempting again his high-earning pre-dive acrobatics, he swung from a noose around his neck. The rope suddenly slipped and tightened around Scott, who remained suspended for several minutes. Again an audience applauded his plight until one observant spectator "leaped upon the scaffolding and cut him down."

Scott was, according to a broadside printed the following day, rushed to Charing Cross Hospital, where "every attention was paid to him, but unfortunately without effect, as life was quite extinct."

Another publisher, in an attempt to capitalize immediately on the accident, reissued a portrait of the poet Robert Burns with a diving scaffold hastily drawn in the background and a caption which read: "Samuel Scott, the Unfortunate American Diver."

The newspapers, in their hasty reportage, issued conflicting accounts of Scott's native origin, marital status, and drinking habits. One account forcefully stated that he was almost totally abstemious but that he had, on this particularly cold day, fortified himself with "a third quartern of gin and water" as a pre-immersion potable.

Some papers eschewed the outrage of public feeling, expressing the brutality, indecency, and degradation of senseless acts which they felt should be disallowed. Opposing journals defended the rights of individuals to participate in public demonstrations and amusements no matter what the consequences.

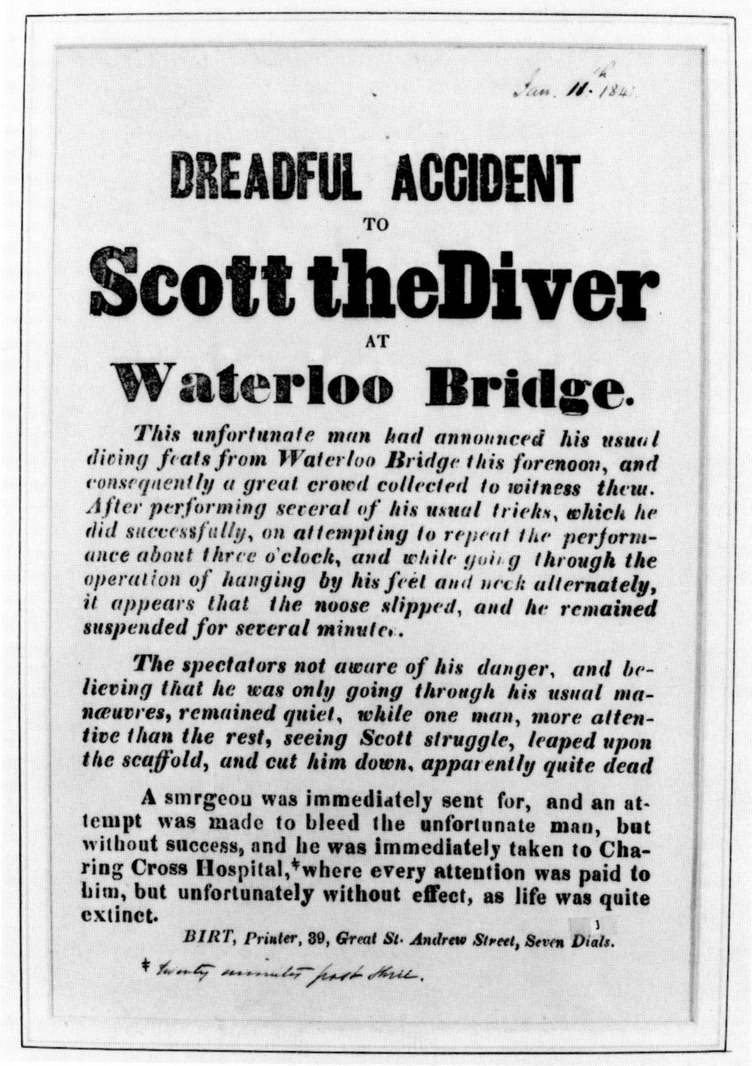

BORN
TO A
DRIER
DEATH
THAN
DIVING

151

SAMUEL SCOTT.
the unfortunate
AMERICAN DIVER.

Robert Burns or Samuel Scott?

Perhaps the most lucid contemporary account, appearing in *Tom Spring's Life in London* on January 21, 1841, called Scott a civil and unassuming fellow but "by no means a particularly intelligent man."

Neither Scott's daredevil diving and rope acrobatics nor his untimely demise was uncommon in the chronicles of irregular entertainment.

In 1546 Londoners saw a fearless Spaniard who, in an attempt to impress King Edward VI, shot headfirst on a taut rope from the battlements of St. Paul's Cathedral to the ground far below. His descent, popular to this day with stunt men and performers, is usually called the "slide for life."

Indeed, as early as 1563, the loss of life from such folly was recorded: "From the top of the spire, at coronations or other solemn triumphs, some for vain glory used to throw themselves down by a rope, and so killed themselves, vainly to please other men's eyes."

Almost four hundred years later, a circus performer called "The Great Peters" featured a spectacular stunt. From a rigging seventy-five feet in the air, Peters waved to the audience and took a swan dive

AWFUL DEATH OF SAM SCOTT,

THE GREAT AMERICAN DIVER,

who accidentally strangled himself while exhibiting his performances on WATERLOO

BRIDGE, Monday, January 11th 1841.— before thousands of Spectators!

Published by Glover & Co. at their popular Print & Caricature Warehouse Water Lane, Fleet Street

*Cartagos was more successful than Scott with his ship-rigging acrobatics
in this Friedlander lithograph, circa 1919.*

toward the ground. Around his neck was a long rope ending in a
noose (the rope covered a layer of special elastic). As the rope stretched
taut a few feet from the ground, the resiliency of the elastic would
break the fall, causing Peters to bounce back into the air, regain his
composure, and gracefully descend to terra firma.

For more than a decade, Peters shocked and thrilled audiences
with his unusual act. Appearing with the Sells-Floto Circus in St. Louis
on October 22, 1943, he was killed when the rope gave way and he
plummeted to his death (see poster in color section).

A FEW WORDS
ABOUT DEATH
AND SHOW BIZ:
Washington Irving Bishop,
J. Randall Brown,
and the Origins
of Modern Mind Reading

Seer's chromolithograph of Bishop.

A FEW
WORDS
ABOUT
DEATH
AND
SHOW BIZ

Washington Irving Bishop was born in 1856; he died in 1873, 1881, and 1889. His act was peculiar. His habits were peculiar. His family was peculiar. His death was *most* peculiar.

On May 12, 1889, noted actors Henry Dixey and Sidney Drew invited Bishop, who was billed as "The First and World Eminent Mind Reader," to dine at the prestigious Lambs Club in New York City. Asked to perform for the distinguished show-business crowd, Bishop responded with an effect he had demonstrated for the czar of Russia.

He left the room in the company of a club member, and requested that an imaginary murder take place in his absence. The group was instructed to choose a murderer, a victim, and a weapon. The "murderer" was to act out the crime and hide the weapon. Bishop was then called back to the room with the chaperone, who attested the mind reader was unable to see or hear what had taken place.

A man who witnessed the "crime" was designated to be Bishop's assistant. The mind reader was blindfolded. He grasped the assistant's left wrist lightly with his right hand, asking the assistant to concentrate on the chosen "victim," but to say nothing. Bishop slowly turned around, then suddenly lurched forward, dragging his assistant as he wound his way through people and furniture. Impulsively he stopped and pointed at someone in front of him. It was indeed the "victim."

Bishop immediately set out again, more excited, awkwardly, erratically charging about the room with his puzzled assistant in tow. In a few moments he successfully located the "murderer" and the "weapon."

An enthusiastic crowd demanded another demonstration. The mind reader decided on a stunt he had done for Governor Fannin of Missouri at the State House in Jefferson City only a few days before.

Clay Green, comedy writer and Lambs Club secretary, was asked to mentally choose a name in the club register. The blindfolded Bishop, with Green in hand, managed to locate the book and point to the selected page. Asking for further concentration from Green, Bishop attempted to write the chosen name. He scrawled the letters

TOWNSEND.

Puzzled, Green announced the correct name as Margaret Townsend. When Bishop's letters were held to a mirror, the name Townsend was revealed!

As the crowd applauded, Bishop, who had grown increasingly frenetic during these tests, fell to the ground unconscious.

Dr. John Irwin, an old acquaintance of Bishop's, was not worried. He assuaged the gathering by explaining Bishop had a disease characterized by the suspension of sensation, muscular rigidity, and the loss of life signs. He was a cataleptic. Indeed, the histrionics which

Henry Dixey, the noted actor-magician
who invited Bishop to the Lambs Club.

alarmed, intrigued, or outraged his audiences were commonplace. The Portland *Oregonian*, reviewing his murder test in that city, said, "Bishop was trembling in every limb and appeared to be bordering on hysterics. The veins on his forehead were swollen and his pulse which before the experiment was 72 now throbbed at 116." Bishop was described variously as "wild-eyed," "entranced," "weasel-like," and "a full-dress coated skeleton." In accounts of his shows, numerous witnesses had seen him collapse, lifeless, as he did at the Lambs.

Bishop soon regained consciousness and was taken to a bed upstairs. Irrationally, he insisted on performing his experiment again. Weak, perhaps delirious, he had the ledger brought to his room and the test was repeated, with Dr. Irwin as the assistant. With difficulty he located the correct page. He was helped to a standing position to determine the chosen name. The strain was too great. Again he collapsed, unconscious.

Dr. Charles C. Lee, who had previously attended to Bishop, was summoned. At 4:00 A.M., when all his attempts to revive the patient failed, he left.

Augustus Thomas, Bishop's advance man, recalled the events of that fateful night in the *Saturday Evening Post*. Thomas was walking down Broadway when a friend reported, "Your star is sick at the Lambs." Thomas ran and "found Bishop in a little hall bedroom on an iron cot where he had been for twelve hours, a tiny electric battery buzzing away with one electrode over his heart and the other in his right hand. He was unconscious. Two doctors sat smoking in the adjoining room, tired with the watch of the night. I looked at the handsome face of Bishop and sat beside him for some minutes. Although he was to every appearance dead, a deeper solemnity suddenly came over his face."

"I think there is a change in your patient," Thomas said to the doctors, who returned to the room and pronounced Bishop dead.

Thomas immediately left for Philadelphia to break the news to Bishop's family.

The following morning Bishop's wife went to Hawkes Funeral Parlour on Sixth Avenue. After viewing her husband through the glass-topped casket, Mrs. Bishop asked that his hair be combed.

As the nervous desairologist stroked the dead man's hair, the comb dropped from his hands and seemed to disappear. It had fallen into the empty brain cavity, which had been opened by an unauthorized autopsy. It was not until this horrible moment that Mrs. Bishop realized an autopsy had been performed. Washington Irving Bishop always carried a note, which he called a "life guard," explaining his cataleptic condition and prohibiting autopsy or the application of ice or electrodes to his body. The papers also left the address of family and lawyers to be alerted if Bishop fell into a trance. *The document was never found.*

Mrs. Bishop began screaming, "They have killed my husband, they've killed him. He was murdered by those doctors . . . to get at his brain."

Why, dear reader, you may ask, would men of science wish to steal the used cerebral cortex of a mere "variety artiste"?

One possibility is that Bishop himself often spoke of having a brain unlike that of other humans. Dr. Irwin's major defense in the hearing which followed was the mind reader's constant talk about an autopsy which might reveal the explanation for his marvelous powers. Bishop had excited the medical world with demonstrations like the following:

On March 6, 1887, two years before Bishop's demise, a committee of men led by New York *World* reporter Henry Guy Carleton (a well-known literary figure who had authored a humorous and damaging exposure of Bishop's act in his newspaper) left the Hoffman House on Twenty-fifth Street carrying an expensive pin loaned for the demonstration by Mrs. Frank Leslie. A short time later, the committee returned, having hidden the pin within a one-mile radius of the hotel.

Washington Irving Bishop was blindfolded with cotton batting, a heavy handkerchief, and a black cloth bag that tied under his neck.

Wrapped around his wrist was a length of number 18 copper wire, which in turn was wrapped around the wrists of three committee men. Bishop was led to the driver's seat of an open horse-drawn wagon. One of the men sat beside Bishop, two behind him. The mind reader asked the men to concentrate on the location of the pin and to hold their hands near his head for a moment. Suddenly the horses bolted, perhaps uneasy because of the large crowd which had gathered in front of the hotel. Bishop gained control of the animals and started out again, this time crossing Broadway.

A second carriage with members of the press, and two others with observers, followed. According to the New York *Sun*, "a crowd of five hundred, including a group of able-bodied and well dressed and apparently normal men, joined in the mob of bootblacks and newsboys which swarmed after him."

The black-hooded figure and his entourage passed the east side of Madison Square to Twenty-third Street. At Fourth Avenue and Eighteenth Street they narrowly escaped a collision with another carriage as Bishop drove close to the curb. The mind reader quickly turned into Eighteenth Street, then onto Irving Place and into Gramercy Park. There, "one well-dressed man, being knocked down by a carriage which was following in the mindreader's wake, jumped up cheerily and limped along with the procession with unabated enthusiasm."

Suddenly stopping the wagon, Bishop disembarked and ran, the committee barely able to keep pace with him, to the Gramercy Park Hotel. In the main reception room, near exhaustion, Bishop stopped in front of a bronze statue on a mantel. Gesturing to the committee to lift the object, he grabbed Mrs. Leslie's pin, which rested beneath the bronze. His blindfold was removed and his pulse rate taken—it was beating at 152 counts to the minute.

Carrying the pin triumphantly, he returned to the Hoffman House accompanied by a cheering crowd.

These and other miraculous stunts promoted the theory that Bishop's brain may have been wonderfully abnormal.

Mrs. Bishop was convinced her husband's missing brain had been stolen in the name of science. Screaming for revenge, she applied for satisfaction at the Lambs and Dr. Irwin's office. Eventually she was calmed and returned to her hotel, the Hoffman House, site of Bishop's earlier triumph.

The tirades issued by the wife were calm, rational, and dignified, compared to those shouted by the mother of the deceased, Eleanor Fletcher Bishop.

Eleanor, for years a controversial figure, now jumped to the forefront in the perverse tale of her son's death. She, too, claimed the doctors had killed her son and stolen his brain.

A FEW
WORDS
ABOUT
DEATH
AND
SHOW BIZ

161

Eleanor embraces her dead son.
Notice the autopsy line visible on his forehead.

She demanded and received a coroner's inquest, which commenced on May 24, 1889. In the days before the inquest Eleanor regaled the press with stories of her own cataleptic tendencies, pleas for more humane treatment of persons only presumed dead, and anecdotes about herself and her son. She tried to persuade the undertaker to chisel her son's gravestone with the words, "Born May 4, 1856—*Murdered* May 13, 1889."

She had a plaster bust made of her dead son, saying, "I want something I can throw my arms around." A few days later she returned to the funeral parlor and tried to prop up her son and embrace his neck. Dissuaded from this notion, she succeeded in having the coffin tilted, and herself photographed with her hand around the casket looking lovingly at her son's face.

In preparation for the inquest, Dr. Irwin, along with Doctors Ferguson, Lee, and Hance, who performed and witnessed the autopsy, were arrested and released on $2,000 bail.

A second autopsy was performed by assistant coroner Jenkins on May 18. Bishop's brain was found—not in the apartment of some pilfering physician, but inside his chest cavity, where it had been placed. Nothing new was determined regarding the cause of death, or the source of his unusual talent.

Finally, after repeated pleas to bury Bishop, Eleanor consented and her son was put to rest at Green Wood Cemetery on May 20. He was placed in the family plot, which contained twenty-eight bodies, many of unknown Civil War victims which Eleanor had generously sheltered.

Although the large gathering of notables expected did not materialize at the cemetery, the bizarre histrionics continued. Bishop's wife and mother appeared with different attorneys (no doubt because Eleanor was now claiming her son's marriage to be illegal). As Bishop's

A youthful Washington Irving Bishop.

body was lowered, the New York *Star* reported, "the poor mother threw herself upon her knees, and clasping the casket in her arms, cried out piteously against the injustice done her boy. She kissed the coffin several times and only by main force [was] induced to allow the work to proceed." This was not particularly unusual behavior for Eleanor. At the funeral of her husband in 1874, she actually threw herself into the grave after the coffin was lowered.

At the inquest, Eleanor and friends of the family attested to Bishop's being pronounced dead on other occasions. Dr. Edwin Biggs delivered powerful testimony. In 1873 Bishop lay lifeless in a trance. Doctors Ford and Leech, seeing no pulsation, no respiration, "no indication of life whatsoever," pronounced him dead. Knowing Bishop's "predisposition to these trances," Biggs refused to give up hope. "There were no other reasons," he said. "He was dead to every appearance, and to every test made." Suddenly, twelve hours later, Bishop awoke with a start. "I gave him some tincture of ammonia and at the end of forty minutes he was apparently none the worse for the attack."

A FEW
WORDS
ABOUT
DEATH
AND
SHOW BIZ

163

Madame M. A. Swett testified to a similar attack and recovery. Miss Irene Orme Jones told of an event in Cincinnati during which two doctors pronounced Bishop dead. Another time, in Boston, a Dr. Kane declared him dead. "With my handkerchief," Miss Jones said, "I closed his mouth and I also crossed his hands, I at the time sharing the belief of the physician." Upon his recovery Bishop told her, ironically, the papers had cut him up, "but the physicians never would."

George Francis Train, a wealthy and flamboyant controversialist who was often seen in patent leather boots and lavender kid gloves, and was called New York's "best known eccentric," interrupted the proceedings. He told the court he had lost twenty-eight pounds by fasting in sympathy for the Bishop family, whom he represented. Train had appeared in an unofficial capacity earlier, displaying proudly the plaster cast of Bishop. On this occasion, asked to testify, he rushed comically to the stand and looking directly at the lawyers and newspaper reporters, said in a very loud voice, "I want to know if I am to be paid for my daily attendance here. I have distributed flowers and dispensed cologne with the purpose of making things as pleasant as possible."

The coroner reproached Train, and advised him to address his remarks to the court. "I will," he said, and again gesturing to the lawyers, added, "I am not stuck on that crowd."

Eleanor Fletcher Bishop related the story of her son's supposed death in Malta to a New York *Herald* reporter. "Several years ago, a short time before the Tay disaster when he was utterly prostrated by the work of saving a number of lives, he was in a trance for three weeks. But the Scottish surgeons were more merciful than these—they spared him."

Dr. E. C. Spitzka, considered the leading authority on catalepsy, testified that there were no positive signs of death. He told of numerous instances of premature burial and of cataleptics who suddenly came back to life.

Section 309 of the New York Penal Code reads, "A person who makes or causes or procures to be made any dissection of the body of a human being, except by authority of law, or in the pursuance of a permission given by the deceased, is guilty of a misdemeanor." Since Bishop's autopsy was performed within twenty-four hours of his death, only the coroner or Bishop's mother or wife could have given permission for the act.

The jury, imaginatively composed "chiefly of dry goods men and jewelers," returned a verdict of not guilty for all the doctors. A mild censure was given to Dr. Irwin for his haste in performing the autopsy.

Outraged, Bishop's mother sought revenge. She spoke to any person or group that would hear her story. From the Manhattan Liberal Club, at the request of Vice President Joseph Rinn (the noted psychic investigator and long-time friend of Houdini) she raised enough money to publish a monograph. Proceeds from this work, she hoped, would help her financial plight. When she attended to her son's funeral in New York, she said her home in Philadelphia was robbed of $30,000. She was forced to give up the house and was now penniless and alone.

The book, surely one of the strangest ever written, is a slim octavo of red cloth, stamped in gold:

HUMAN VIVISECTION OF
SIR WASHINGTON IRVING BISHOP
THE FIRST AND WORLD-EMINENT
MIND-READER

The title page reads:

*A mother's life dedicated and an appeal for Justice
to all Brother Masons and the generous public.
A synopsis of the Butchery of the late
Sir Washington Irving Bishop (Kamilimilianalani)
a most worthy Mason of the thirty-second degree,
the mind reader and philanthropist by
Eleanor Fletcher Bishop, his Broken Hearted Mother.
Philadelphia, 1889.*

The few copies examined of this now rare book contain only three photographs numbered, perhaps not strangely, 21, 22, and 23. The first is a standard portrait of Bishop at 21 years old, the second of a hirsute Bishop at 33, his suit bedizened by peculiar ornaments and medals, and the last, the funeral-parlor picture of Bishop in casket embraced by his mother, the autopsy line clearly visible on her son's forehead.

In addition to Bishop's story, the book related other cases of supposed premature burial, a very real concern in the Victorian era. As foreign as this excursion may seem, peer with me into the caskets of another time:

Baron Larry, a doctor demonstrating to students "how muscular contraction can be produced in a corpse," plunged his knife into the breast of a supposed cadaver, only to have the patient sit up, open its eyes, and groan.

Cardinal Espinosa, the prime minister to Philip II of Spain, was cut in preparation for embalming. He sat up and "grabbed the knife of his startled dissector before finally expiring."

Count Karnice-Karnicki, a doctor of law and chamberlain to the czar of Russia, attended the burial of a young Belgian girl who came alive when the first shovelful of earth was thrown on her coffin. Haunted by the girl's screams, and to prevent the repetition of such a tragedy, he invented a device similar to many patented in the period: a long tube extending six feet above ground and three and one-half inches wide was placed in the coffin. The tube led to a hermetically sealed box which could not be opened from the outside. Inside the coffin a glass ball several inches in diameter was attached to a spring which connected through the tube to the box above ground. The ball was placed on the deceased's chest. The slightest breath or movement

A FEW
WORDS
ABOUT
DEATH
AND
SHOW BIZ

165

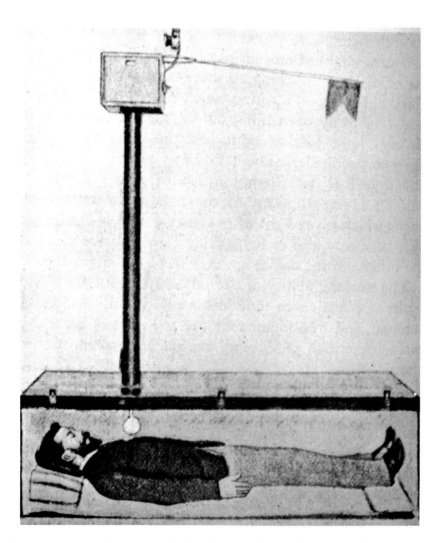

An invention from Premature Burial, How It May Be Prevented, *London, 1905.*

would release the spring, admitting light and air to the coffin. At the same time a flag would extend four feet from the outside box, and a bell would ring for thirty minutes. The tube was built to amplify any sound coming from the coffin, and an electric light was ignited in the casket below. Such were the fears and concerns of the nineteenth-century populace.

Eleanor Bishop's relentless pressure forced New York District Attorney Delancy Nicoll to review the case. In June 1889, Irwin, Ferguson, and Hance were indicted to stand trial by grand jury.

In September of 1889, before the trial, Dr. Ferguson again made headlines. The New York *World* reported that he "made an autopsy before the arrival of the coroner," upon the body of young Frederick Doty, who was found apparently dead in a cab as the result of a fall while intoxicated. Doctor Ferguson was reported admitting that he had no actual authority for his action, but made the autopsy to "satisfy himself that Doty was dead." The *World*, outraged, labeled Ferguson a "lightning autopsist" and a "sort of scientific Jack the Ripper," an epithet quickly adopted by Eleanor Bishop.

Dr. Irwin's trial began three years later on June 28, 1892. The jury was unable to reach a verdict, nine members voting for conviction, three for acquittal. Irwin was set free. The following year the charges against Hance and Ferguson were also dropped.

If premature burial was a concern of the times, so too was Spiritualism. A quasi-religion founded in 1848, it was originally based on the strange rapping noises produced by the so-called mediumship of Kate and Margaret Fox, young daughters of a New York State farmer. The raps were interpreted to suggest that spirits, dear departed souls who had shuffled off to the astral equivalent of Buffalo, were trying to communicate with loved ones left behind.

Eventually the Fox sisters confessed their fraud and demonstrated how they were able to produce rapping noises, loud enough to fill a large theater, by merely cracking their toes with no perceptible movement.

Their confession, however, was ignored and Spiritualism grew. It attracted philosophers, scientists, and millions of devotees who attended séances searching for supposedly psychic phenomena to justify their belief in the hereafter.

Eleanor Bishop was a practicing medium; her husband, Nathaniel Bishop, was a Spiritualist. Their son was raised in that philosophy.

Throughout her life Eleanor laid claim to enormous wealth and high position. She was neither rich nor regal. She dropped names like

An artist's representation of a typical Victorian séance from
Harper's Weekly, *December 30, 1871.*

rain; not the least of which was her son's. She claimed that Washington Irving, the author, was the boy's namesake. There is no evidence to support her statement, and it is likely her son's given name was Wellington, not Washington Irving.

Eleanor was an unimportant actress and opera singer; Nathaniel has been described both as a hard-drinking ne'er-do-well and as a wealthy and important lawyer. Eleanor tried to divorce Nathaniel in 1867, claiming her husband attempted to murder her. Although they had been separated for seven years, she caused the aforementioned furor at Nathaniel's funeral in 1874. Two days after the interment she demanded the body of her husband exhumed, claiming he had been poisoned by unnamed people who had also taken property which legally belonged to her (a recurrent theme in Eleanor's life). The examination of the body showed no such evidence. The bill for exhumation and reburial was never paid.

Young Bishop grew up with his mother in New York and Philadelphia and was present while she conducted séances. Her most distinguished sitter was Cornelius Vanderbilt, who, it is said, wanted tips on the stock market rather than conversation with departed relatives who had bored him unmercifully in life.

After Vanderbilt's death, relatives contested the will, claiming the commodore was under the influence of Mrs. Bishop (to this author, at least, *certain* proof of an unsound mind). Eleanor appeared at the hearings, which resulted in a redistribution of the family fortune.

However peculiar were the early actions of Eleanor Fletcher Bishop, in the years after the death of her son she became truly mad.

In 1907 she married Count Lucas Langdon Nicholas, a Russian nobleman and grandson of Czar Nicholas. She moved into his baronial home in Montpelier, Vermont. Soon, to the chagrin of every society mother, the count left Eleanor and ran away with the maid. Shortly thereafter, a gang of roughs in her husband's employ, said Eleanor, ransacked her house "like murderous Indians." They destroyed the house and left Eleanor "lame, bruised, half-blind and ruptured." She was found, she said, in the snow, homeless and penniless. She began to plead for justice and remuneration, claiming to be the cousin of the late prime minister of England William Gladstone. She was also a friend, she insisted, of Abraham Lincoln, who, along with the New York *Herald*, dubbed her the "Florence Nightingale of America" for her help to soldiers during the Civil War.

She raved that Presidents William McKinley and Theodore Roosevelt had agreed to aid her recover lost monies. Carlos Butterfield, she said, became her adopted half-brother when she saved him from suicide. In return, Eleanor believed she was to be the recipient of a $24-million claim against the government of Mexico. President Wilson, she assured friends, had demanded Mexico pay her claim, with interest.

Eleanor recounted how she saved boatloads of British subjects in a mid-ocean tragedy by the use of her psychic powers. She received a priceless string of pearls from the wife of Arctic explorer Sir John Franklin for her help in yet another boat rescue. From another adopted son she expected an interest in a Salt Lake City gold mine.

She called herself Countess Lucas Langdon Nicholas, but insisted her relatives set fire to her home and poisoned her water.

Harry Houdini came to her aid. He sent her money (she insisted it was a loan) and received in return much of Washington Bishop's memorabilia for his enormous collection. But even Houdini was unable to keep up with Eleanor's more and more frequent rantings and pleas for money.

When Eleanor, perhaps mercifully, died in January 1918, Houdini learned he was to be beneficiary of her non-existent $30-million estate.

Although later events would strengthen the theory linking mental imbalance to heredity, Bishop's early life seemed normal enough. He was an uninspired student at St. John's College and later, equally restless as an employee of Hudnut's Drugstore.

It was not until he joined the troupe of stage medium Anna Eva Fay that his spirit ascended.

A FEW
WORDS
ABOUT
DEATH
AND
SHOW BIZ

169

Miss Fay, called the "Indescribable Phenomenon," was a small-town Ohio schoolgirl who became the leading psychic performer in America. "There is no living person who has created such a furor in the Spiritualistic world," said magician and author H. J. Burlingame in 1891. "A slender, almost fragile creature, grey eyes, flaxen hair, always richly dressed, and with a score of rings set with glittering diamonds, she invariably has made a most bewildering sensation. No woman ever trod the stage who possessed more confidence in herself and her language, than this little, vivacious, almost enchanting personage."

Bishop worked for Fay and eventually became her manager. Over and over he witnessed her perform her most famous effect, the cotton-bandage test. She was firmly tied, hands behind her back, to a wooden post. Another piece of bandage was tied around her neck and fastened to the post. Her feet were similarly bound. A curtain was drawn, concealing her from the audience, and "manifestations" commenced. Tambourines and guitars played, glasses of water were drunk, bells rang, buckets moved. When the curtain was opened, Fay was seen motionless in the same bound position. The knots were checked and found intact by the same audience committee that had tied her. Even with a volunteer placed beside her the phenomena continued.

In April 1876 a complete exposure of Fay's act appeared anonymously in the New York *Daily Graphic*. On May 18 of the same year, Washington Irving Bishop made his debut as a performer at Chickering Hall in New York. Not only did he duplicate the stunts of Anna Eva Fay, he exposed them. It was Bishop who wrote the unsigned article in the *Graphic*.

He felt justified in these actions, he claimed, to warn the public of the evils of fraudulent Spiritualism. He later concocted the story that he was urged to join Fay's troupe and gain evidence for his exposure by a former surgeon general of the United States, William A. Hammond. Ironically, his mother was conducting séances during the period he was exposing them.

Even if Bishop's motives were suspect, his success was not. The hall was packed, the New York papers were filled with praise. Typical was the New York *Evening Post*, which stated, "One of the most remarkable entertainments ever given in this city took place last evening in Chickering Hall. . . . The whole entertainment was in the highest degree satisfactory. Mr. Bishop's manner of performing the tricks he undertakes is far superior to any professional 'medium' who has performed in New York within our recollection."

He did Fay's cotton-bandage test in full view of the audience. He showed how he was able to tie a ring placed in his mouth onto a cord suspended from his neck, even though his hands were tied behind

Fourteenth Street Theatre.

WEEK COMMENCING Monday, March 12th.

Special Matinee on Friday and Saturday at 2:30 for
Ladies Only. No Gentleman Admitted.
Matinee on Sunday at 3:00 for Everyone.

Evening Prices, 25c & 50c. Matinee Prices, all Seats 25c.

ANNA EVA FAY.

◄ PROGRAMME. ►

SPECIAL NOTICE.
Read carefully. Everything done is the result of natural causes.

SPECIAL EXPLANATION TO THE PUBLIC.
MISS FAY wishes it distinctly understood that the results produced,
especially in the "Somnolency" and "Materialization," are wierd and bewildering, but the forces and means employed, although at present not
thoroughly understood by the mass of people, are perfectly natural, and may,
at some future day, be utilized by scientific workers.

PART FIRST,
**Anna Eva Fay will introduce many Novel Features in her peculiar line of
☙ Cabinet Experiments. ❧**

MISS FAY having appeared for nine consecutive months at the Queen's
Concert Rooms, London, and later for three weeks at the Crystal Palace.
For three months Miss Fay was the guests of Prof. Wm. Crooks, F. R. S.,
No. 20 Mornington Road, W. C. During that time Prof. Crooks built the
Galvanometer, an electrical machine to test physical demonstration.

During Parts First and Third, in which Miss Fay appears, and during which she is at such
a high mental strain, it is necessary for her to have a complete release from the same some-
time during the performance, consequently the following will be introduced in

PART SECOND.

MR. WETHEREL RHOADS'
ROYAL ENGLISH MANNIKINS
Harry D'Esta, Wm. W. Rhoads, L'Mai D'Esta, Manipulators.

No intermission between Part Second and
PART THIRD.

The entertainment will close by placing Miss Fay in a Hypnotic Condition and she will
give her weird and startling vistons of what she sees and hears in Hypnotic Dreamland by

"SOMNOLENCY."

SPECIAL NOTICE—Miss Fay receives hundreds of letters and is obliged to employ two
secretaries to assist in her correspondence. Letters regarding "Somnolency" will not be
answered unless they contain an envelope properly addressed and stamped for the reply; even
then no reply will be sent to letters deemed silly or unimportant. Even when the above conditions are complied with it may be several days before a reply can be sent. Don't write
unless it is important. Letters are answered as a matter of courtesy. Send all communications
to the PLANTER'S HOTEL. No one received in person at the hotel.

MISS FAY "DREAM BOOK"

In the hands of the publisher now, is a book that Miss Fay has
compiled from years of experience interpreting all dreams, which are
alphabetically arranged, with full directions as to how to put yourself
in a somnambulist state to receive the benefit of your living nights.

BYRON'S QUOTATION.
"WE LIVE BY NIGHT, AND NOT BY DAY."

When you write your letter to Miss Fay to the Planter's Hotel,
enclose twentyfive cents for one of these books.

C. Schreiner Printing Co., 810-12 N. 15th St.

A later playbill of Anna Eva Fay.

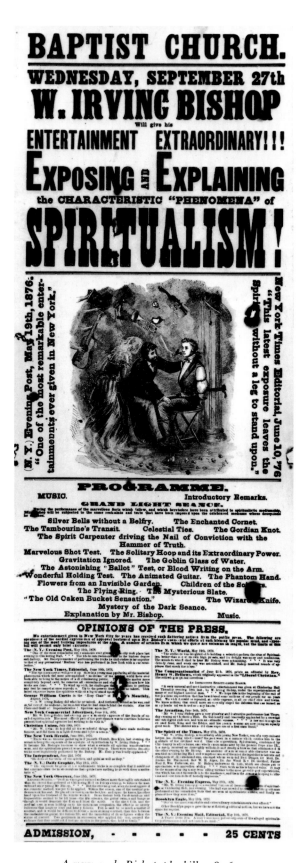

A very early Bishop playbill, 1876.

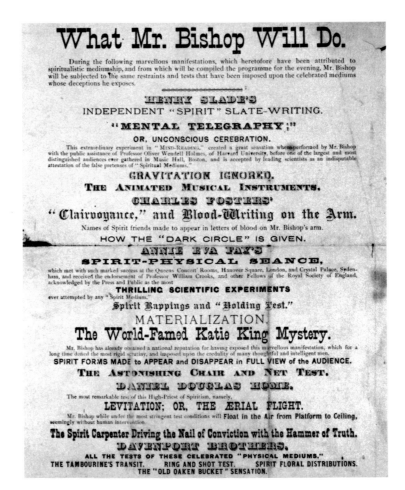

*Bishop takes on Anna Eva Fay, Daniel Dunglas Home,
and the Davenport Brothers. From a program, circa 1877.*

him. Using physical movements which even the *British Medical Journal* classified as abnormal, Bishop showed how by throwing out his shoulder blade, he was able to move his arm farther up his back than was thought humanly possible. Twisting his left hand around the post to which he was tied, he managed to reach his mouth and thread the ring on the cord necklace. It was an exhausting effort which never failed to win the approval of the audience.

Bishop also exposed supposedly "clairvoyant" demonstrations of Fay, as well as the methods of other mediums, either nationally famous or local pretenders, in the cities that he played. He even exposed the acclaimed "second sight" act of magician Robert Heller. He wrote a four-part article for *Leisure Hour* magazine in which he showed the workings of the séance room and gave advice for a more rational approach to examining supposed "phenomena." He elicited the thanks and support of scientists who would later fight Bishop's own claims of paranormal ability.

A FEW
WORDS
ABOUT
DEATH
AND
SHOW BIZ

173

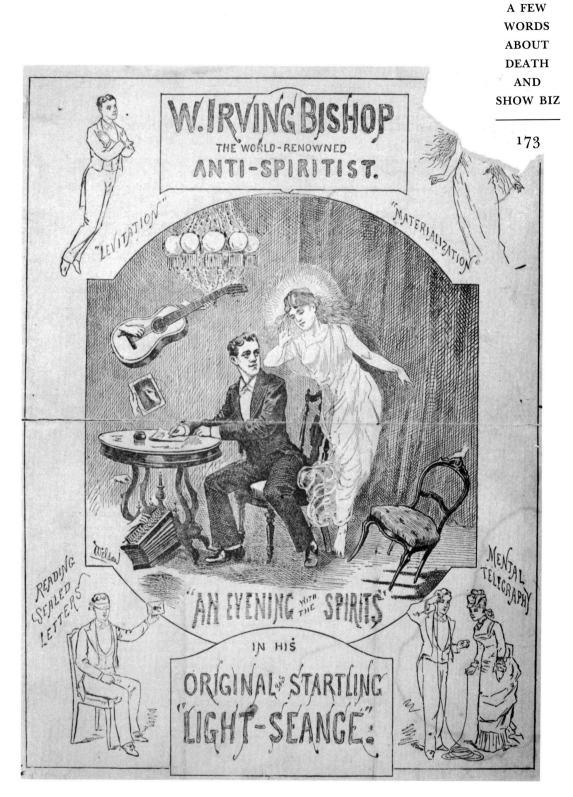

The back cover of the Bishop program on page 172.

The famous American humorist Josh Billings (Henry W. Shaw) praised Bishop's work in a typically amusing style:

Bishop mi Dear,
    I regret (i may say that I fairly mourn) that I kant be present to witness yure expozure ov spiritualism in St. James Hall, London. Altho not present in the flesh (mi aktual weight iz 186 pounds) in spirit i shall be thare, (mi spirit, on this particular matter weights 642 pounds) the whole ov which you are welkum to. Thar are a fu spiritualists who i pitty, theze are the phools—thar are a greater number whom i dispize, theze are the frauds, and ded beats ov the profeshion—Enny man who kan bring a kounterfitter to justice. Enny man who kan beat a Thimble Rigger at his own game, Enny man who can probe a *Three kard monte wretch*, and dispoil him ov his little joker, i look upon az a child of genius, at work in the vineyard of truth, and morality. The only spiritualism that haz suckceeded yet iz the kind that haz got the most fraud in it.

> Good bye Bishop
> Yures unto deth
> Josh Billings

It was the exposure of a professional's act that launched his career, and the duplication of another's that won him fame.

Bishop, the "First and World-Eminent Mind-Reader," actually learned his craft from watching J. Randall Brown, who developed the modern thought reading act in the 1870's.

Jacob Randall Brown, the son of a prosperous miller, was born in St. Louis on October 28, 1851. He claimed to discover the "gifts" which were to form the basis of his act while playing hide-and-go-seek as a schoolboy.

Brown moved north in 1872 and landed a job as a reporter on the Chicago *Inter-Ocean*. An assignment covering séances for his paper led to demonstrations of his own talents for fellow reporters. While Brown was chaperoned outside, a reporter chose one of a group of sixteen identical vials. Brown returned blindfolded. He took the right hand of the participating reporter and placed it to his forehead. Without any verbal communication he identified the chosen bottle. Using the same method he located a penny hidden on an empty chair, and with children's alphabet blocks spelled out a word thought of by a volunteer. On the advice of Frank Palmer, his managing editor, Brown demonstrated his skills at Rush Medical College. The positive publicity he obtained from that performance led to local engagements and, soon thereafter, a professional career.

A FEW
WORDS
ABOUT
DEATH
AND
SHOW BIZ

———

175

Dr. George Beard first saw Brown at Sturtevant House in New York in July of 1874. Brown was causing a sensation with his demonstrations of "mindreading." Said Beard, "For weeks this young and unknown adventurer, without education, without a history, held the American people by the nape of the neck, controlling the press as absolutely as a Napoleon or a Czar." Dr. Beard coined the term "muscle reading" to explain the methods of Brown and others who later performed similar stunts.

In subsequent articles in the *Detroit Lancet* and *Popular Science Monthly*, and a monograph entitled *The Study of Trance, Muscle Reading and Allied Nervous Phenomena*, Beard outlined the physiological princi-

*J. Randall Brown
on the cover of*
The Art of
Mind Reading.

ples used by Brown: "The power of detecting, through physical contact, very slight and delicate muscular tensions and relaxations that result from the unconscious action of mind or body."

The concept of involuntary muscular response had already been suggested by scientists like Michael Faraday to account for table-tipping and other supposedly spiritualistic séance phenomena. Brown's tests, however, were more interesting to scientists because no apparatus was involved.

Brown was tested by the faculty of Yale University in October 1874, and thereafter numerous doctors and psychologists (such as

A blindfolded Brown chooses letter cards.
From The Art of Mind Reading.

Jastrow and Dessoir), and societies for psychic research, investigated the mind reader's techniques.

Beard said that in spite of his "adulteration with charlatanism," Brown was "of immortal service to psychology."

As the investigations and exposures of Brown did not denigrate his skill, and as he received tremendous publicity, his career flourished.

Bishop, whose performing career did not begin until 1876, never included "contact" or "muscle reading" stunts until after he saw Brown at Chickering Hall in 1877.

According to unpublished records of C. A. George Newmann, an important mind reader and historian who knew Brown in his later years, Bishop and Brown became friends. Although Bishop never worked for Brown, he did learn the contact technique from him and in return showed Brown some new mediumistic stunts. These séance effects were added to Brown's show, for the most part performed by his wife, Lillie May, who appeared on the bill as a medium, doing the cotton-bandage test and similar stunts.

Brown was described as an attractive man of medium height, slender, and with large, expressive, hard eyes. He had long, nut-brown hair, which occasionally was tied back with ribbon.

Brown's career was not without controversy. The magic press was annoyed when Brown called himself "The White Mahatma," a title then used by Samri S. Baldwin, a clever and inventive performer. Baldwin, who also did contact mind reading in the 1880's, may have been the first performer to do a stage escape from handcuffs, and he developed the modern "question answering act" based on an important method of gathering information to feign clairvoyant powers. Baldwin countered by calling himself "The *Original* and *Only Real* White Mahatma."

On June 10, 1889, the New York *Herald* reported that Brown had done an impressive test the previous evening at the Bijou Theater. A wire was stretched between the mind reader at the theater and the Western Union telegraph office some blocks away. There, a Professor Cromwell held the wire to his head and thought of a number. Brown, holding the other end of the wire at the Bijou, correctly announced the number: 742.

Brown had done a similar stunt for the Yale professors many years earlier. The results of the Cromwell test would have successfully rebuffed Dr. Beard's hypothesis of muscle reading, but the wire test was suspect, it being thought that a confederate was employed.

A FEW
WORDS
ABOUT
DEATH
AND
SHOW BIZ

———

177

Samri S. Baldwin, "The Original *and* Only Real *White Mahatma."*

*Baldwin's wife, Kitty, was sometimes billed as
"The Rosicrucian Somnambumancist."*

After a temporary retirement due to the physical demands of his profession and the inability to secure lucrative engagements, Brown in 1886 again found success. He performed in Europe, India, the Orient, and Australia. In 1902 he used the billing "The great, the only, the original white Mahatma." He invented not only the technique, but many of the presentations used by Bishop and other mind readers. Apparently, however, he never had the showman's flair or the histrionics, real or contrived, that made people talk about Bishop.

Brown's final days were spent in his home in Minneapolis. He died at St. Mary's Hospital on July 4, 1926, at the age of 72. His last words were "Take me out of here!"

By the end of 1877 Bishop had successfully added contact mind reading to his act. He realized that by going to Europe he would avoid comparison with Brown, and indeed, steal his thunder. Calling himself the "World's First Mind Reader," he entered Great Britain as a lion. He was to leave much less nobly.

Scientists, doctors, and psychic investigators in England and Scotland were fascinated by Bishop's prowess. He received from the press much the same attention accorded to Brown in the States.

Bishop managed to convince many people that he was a man of means who merely demonstrated his abilities to a curious public in the aid of science.

A *Daily News* correspondent, in describing Bishop's mind reading, reported on May 11, 1881, "It is fair to say Mr. Bishop appears to be a perfectly disinterested person. He is not seeking to make money by his discovery."

Bishop fueled the "independently wealthy" image by accepting shows (or wagers to test his ability), with the proceeds—less expenses, of course—going to charity. On one occasion, proudly mentioned by Mrs. Bishop in her monograph, her son performed for the Victoria Children's Hospital in Chelsea. Two letters from W. C. Blount, secretary of the hospital, profusely thank Bishop for his offer of "the entire proceeds" of his show at St. James Hall, June 2, 1883.

A FEW
WORDS
ABOUT
DEATH
AND
SHOW BIZ

179

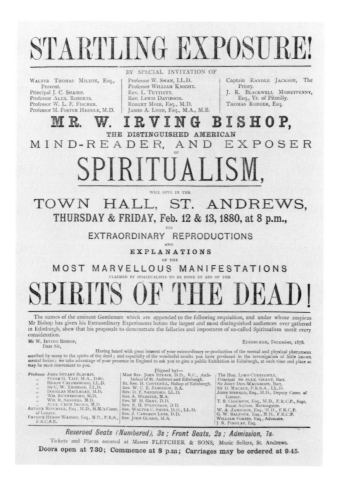

Program of Bishop in Scotland, 1880.

According to J. N. Maskelyne (the most well-known and well-respected magician of the period), the hall was packed and about £300 collected. The mind reader presented Mr. Blount with a check for *net* profits amounting to less than £19. Bishop's generosity was refused by the hospital.

Bishop impressed well-known scientists Dr. Carpenter and Professor Huxley with his demonstrations (although Huxley later claimed a letter praising Bishop was not written by him). Professor E. Ray Lankester and other notables witnessed the mind reader at the home of C. A. Drake in London, May 1881. Bishop located a small box in his usual style, charging through rooms, upsetting furniture, "in the manner of a dog chasing a cat." Other tests were less successful, but he impressively responded to a challenge by Lankester. The professor told Bishop he was suffering from a pain, and asked the performer to locate it. Bishop indicated a spot on Lankester's cheek corresponding to the location of the professor's toothache.

In a May 14 article on thought reading a *Daily Telegraph* reporter called Bishop a new Katterfelto (comparing him to the famous eighteenth-century quack magician). Claiming Carpenter and Huxley "decidedly premature" in their rather credulous certification, the reporter was not convinced mind reading was possible, but he amusingly shuddered at the thought. "With Mr. Bishop's art extended we should all have windows in our breasts and spies could peep into our opened hearts. Whist would receive its death blow and poker, one of the best round games invented, would be simply impossible."

Lankester, who had earlier exposed the well-known medium Henry Slade, was also unconvinced. Articles in the prestigious journals *Lancet* and *Nature* (much like Beard's findings in America) explained Bishop's methods as dependent on involuntary muscular response.

Bishop retaliated by performing tests which involved no contact. His helper would extend one hand at waist level, the other just below the shoulder. Bishop would place his right hand between (but not touching) the helper's hands, and successfully complete his demonstrations.

The premier issue of the *Proceedings of the Society for Psychic Research* discussed the Bishop methods. They felt results of the non-contact tests were not significant due to the proximity of performer and helper, and to Bishop's frenetic "wiggling" gestures throughout the experiments. In spite of the committee's skepticism, Bishop had, by physically removing himself from his assistant, opened an important door in the development of the thought reading demonstration.

One of the problems with Bishop's act, and indeed the idea of all such tests as theatrical entertainment, is the impossibility of guaranteed success.

It was Bishop's misfortune to have one of his least successful performances at London Polytechnic Institute in May of 1881. Among those in attendance was Henry de Pré Labouchère, a Member of Parliament and the owner and editor of the magazine *Truth*.

Chosen to sit with the committee on stage, Labouchère likened the experience to a minstrel show: "I felt like an Ethiopian serenader and expected every moment Mr. Edward (the chairman) to address me as 'Massa Bones' and propound a conundrum to me."

Labouchère was asked to concentrate on a word, which, in spite of the editor being dragged around the stage with Bishop "like two carriages attached to one engine," the mind reader was completely unable to discern.

A FEW
WORDS
ABOUT
DEATH
AND
SHOW BIZ

181

J. N. Maskelyne.

Calling him a clever conjurer who *sometimes* succeeds, Labouchère took Bishop to task in his journal, stating, "He can no more see what is passing in another person's mind . . . than I can."

In spite of frequent attacks, Bishop's fame and pocketbook flourished. In May of 1883, Labouchère issued a challenge. He wagered £1000 that Bishop would be unable to thought read the serial number of a bank note sealed in an envelope. Bishop accepted, knowing that *he* was to forfeit only £100 if unsuccessful. The performance was to benefit the Children's Hospital previously mentioned.

Bishop and Labouchère were unable to agree on an impartial helper for the test, and so the owner of *Truth* withdrew his challenge. Bishop, faced with a well-publicized event, proceeded with the show. After refusing the sealed bank note of Professor Lankester and others in the audience, Bishop took the hand of Colonel Stratham of the 20th Lancashire Rifle Volunteers. Asking the colonel to think of the numbers

Unthan, the Pedal Paganini. A one-sheet lithograph by Jesus Del Valle.

Original gouache self-portrait of Miss Biffin, done in 1842 with the brush held in her mouth, supported by her shoulder. The lithograph struck from this portrait is shown in the text in its various states.

A woodblock print showing the remarkable skills of Madame Hanakawa.

LES SERINS SAVANTS.

The escapades of trained canaries.

LE CHEVAL ARÉONAUTE

The ascension of Testu-Brissy with the aeronaut horse. The illustrations of the canaries and of Testu-Brissy are hand-colored engravings by Dugourc from Les Animaux Savants, *1816.*

Rithlow, the equestrian escape artist. A Friedlander one-sheet lithograph of 1908 notable for the peculiarity of language and the performance it represents.

A Courier one-half-sheet lithograph featuring the swinging horse from D. M. Bristol's Equescurriculum, 1888.

An early Friedlander lithograph (1880's) featuring the antics of a tightrope-walking mule named after Blondin, the first man to cross Niagara Falls on a high wire.

An Illinois Litho. Co. one-sheet poster of the Great Peters made a dozen years before he fell to his death in 1943.

A Seer's one-sheet lithograph designed by the famous poster artist Matt Morgan, signed by
Eleanor Fletcher Bishop (as Countess Nicholas) to Harry Houdini.

A Strobridge one-sheet lithograph for LaRoche, printed in America for the
Barnum & Bailey tour of France, 1902.

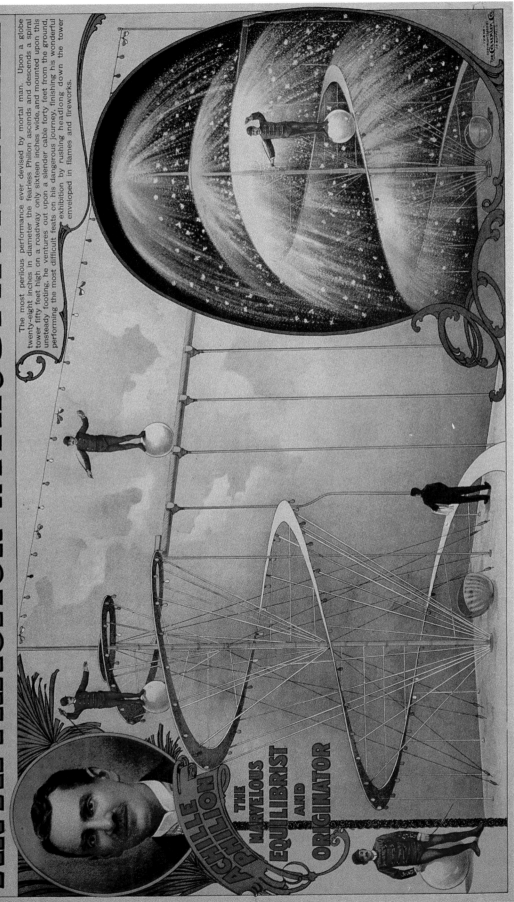

AN ATTRACTION WITHOUT A PARALLEL

The most perilous performance ever devised by mortal man. Upon a globe twenty-eight inches in diameter the fearless Philion ascends and descends a spiral tower fifty feet high on a roadway only sixteen inches wide, and mounted upon this unsteady footing, he ventures out upon a slender cable forty feet from the ground, performing the most difficult feats on his dangerous journey, finishing his wonderful exhibition by rushing headlong down the tower enveloped in flames and fireworks.

ACHILLE PHILION

THE MARVELOUS EQUILIBRIST AND ORIGINATOR

A Courier one-sheet lithograph featuring Philion's spiral ascent in 1899.

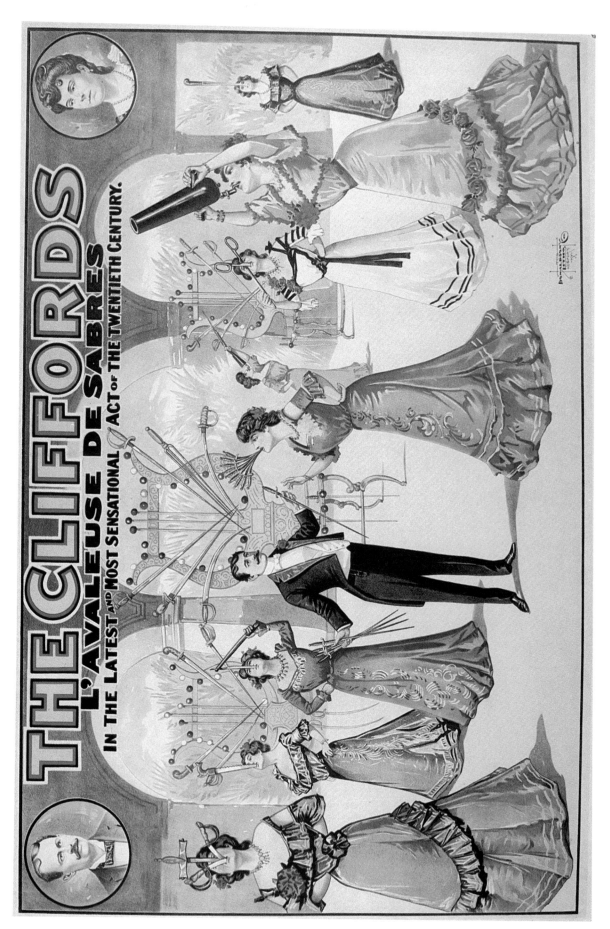

A one-sheet Donaldson lithograph featuring the remarkable Edith Clifford.

An early nineteenth-century Irish hand-colored caricature of the incombustible Signora Girardelli.
Strangely, it features her in two of Chabert's signature stunts: amidst a blaze of fireworks and in an oven.

Kar-mi, a three-sheet National lithograph portrait.

The Victorina troupe (relabeled Kar-mi) featuring the swallowing of an electric light bulb, which could be seen to shine through the body. A one-sheet Donaldson lithograph.

Hans Rohrl, the living hydrant. A Friedlander one-sheet lithograph of 1921.

The Human Aquarium at the Circus Busch, circa 1912.

on a bill supplied by Colonel Trench, Bishop proceeded to write figures, one at a time, on a large blackboard. He was successful. An enthusiastic audience cheered, and a balloon in front of the theater was sent skyward to signify victory.

Bishop took full credit for successfully completing the Labouchère test, even though the challenge had been withdrawn.

Bishop then published a fake issue of *Truth*, resembling the actual magazine in layout and typography (much like today's *Harvard Lampoon* parodies), to extol his virtues, and denounce Labouchère and magician J. N. Maskelyne. Bishop accused Maskelyne of collusion with Labouchère in a plot to discredit him. The magician, Bishop said, "I unqualifiedly stigmatize as a man devoid of honorable instincts . . . with the proofs of infamy in my possession I can hold John Nevil Maskelyne criminally liable and make justice punish him heavily for his villainous conduct. On the odium of public opinion do I crucify this villainous brace of scoundrels."

A FEW
WORDS
ABOUT
DEATH
AND
SHOW BIZ

———

183

*An early Maskelyne & Cooke playbill featuring
their version of the Davenports' stunt.*

Maskelyne was equal to Bishop's challenge. An experienced performer, court battler, and old hand at advertisement and promotion (twenty years earlier Maskelyne had launched his own career exposing the "spiritualistic" phenomena of the famous Davenport Brothers), Maskelyne sued Bishop for libel. The well-publicized case commenced in January 1885. Bishop did not even appear. The jury awarded Maskelyne £10,000 damages, in those days a staggering sum. He did not receive payment, as Bishop had left England, never to return.

On the Continent, Bishop drew packed houses, rave notices, and the attention of royalty. His shows were witnessed by the kings and queens of Romania, Greece, Sweden, and Norway. He was most successful in Russia, where he received the acclaim of Czar Alexander III and his wife, Maria Feodorovna.

Bishop, who was a master of adapting to new-performance situations, added to his repertoire: Having a famous painter concentrate on the features of a well-known individual, Bishop was able to draw a marvelous portrait of the thought-of subject. Both his mind reading skill and artistic talents received praise.

On another occasion Bishop was able to divine a musical composition thought of by the audience. Not only did he identify the piece, but he played it, apparently in commendable fashion, on the piano. (Bishop was also known to take credit for skilled composing ability, even though he had no specific training in music. In 1910, in the *Magician's Monthly*, Henry Byatt recalled how Bishop bought lyrics from one person, and music from another. Bishop told each collaborator he had written the other half. He apparently published a number of tunes this way.)

Bishop returned to America. After some initial setbacks, due most likely to management problems and the backlash of the Labouchère controversy, he again blazed forward as the result of his blindfold carriage drives.

Arriving triumphantly in Boston in November 1886, Bishop was soon to face the most serious exposure of his career.

On November 30, he appeared in what he claimed would be his "last performance prior to his retirement from public life." Among those in attendance was young Charles Howard Montague, an enthusiastic viewer of Bishop's private entertainments, and the city editor of the Boston *Globe*.

Freely admitting prejudice stemming from a pre-show rebuff by a typically nervous and insensitive Bishop, Montague still praised the performer, but took an impassioned interest in the discovery of his methods.

A FEW
WORDS
ABOUT
DEATH
AND
SHOW BIZ

185

In the eight days following the show, Montague attempted Bishop's experiments for some fifty of his friends. He was remarkably successful, and getting better, it seemed, with each new attempt.

On December 19, a long two-part article entitled "The Secret" appeared in the *Globe*. The preliminary report, by D. J. McGrath, told of a splendid performance by Montague for some twenty-five or so invited guests. Montague successfully located hidden pins and coins; he duplicated Bishop's "murder mystery" by identifying an assailant, a victim, and a murder weapon. He played note by note (but admittedly without the musical skills of Bishop) a song thought of by a young lady. He duplicated a geometric design drawn by one of the men, and was even able to locate objects by "non-contact" methods, although in close proximity to his helper.

Montague wrote the second part of the article. He praised but demystified Bishop's act: "Mr. Bishop would have us infer that he does not know how he does it. I know how I do it, and I am rather of the opinion that his self-consciousness is not a great way behind my own. It is very difficult for me to believe that so expert a student of the sensations of other people should be so poor a pupil in his own case."

Montague related the pattern of his experiments, the results, and his analysis of the techniques employed. He concluded that success was possible "very largely on interpreting the unconscious impulse of the subject to go toward the place where he has fixed his mind."

The December 21 issue of the *Globe* carried the headline BISHOP READS, NOT MINDS BUT THE GLOBE'S EXPOSE. In a long rebuttal, Bishop took Montague to task for not sharing his credit in performing such feats with "Almighty God." Calling the editor's witnesses "eager sympathizers," Bishop asserted "that Mr. Montague could not go before an audience of 3,000 strangers and do a single one of the things of which he tells."

As the debate in the newspapers continued, Montague countered Bishop by performing successfully for the Boston Press Club, the local Society for Psychic Research, and the Somerville Cycle Club.

Bishop, who was in Washington, D.C., during the Montague experiments, returned to Boston for an appearance at the Music Hall on January 4, 1887. Bishop confronted Montague, who was in the audience, and addressed him warmly. Perhaps the presence of his rival encouraged Bishop to do an unusually good show. He concluded his very successful performance with the difficult reenactment of a tableau. With Bishop in another room, three volunteers were asked to create a scene, with each person taking specific actions and positions on stage. The volunteers were then led back to their seats and Bishop returned to the auditorium. He quickly determined the participants and brought them back on stage. After many false starts, with Bishop growing increasingly frenetic, he placed two men on the floor, one supporting the other. The third man was placed standing up and holding the wrist of the man being helped on the ground. Bishop correctly announced the tableau as a doctor taking the pulse of a sick man being helped by a friend.

In the next day's paper Montague pronounced Bishop "an exceedingly clever and exceedingly interesting . . . remarkable man." Montague wasn't your ordinary meat-and-potatoes man himself. He successfully accepted some professional engagements, the most important at Dockstader's Theater in New York, while Bishop performed at nearby Wallack's. Montague's appearance, before thousands of strangers, was a complete success. The box office receipts were donated to charity.

Montague had no intention of abandoning his writing, and soon retired from the stage, having most emphatically "made his point." He received many letters unfavorable to Bishop. Magician Henry Hatton wrote to say Bishop was a fraud. He mentioned the articles on mind reading in *Truth* and *Popular Science* and discussed the prowess of Judge Blydenburg in similar tests.

Dr. J. J. Miller wrote to extol the virtues of Helen Knapp of Chautauqua County, New York, who he claimed did stunts like Bishop's years ago. John Babson, who had known the family since Bishop was a child, wrote an extremely damaging letter. He called Eleanor the "greatest *vixen* who ever made man's home a hell . . . [She] has been mixed up in more ridiculous and notorious affairs than any ten women you can name." Wellington (not "Washington," he emphatically stated) Irving Bishop was a "supreme fraud" who would benefit from "one or two good horsewhippings."

Montague tactfully never published these letters.

Although Bishop survived the Montague ordeal, his last few years were marred by family and personal problems.

Before the mind reader left Washington for his Boston date, Anna Eva Fay, the medium he exposed years before, told the papers, "I can read Bishop's thoughts. He is thinking of what that girl in Peoria will say when she finds out he has come back from Europe and married another girl."

In fact, Bishop had met the beautiful Helen (Mack) Loud, then the wife of millionaire Boston broker Thomas J. Loud, on the passage to Europe. In Scotland, even though both were married to other partners, they were wed in a civil ceremony.

Mrs. Loud secured a divorce from her husband. Bishop, it seems, did not mention his previous marriage to Helen. The first Mrs. Bishop took their infant daughter and successfully filed for divorce on grounds of desertion.

Bishop and Helen were officially united in Boston, where they took up residence in a fashionable home.

A FEW
WORDS
ABOUT
DEATH
AND
SHOW BIZ

187

In March of 1888, with Bishop still in the midst of the Montague upheaval, Helen made her way, or was abducted (the newspapers were unsure), to Detroit.

She wired Bishop, asking for a rendezvous in Buffalo or Albany, assuring she had "much to reveal."

Bishop responded by declaring Helen had deserted him while he was at death's door. A series of telegrams served only to further confuse events. Bishop thought his wife was insane, the victim of foul play, or under the control of Thomas J. Loud.

Helen, claiming that Bishop was a cocaine addict who beat her unmercifully while under the drug's influence, obtained a divorce on March 27, 1888.

A few days later Bishop remarried his first wife, and once again took to the road.

Obtaining release from the famous theatrical manager Charles Frohman, Bishop signed with the equally august M. B. Leavitt. He was booked into the Metropolitan Temple in San Francisco after a private engagement to create interest at the Palace Hotel. Bishop was very successful both in the Bay City and on a subsequent tour of the West Coast.

While Leavitt paved the way for a tour of Australia, Bishop, in the company of singer Harrison Millard, with whom he would share his show, left for Mexico City.

A well-received private showing for President Diaz, his wife, and local dignitaries led to successful engagements in Mexico City, Guadalajara, Guanajuato, and Vera Cruz.

Bishop was not so fortunate in Cuba. Appearing at the Tacón Theater in Havana, the mind reader was harassed by hecklers (who may have been sent by a jealous rival theater owner) and an unsympathetic audience. When Bishop presented his musical thought reading, the crowd became hostile. Why, they asked, was Bishop unable to play Cuban tunes instead of American or Italian themes? Bishop flatly refused audience intervention in his show. The theater censor ordered the curtain dropped and fined Bishop for failing to meet the terms of his advertisements. Characteristically, Bishop managed to get out of both the fine and Havana.

Bishop returned to the States via New Orleans in December. About this time a tongue-in-cheek article in the Chicago *Mail* told of Bishop joining forces with Mr. Yerkes, president of the city's street railway. The performer announced he would move to Chicago to assume the direction of the Yerkes Mind-Cure Institute. Bishop's main function was to provide a cure for "coldi-streeto-caribus" (i.e., cold streetcars). By the power of positive thinking and the creation of mental furnaces, Bishop was to insure more comfortable rides for the passengers from November to April. "When people enter a streetcar today," said the *Mail*, "they do so laboring under the fear that they may be frozen to death before they ride ten squares. Bishop, seated in the crematory (the engine room), exerts his will power—wills that the passengers shall be warm . . . his will power, being stronger than that of the passengers, triumphs."

Back in San Francisco, Bishop departed for the Leavitt tour of Australia. He never passed Hawaii. In Honolulu Bishop met and fell in love with Mabel Clifford Taber, a New Bedford girl who was visiting her uncle's sugar plantation. Mabel, dubbed Kapoauilani ("the flower of heaven") by King Kalakaua, was a great beauty and favorite of island society. Bishop took Mabel and returned to the States in preparation for yet another wedding.

As the reader may well imagine, the details of Bishop's private life, made more puzzling by contradictions in the contemporary press, leave many questions for researchers. One reason for the confusion is Bishop's almost certain involvement with drink and drugs. Harrison Millard, in an attempt to dispel the rumor that Bishop was a drunkard, reported to the New York *Herald*, "Bishop has often been accused of being addicted to alcoholic stimulants but such accusations are unjust, though not unfounded. I don't believe it was possible for any man to make him drunk." Millard related how Bishop was able to consume whole bottles of potables so strong one glass would send a normal man into an impromptu cakewalk.

He told of taking "tekila" with Bishop in Vera Cruz. "One glass was enough for me for the rest of my life, while Bishop took twelve glasses in my presence, at one sitting—and it hardly dazed him." Bishop, he said, "had no morbid appetite for liquors, whatever he might have for other exciting drugs."

Helen, it will be recalled, divorced Bishop citing cocaine abuse as a major cause. Leavitt, in his memoirs, spoke of a tour with large ticket sales, "but it made no difference," he stated, "how much money Bishop earned, his expenditures were in excess of his income, and as a consequence of this, he was always in my debt." While this may only pass as circumstantial evidence, the Chicago *Herald* was considerably more specific. In an article entitled "Bishop's Pet Tipple, Cognac and Absinthe His Disease," it was stated that Bishop was the victim of liquor and drug habits and almost constantly affected by their use. "When in California," it continued, "Bishop became violently insane from the use of alcohol, cocaine, and morphine, and he was confined for some time in an insane asylum near San Francisco." Although this is the only reference uncovered dealing with Bishop's asylum stay, it does not seem particularly farfetched.

Resiliently, Bishop was to bounce back from his troubles and enjoy success in St. Louis and Minneapolis (where he made front-page headlines by staying the execution of the Barrett Boys, railway employees convicted of murdering a passenger. Bishop delayed the verdict, attempting to discover the boys' guilt or innocence by his mind reading powers.)

After performing for the governor of Missouri, Bishop arrived in New York to work out details of a forthcoming tour with noted cornetist Jules Levy in May of 1889. His career was flourishing again when he arrived for his ill-fated evening at the Lambs Club on May 12.

Bishop was a young and talented artist whose successes and indulgences were compacted into an incredibly short period of time. He hobnobbed with royalty, lost lawsuits, cowered out of countries, enjoyed wealth, fame, and beautiful women. He had suffered through divorces, addictions, and three deaths by the age of 33.

Bishop and J. Randall Brown spawned a fascinating group of performers whose acts and exploits continue to the present day.

Stuart Cumberland (Charles Garner) was their most famous contemporary rival. He first witnessed Brown's mind reading in Australia and later went to work for Bishop. He had an impressive roster of supporters, which included, according to his brochure: "From upwards of one thousand famous Divines, Statesmen, Scientists and others who have given Mr. Cumberland their moral support in his crusade against the follies and shams of modern spiritualism." He often worked for royalty and authored numerous books, the most well-known of which were *A Thought Reader's Thoughts* (London, 1888) and *People I Have Read* (London, 1905). Cumberland was almost as impressive a name-dropper as Bishop. He abounds in anecdotes of thought reading the rich and famous like Prime Minister Gladstone and Kaiser Wilhelm. He traced a map of Congo exploration known only to African explorer H. M. Stanley. With a hungry monkey holding Cumberland's wrist, the mind reader found a hidden orange thought of by his simian subject. For his New York debut, Cumberland presented a dramatic version of the number test. Holding the hand of the impresario Major Pond, who concentrated on a chosen number, the mind reader stroked his own bare arm and the thought-of figures appeared as if written in blood. Cumberland died in his native London in 1922.

Britishers James Edwyns and Alfred Capper did similar stunts and were also successful. Edwyns called himself "Champion of the World in Thought Reading" and claimed Bishop and Cumberland allowed him "undisputed possession" of the title, but I can find no supporting evidence for this honor. Edwyns conducted mind reading tests with contact, non-contact, and while connected to a helper holding an ivy twig.

A FEW
WORDS
ABOUT
DEATH
AND
SHOW BIZ

189

Capper, who was better known, authored *A Rambler's Recollections and Reflections* in 1915. He also attracted an illustrious audience, including the Prince and Princess of Saxe-Weimar, the Marchioness of Lorne, Sarah Bernhardt, and Oscar Wilde. Apparently realizing the tenuous nature of his demonstrations, he also featured dramatic recitals and musical sketches in his show.

Lucy de Gentry, according to Burlingame, "performed the same experiments that Bishop and Cumberland did . . . but quicker and with more brilliant success." She was Russian by birth and popular on the Continent. Her favorite method of operation was to be linked to her helper by holding only a handkerchief or a ruler. Unlike Bishop, whose movements were frenetic, de Gentry was known for her graceful and dignified presentation.

*A portrait
of the mentalist
Stuart Cumberland,
circa 1888.*

Theodore Pull, a contemporary American mind reader, apparently thought histrionics was a key to Bishop's success. Pull chewed on a piece of soap, which enabled him to foam at the mouth during his performances.

Detroit, inexplicably, was the spawning ground for a number of important early mind readers. Corey, Carl King, and Eva McCoy all provoked medical and scientific interest. McCoy, a twelve-year-old orphan, was discovered in Michigan by magician Alexander Herrmann, who brought her to perform at his theater in New York. He was particularly impressed with her three-helper test. McCoy attempted to find a pin stuck in the bottom of a cane chair. "The man who placed

Bishop and Cumberland satirized in sheet music of the period.

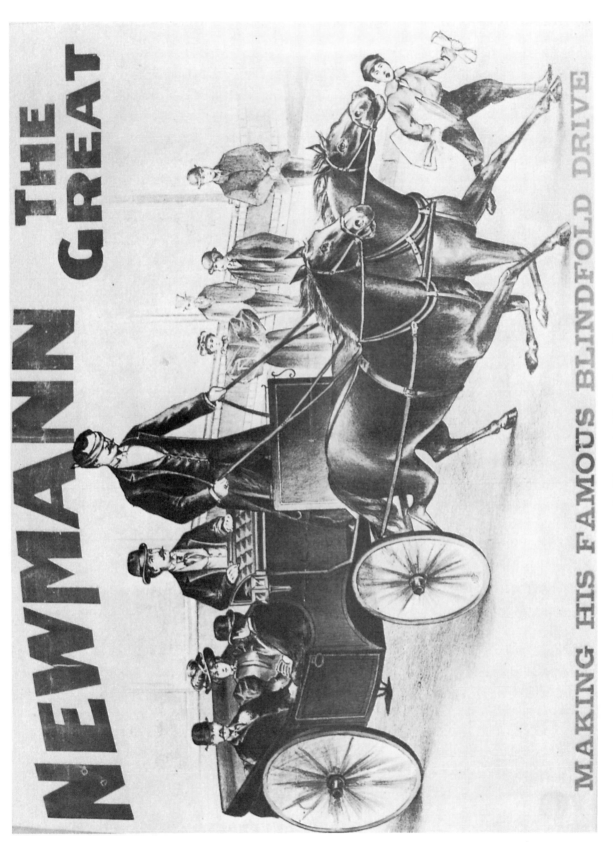

A two-color lithograph of C. A. George Newmann.

it there joined hands with another man who was not in on the secret, and this second man linked to a third who was also ignorant of the object of the search." Taking the third man's hand, the young girl successfully located the object.

Maud Lancaster, an English woman who performed at the Casino Theater in New York, was very important in the development of the thought reading act. When she did the hidden pin test (reported the New York *Herald* on December 2, 1893), she did not use contact, nor did she single out a helper in close proximity. Blindfolded, she returned to the room where the pin had been hidden, and "with hands waving she started in an uncertain way about the room. She fingered backs of chairs, passed her hands over the shoulders and arms of men and women . . . after an incessant search of five minutes, she drew the pin from its hiding place." She also duplicated the murder mystery, and other standard presentations, with her decidedly different and impressive non-contact techniques.

C. A. George Newmann, the Minnesota-bred hypnotist, mentalist, and historian, thought he was the first performer to do non-contact stunts, in 1896, but he was unaware of Bishop's and Montague's non-contact achievements. He heard of Maud Lancaster only in his later years through Joseph Rinn. Newmann was apparently the first performer to do the blindfold carriage drive without contact.

Newmann had a long and successful career, largely in rural America. He left his mark both as a performer and as an important collector and chronicler of material on early mind readers and magicians.

Dietrich Neuman, a Russian contact reader, impressed New York newspapermen with a charity appearance for the benefit of the Sick Baby Fund at the Herald Square Theater. Neuman located a penny hidden by reporters in nearby Hammerstein's Olympia Roof Garden. Neuman's three-sheet posters featured the peculiar slogan "Washington Irving Bishop (Deceased) Outdone."

Mind reading demonstrations, for a time, became almost a society party craze. Marshall P. Wilder, the well-known hunchbacked humorist and actor, demonstrated his skills at fashionable New York parties. (He had earlier accompanied Bishop on his blindfold drive to the Gramercy Park Hotel.)

Fanny Brice, according to Orson Welles, used her forceful personality coupled with keen interpretation of visual clues to successfully do non-contact stunts for her friends. Welles saw her on numerous occasions "unfailingly" perform these demonstrations. She was precise enough to determine a single thought-of book amidst an entire bookcase of volumes. After teaching Welles some of her techniques, he asked her how she ever learned her skills. "Oh," she said, "I just do these things, darling."

A FEW
WORDS
ABOUT
DEATH
AND
SHOW BIZ

———

193

In 1928 a German, Axel Vogt, performing under the name Hellstrom, appeared at a magician's conference in Lima, Ohio. He caused a sensation with his apparent ability to read minds. Ohio mentalist and publisher Robert Nelson coined the word "Hellstromism" and issued a booklet to explain its techniques. This angered C. A. George Newmann, who, in a rebuttal pamphlet, insisted that Hellstrom was an exponent of contact mind reading, incapable of *non*-contact experiments, and a mere shadow of the originator of the art, J. Randall Brown.

A portrait of the humorist Marshall P. Wilder.

There is little doubt that Hellstrom was considerably less interesting than Eugen de Rubini, a Moravian non-contact mind reader. For a brief time, though, Hellstrom fascinated the public with such stunts as finding a long lost cigar-store Indian in Colon, Michigan (accompanied by magician Harry Blackstone). One hopes these gentlemen did not swear on a stack of Bibles to the legitimacy of this experiment.

Rubini made headlines in the 1920's, winning the endorsement of Harry Houdini and other notables. In one test he found a set of keys hidden by author Sinclair Lewis in the clothing of Lewis' wife, Dorothy. He found the keys by walking toward Dorothy with Sinclair mentally guiding him but walking five feet behind Rubini. In one of the most impressive of all mind reading tests, Rubini was asked to repeat a series of actions which took place while he was in another room. Rubini was expected to locate a specific cigarette, extract a

toothpick which had been inserted therein, replace the toothpick, and break the cigarette and toothpick simultaneously. Rubini entered the room. Not a word was spoken. Staring at a woman who was to mentally guide him, Rubini, with no contact, exactly reconstructed the convoluted actions.

If one is to rule out the possibility of confederacy or collusion in such tests (and many psychic researchers, it should be noted, *do not*), there is much to consider. Clearly involuntary muscular response cannot be a completely satisfying answer for such phenomena.

Even with the aid of subtle visual, tactile, or auditory clues which may be unconsciously imparted to the mind reader, it is possible to see why many people would consider the skills necessary to interpret such data with miraculously specific results as an "extra-sensory" ability.

Harry Price, the controversial British psychic investigator and book collector, studied the work of four impressive mind readers. Price saw Erik Jan Hanussen (né Hermann Steinschneider), the fascinating psychic and occultist to the high-level Nazis, who may have predicted the Reichstag Fire. Hanussen had an unusual semi-contact technique involving a gold ball. Before he could be brought to Price's National Laboratory of Psychic Research for investigation, he was murdered (most likely by the Nazis) on April 7, 1933.

Maloitz, a Dutch opera singer (Moische Blitz) turned mind reader, was impressive in both contact and non-contact tests, but would not subject himself to Price's laboratory studies without pay.

Marion (Josef Kraus), a native of Prague born on October 15, 1892, was studied at length and was the subject of a publication by S. G. Soal entitled *Preliminary Studies of a Vaudeville Telepathist*. Price and Soal concluded that Marion gathered "indica" (generally physical clues from body movements) from the people who witnessed his non-contact tests. When the helpers were screened from Marion by a "sentrybox" device, he was unsuccessful in locating hidden objects.

Price also tested McIvor Tyndall. Then an old man, he had made his living as a mind reader, learning his craft from watching J. Randall Brown in the 1880's. Tyndall was a mysterious fellow who edited an occult magazine called the *Swastika Journal*. He lectured on spiritualism and against liquor. Some think he may also have been Paul Alexander Johnstone, another mind reader and one of the first to perform the blindfold drive, but they were, in fact, different men.

Price called these performers "hyperaesthetes." He claimed they were abnormally sensitive to clues gathered from a helper's clothes, speech, movement, temperament, etc.

The blindfold drive continued to be an important feature in the acts of mentalists and magicians, who in keeping up with the times performed it on bicycles and in automobiles rather than in horse-drawn carriages. This act still survives. In modern times, however, the drive is an attempt to show "eyeless vision" (the ability to see while blindfolded) and somewhat shamelessly to garner publicity, rather than to locate an object hidden by freely selected audience members. Perhaps the one performer who was able to elevate "eyeless vision" to an art was Kuda Bux. Born in Kashmir on February 17, 1905, he astounded both scientists and magicians with his convincing demonstrations. After a long and remarkably publicized career, he died on February 5, 1981.

As early as 1909 an innovative, blindfolded Emil Knudson piloted a steamer through busy Copenhagen harbor; but for sheer promotional brilliance, none topped El Dorado the magician. Performing with his "VOD-VIL" entertainment company in the rural Midwest, El Dorado provided:

> *Special Added Attraction at 4:00* P.M.
> *Lovely Miss Arden of Hollywood Will Drive*
> *a New Tractor Over the Streets of Remington*
> *While She Is Completely Blindfolded.*
> *Tractor courtesy of Holderly Implement Co.*

A FEW
WORDS
ABOUT
DEATH
AND
SHOW BIZ

197

A Friedlander lithograph of Hanussen.

Kuda Bux heads up a mixed variety bill in the 1930's.

In the 1950's Hungarian Franz Polgar added a clever innovation to the mind reading act. He had local promoters hide his paycheck in the auditoriums where he performed. If he was unable to find his check, he would forfeit payment. Among the peculiar hiding places where he discovered his well-earned wage were a police chief's gun barrel, a hollowed-out tennis ball, and a young woman's brassiere.

Earlier, a medicine showman, Arthur Hammer, used the hidden-object test to avoid paying for sales licenses in the towns where he sold his goods. He would wager a city official that he could locate a personal object hidden by them. If he was successful (and he almost always was), his license fees would be waived.

Lev Schneider, an elderly, heavily bespectacled recent Russian immigrant, is one of the few current performers to do an act based exclusively on contact mind reading.

In recent appearances on the David Letterman television show Lev used his considerable talents searching for objects while pitted in a test for speed against electronic tracking devices and bloodhounds.

Anachronistically, he evokes the memory of Washington Irving Bishop as he babbles to himself and pushes through theater aisles and hallways in a frenetic attempt to succeed. With a translator to interpret the host's questions, and a tall, gawky volunteer in tow, many spectators believe they are witnessing a comedy sketch with hired actors rather than a fascinating skill with a hundred-year-old history.

And with Lev in an absurd chef's hat groping wildly to find the hidden ingredients so Letterman can prepare beef Stroganoff, who can blame them?

A FEW
WORDS
ABOUT
DEATH
AND
SHOW BIZ

199

LAROCHE:
The Sisyphus
of the Circus World

Friedlander lithograph of LaRoche at the Circus Strasbourg.

LaRoche's art required the most physically demanding precision imaginable. But unlike that of most highly skilled acrobats and contortionists, LaRoche's art was concealed. He reached the climax of his act before the audience had even realized a human being was involved. They watched as a metal sphere just over two feet in diameter was placed at the bottom of a long spiral track. The ball moved, as if by magic, slowly and smoothly up the perilous incline. Almost twenty-four feet in the air, the ball stopped at the summit of the structure. A pistol shot rang out and hands holding flags emerged through holes in the ball. For the first time the audience realized the ball was maneuvered from the inside, not the outside.

Descending ominously, the ball traveled back down the spiral and settled on the ground. The hemispheres split and the mode of power was revealed—LaRoche, a full-sized man, emerged from his metal prison to a tumultuous reception.

It is almost impossible to convey the impact this had on the audience. "There are acts," said circus veteran Jim Brent, "which bring great bursts of applause at the time of their performance and are little remembered afterwards. The ball act was not of this group; it belonged to that elect [class] which by sheer novelty or brilliance becomes legendary—the kind of act an audience speculates over, and argues about long after."

Not only the act, but the man as well are subject to speculations and arguments a century after their initial appearance.

LaRoche, who was born Leon Rauch in Austria on November 18, 1857, was at least as mysterious as the ball which brought him fame—such fame that he was even the thinly veiled hero of a novel, *The Golden Ball*, written by Ruth Manning Sanders (London, 1954), and the inspiration for a children's toy depicting his act. The details of his life are cloudy and confused, the truth more difficult to obtain because of countless stories which are still told about him. Apparently a frail and moody child, Rauch was a loner. He was subject, throughout his life, to haunting hallucinations. When he was thirteen, in the midst of one such frightening vision, he ran away from his parents' home. It was on this fateful trip that he met a traveling conjurer from whom he quickly learned the rudiments of legerdemain and with almost unbelievable speed added the skills of acrobatics, contortionism, and equitation. He began to perform under the name of "Soni" and enjoyed considerable success, predominately as a trick rider with the Royal Circus of Budapest and Cirque Sidoli. Rauch's departures from both of these engagements were sudden and mysterious. He then joined a small and undistinguished family circus in Romania which, through his incredible skill, he quickly built into a fine show.

Legend has it that, in the small town of Jassy, outside the circus entrance, a Turk exhibited a game of chance. A small ball was dropped

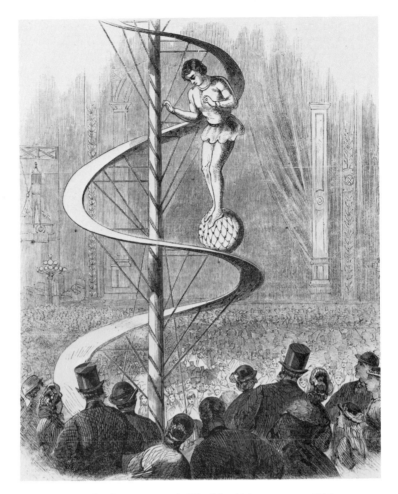

Ethardo, from Harper's Weekly, *February 10, 1866.*

down a spiral incline and landed at random on one of several numbered squares. LaRoche was angered to find that this game was stealing his audience. Within eight days, inspired by the Turk, LaRoche introduced his own spiral and the Mysterious Ball.

According to Bob Bramson, LaRoche's grandson, the real inspiration for the ball act most likely came from Ethardo, who in 1865 delighted Londoners by ascending a spiral while balanced atop a large ball. Ethardo, who was born in Italy in 1835, was successful with his novel act both in his native land and in England, where he made his debut at the Crystal Palace and went on to work in variety theaters. Standing on a thirty-inch ball made of wood and iron, he traveled up a foot-wide track some fifty feet in the air. Ethardo inspired numerous imitators such as Lady Alphonsine, who featured the spiral in France, and Achille Philion. (When the then small-time circus entrepreneurs, the Ringling Brothers, played Chicago for the first time in 1895, Philion was hired as an additional attraction to generate publicity and draw

LAROCHE:
THE
SISYPHUS
OF THE
CIRCUS WORLD

205

spectators. The globe-walker moved up a fifty-foot spiral, then out onto a long cable roadway, and finally descended amid an elaborate shower of fireworks.)

In Boston, Etienne Buislay featured his spiral mountain, which was glowingly described in his playbill:

A slender pole resting on the center of the parquette and reaching above the fourth gallery—around it like a screw twines a thin, flexible board, as wide as the palm of the hand. That is the Mountain the acrobat has to ascend. On this narrow pathway stands a thirty-inch white sphere, spangled with blue stars. Etienne jumps lightly upon the centre of that miniature globe—there, with folded arms, by an almost imperceptible motion of the feet, he gives the needed impulsation and then begins the ascent. Everybody, breathless and with palpitating hearts, fix their gaze on him, thinking that a disaster is inevitable. Look at him! The globe has stopped! Almost his whole body bends over the abyss! "He

A "BLAZE OF TRIUMPH"!!

(With Mr. Punch's Compliments to Mr. Cross.)

The ball act inspired political satire. This illustration is from Punch, *July 10, 1875.*

is falling!" is the universal cry. Poor fellow! Some ladies retire in haste; others cover their faces or faint. A mere illusion. The acrobat keeps radiantly on his sphere, winding up the dangerous path, and thus he reaches the summit, but this is comparatively easy. He must return. Now he moderates the rotation of the sphere and brings under control the unruly centrifugal force which attracts the globe to the abyss. There he stands, hanging rather than resting on the centre of the sphere, his legs doubled, his body bending backward, his head forward. He descends slowly, calmly, while the spectator, not daring to accompany him farther, turns away his face; and after recovering from such an overwhelming sensation, the first question asked is, what is the gift, the talisman, the superhuman means which has endowed this man with wonderful power.

The popularity of these dangerous acts continued with Minting the Marvel, who ascended the spiral on a unicycle, and Leonce, who preferred a more conventional two-wheeler—but made his winding, upward journey on a spiral incline that became consumed by flames.

The success of LaRoche led to numerous imitations and variations of the ball act. Even on the Barnum & Bailey Show, where he won his greatest acclaim, LaRoche was involved in strange promotions. On the 1897 show he appeared in a "Dueling Banjos" of mysterious balls. "Two rival wonder globes together with champion tumbling artists" featured LaRoche and "Nevada and his curious remarkable sphere which by an unseen force rolls along a horizontal wire."

Even though LaRoche may have been working *inside* the ball as early as 1879, the first documented public appearance of the attraction was by the clown Lepère, who created a sensation at the Folies-Bergère in Rouen in 1889 and at the circus at the Champs Élysées in Paris in 1890. Lepere's ball rolled up a straight incline to a platform about five feet off the ground and then rolled down the other side. The ball settled on a cushion and Lepère was found inside.

LaRoche's initial spiral track was twelve feet high and he soon perfected the act with a twenty-four-foot tower. By the late 1890's, he advertised the stunt using a tower fifty feet high. The danger of the experiment was of course greatly increased—it was said that the physical exertions needed to move the ball were much more difficult on the way up, but far more dangerous on the descent. Twice during his career, in Glasgow and Madrid, the ball derailed and fell from the track, causing LaRoche serious injuries.

The "Wunderkugel" or "Bola Misteriosa" act made LaRoche a legitimate star. He appeared as a featured attraction in European circuses, then with Barnum & Bailey in America, and ultimately back

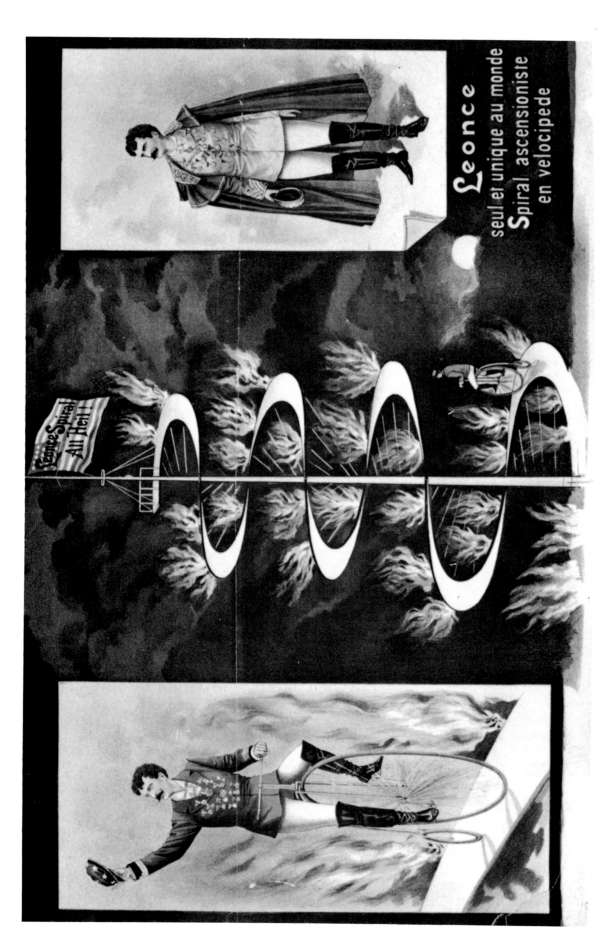

The Centrifugalkugel, yet another strange ball act from 1913.

LAROCHE:
THE
SISYPHUS
OF THE
CIRCUS WORLD

———

209

on the Continent. He was a remarkable fellow, who in the course of his travel mastered nine languages. A. H. Kober, the circus historian, said, "The refinement of his manners and of his language struck everybody . . . the surprising discovery was made that a variety star could be a gentleman."

Nevertheless, he was still plagued by the visions which prompted his sudden irrational behavior. Apparently a vision of his own death while inside the ball induced his retirement. He settled in Berlin, ostensibly to spend more time with his wife and daughter.

Although the act made him a wealthy man, he was ruined by his investment in German bonds during World War I and forced to take a job as a night telegrapher. There he was found by the circus impresario Sarrasini, who lured him out of retirement. LaRoche, then in his sixties, having not performed for thirteen years, was again a tremendous attraction. He worked happily for the next five years, living minimally while sending most of his money home to his family. On a ship leaving South America in 1923, apparently in the throes of one of his dreaded hallucinations, he suddenly jumped overboard and was lost at sea.

The operation of the ball, although imitated, has never been fully explained. Theories about double balls and mechanisms to keep the ball on track have been proposed, but Bramson and others state that the apparatus was completely ordinary. The ball was a hollow sphere hammered out of steel with not so much as a handle inside. After an initial mishap, LaRoche punched holes in the metal, so he could see the track. The skill to move the ball up the long spiral, constantly shifting the center of gravity forward but not from side to side, was considerable. My favorite theory is that the movement came from a secret system taught to LaRoche by Transylvanian rabbis.

Lepère, the originator of the rolling ball act.

Over the years there have been numerous attempts to revive the act. Miss Browell at Cirque Pindar in the 1930's emerged from the ball after it had been pierced with swords, as in the standard magical illusion. Pastelli and Richard Hardner both did the act in the 1950's. Jim Brent and Tom Arnold presented it as an enormous snowball moving upward along a Christmas tree, while LaRoche's daughter, Gertrude, performed with the original apparatus, although somewhat shortening the spiral.

Don Oscarez, born in Poland, performed an unusual act inside a glass ball which was based on his favorite circus movie, *Die Glaserne Kugel*. In the film, a glass ball rolled down a tower, on a track, into a loop-the-loop, then flew through the air and landed in a net. While working as an electrician in Cirque Belli, Oscarez sold his watch, bicycle, and accordion to pay for the construction of a similar apparatus. After a successful debut in Hamburg on a twelve-meter-high steel tower, the

Gertrude LaRoche Bramson is seen standing next to a slightly shortened version of her father's original apparatus.

LAROCHE:
THE
SISYPHUS
OF THE
CIRCUS WORLD

211

The infamous series of Camel cigarette ads infuriated magicians by
exposing their secrets. This one featured the mysterious ball.

act was performed over five hundred times. Forty-five times, however, the ball crashed—providing its passenger with light injuries. On May 30, 1950, at Zirkus Bugler, in Dortmund, Oscarez suffered a terrible accident. The ball and its occupant wound up in pieces. It took three years to put the man back together. Upon his recovery, the indomitable Oscarez became a street construction worker until he had saved enough money to rebuild and perform his act again.

A masked German called Geroku (Peter Gatz from Hamburg), who looks more like a professional wrestler than a circus acrobat, currently performs the routine in a bizarre science-fiction setting. While the performance is still fascinating to watch, one senses somehow that this choppy trip up and down the spiral lacks the mysterious grace of LaRoche's original artistry.

ARTHUR LLOYD:
The Humorous
Human Card Index

An early advertising card.

Wearing a mortarboard cap and gown, Arthur Lloyd took his place, not behind the podium of a university graduation exercise, but in the center of the vaudeville stage.

He asked the audience to mention any playing card. Upon their response, without looking, he then quickly produced it from his coat pocket. He followed with a second requested card, then a third. The ease with which he filled these requests hinted at some remarkable skill, but to aficionados of card magic, Lloyd, although competent, was far from unique.

Continuing, however, Arthur Lloyd then asked the audience to participate in what was, by a quick change of word, one of the most unusual of all stage entertainments. Instead of playing cards, Mr. Lloyd asked the audience to mention *any* sort of card, in fact, *any item printed on paper*, which could be kept in a pocket.

With the same ease, and still without looking, Lloyd produced on demand an insurance policy, a war bond, a pawn ticket, alimony papers, a bus transfer, a license to sell opium, and a sign which said ROOMS TO LET; an Irish sweepstakes ticket, an admission card to the White House, a paper aspirin packet, a pass to the Colombian exposition, and a ringside ticket to the Jack Dempsey–George Carpentier championship fight.

Membership cards were a specialty. Lloyd had thousands of them—for ostrich farms, cemeteries, the Communist party, the Green Bench Sitters Association, and even one for the Society for the Prevention of Disparaging Remarks about Brooklyn.

According to Robert Ripley, who featured Lloyd in his "Believe It or Not" column on June 14, 1936, the "Human Card Index," as he was billed, carried fifteen thousand items. His clothing was estimated to weigh between 45 and 110 pounds.

Lloyd was born in Medford, Massachusetts, on November 5, 1891, but grew up in England. His father, a Welsh brass finisher, died at an early age. Arthur made his initial appearance as a magician at age sixteen, beginning his career to support his widowed mother. According to a February 11, 1939, article in the English entertainment paper the *World's Fair*, Lloyd came to every show of well-respected conjurer Herbert Brooks and soon thereafter made his debut on the stage. Brooks, a masterful showman, featured the "any-playing-card-called-for routine," which suddenly appeared in the show of the young Lloyd. Whether it was a yearning to be different, or simply a business necessity, Lloyd soon expanded his act into the unique entertainment that he presented for most of his life.

His act provided much comedy, some of it obtained by "assistants" planted in the audience to ask for a particularly humorous item at just the right time. The act also included a feature which helped him get return business. If you stumped Lloyd, he promised to have the item

ARTHUR
LLOYD
—
HUMAN
CARD
INDEX
—
CARRIES
15,000
CARDS
IN HIS CLOTHING.
HE CAN PRODUCE ANY CARD ON REQUEST
HIS GOWN-LOADED WITH CARDS-WEIGHS 45 POUNDS

Lloyd featured in Ripley's "Believe It or Not," June 14, 1936.

you requested the next time he played your city (and he would often mail you a photostat when he obtained it). As the following letter will illustrate, this was often more difficult than it seemed.

November 28, 1945

Mr. Arthur Lloyd
210 Avenue of the Americas
New York 14, New York

Dear Mr. Lloyd:
    Your letter of November 26 addressed to the president of our company, Mr. George Waite, has been referred to the writer for reply, with the required recommendations.
    As you can understand, the Caterpillar Club is an exclusive organization, the requirement for enrollment being

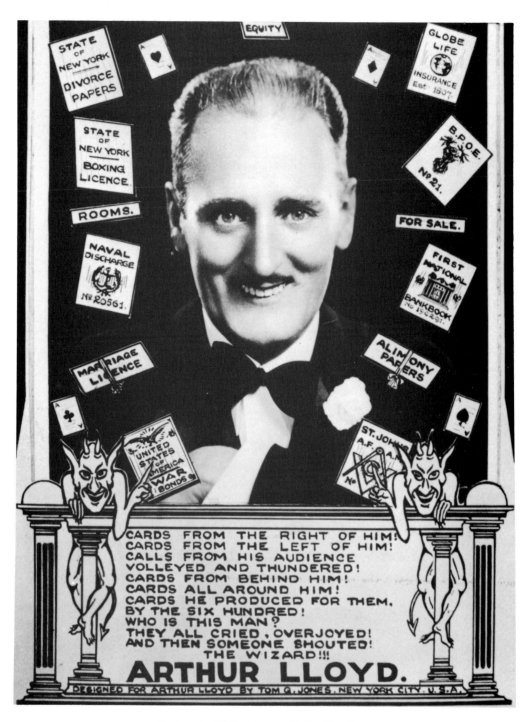

Cartoon publicity photograph for Lloyd's act.

A sampling of actual cards from Lloyd's pockets.

the act of using a parachute to escape from disabled aircraft, thereby saving one's life. For the protection of the members who have qualified for enrollment by saving their lives in this manner, the Caterpillar Club insignia and membership card are restricted to members only.

Therefore, we would not be in a position to furnish you with a card bearing your name but, upon due consideration, it is deemed in order to furnish you for the use described in your letter a sample card, and you will find it enclosed herewith.

Wishing you continued success, we are,

Cordially yours,

IRVING AIR CHUTE CO., INC.

G. C. Krull, Recording Secretary

CATERPILLAR CLUB

I have had an opportunity to examine the clothing, cards, and lists of Lloyd, which now are part of the collection of Chet Karkut in Connecticut. Lloyd used more than forty pockets, which held the thousands of items he carried. The material was divided into sections—

licenses (marriage, pharmaceutical, liquor), gambling tickets (derby, sweepstakes, lottery), sporting events (baseball, boxing, football), office forms, hotel stationery, portraits of monarchs, and on and on. But these provide no real clue to his method of operation. Sometimes a pocket contained one whole section, but sections often had subdivisions and sometimes those subdivisions had subdivisions. Later in his career, Lloyd was flexible enough to refine his act for specialty groups. When working before lawyers, for instance, he would stock his coat with an assortment of briefs, contracts, warrants, depositions, and legal journals. He was able to do the same thing for accountants, doctors, stockbrokers, etc. An attempt to analyze how he produced a specific item within a given category forces one to the amazing conclusion that show business' most famous anal-retentive *had* no system—he simply knew where each of the thousands of cards in his pockets was located.

THE
HUMOROUS
HUMAN
CARD
INDEX

219

ENTEROLOGY:
Getting into Boxes, Bottles, and Trouble with Seamus Burke and Others

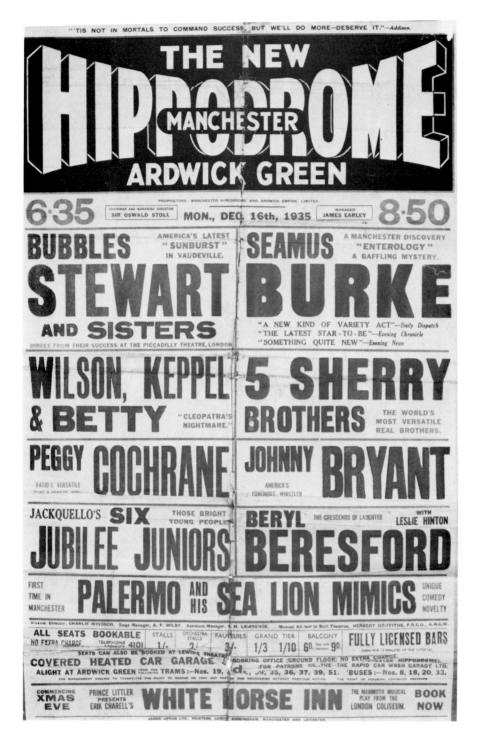

The rumors linking Burke and Bubbles Stewart were purely fictional.
From a playbill for Burke's initial appearance in 1935.

Houdini and other escapologists made a career of getting out of boxes, bags, and bonds. Seamus Burke earned a living getting *into* them. He was the world's only "enterologist."

In the winter of 1935, the *Catholic Herald*, a Manchester, England, newspaper, received a letter from Burke, stating that he was capable of accomplishing three unbelievable stunts. First, he claimed he could enter a thoroughly examined trunk which had previously been locked, encircled with rope, and sealed with wax. Next, he could appear inside a sealed tissue bag handed to him *after* he had been bound, mummy-like, from head to foot, with more than one hundred feet of stout rope. (The sealed bag, naturally, would be examined both before and after the demonstration.) Finally, Burke insisted he could be bound securely to a chair with a sealed bag draped on his shoulder, and in a moment, would be found, still tied to the chair, within the sealed sack. Miraculously, each stunt would take less than one minute to accomplish.

The *Herald* editor sent a representative to investigate.

"Burke can do exactly what he claims," wrote the gullible reporter, "as proven by my testimony, and the testimony of the other independent witnesses, and neither the sack nor the trunk contains the mechanism of a trick. Burke has never been at any time a frequenter of other cinemas or theatres. Showmanship and trickery can be entirely disregarded. There is, on the other hand, quite definite proof of psychic experience in Burke's life."

Undaunted by numerous earlier rejections from the press and various theater owners, Burke took his *Herald* story to James Earley, manager of the New Manchester Hippodrome. Soon after, auditioning for the manager, Burke made his debut as the headline act of an all-star variety bill that included "Bubbles Stewart, America's latest sunburst," "Jaequelle's Six Jubilee Juniors," and "Palermo and his Sea Lion Mimics."

As unlikely as his act, or his sudden rise to stardom, was Burke's account of the origins of "enterology."

Late one night in 1935 in a Manchester attic apartment Burke arose in a trance-like state. Having never before produced so much as two straight lines, he nonetheless took pencil in hand and began to draw. The pencil seemed to move of its own accord and soon strange pictures of faces, birds, eyes, and insects took shape. In this trance, he produced another picture. Then another. In the morning Burke was surprised upon awakening to find that almost fifty of what investigators of the paranormal like to call "automatic drawings" were completed.

Although the pictures seemed, to be charitable, childish, Burke looked upon them as the product of some divine agency. So impressed was he with his newly found talent, that he sent his artwork to a celebrated if eclectic group consisting in part of Mahatma Gandhi, General Montgomery, Pope Pius XII, King George, and Adolf Hitler. He claimed to have received thank-you notes from each of the recipients, and a papal medal and apostolic benediction from the Pope.

Although Burke was never again to be blessed with psychic doodles, a few weeks later he was awakened by a strange dream. He had recently been fired from his job as an elevator operator at the Midland Hotel, and, though an illiterate until the age of twenty, he had begun to support himself by writing a series of stories for small English magazines. The hero of these tales was a "little henpecked man by the name of Killboggan, who was always planning crimes and robbery, and each time, as he was on the point of success, he always failed in some mysterious way." In Burke's latest story, Killboggan was to enter a bank vault and make off with a sack of large bills only to find he had mistakenly stolen a batch of canceled checks.

Burke was searching for a way to get Killboggan into the vault. He thought of having an accomplice place Killboggan in a locked trunk, ostensibly containing rare books, and having the trunk placed in the vault overnight. Killboggan would wait for the bank to close, open the trunk from the inside, get the money, and return to the trunk. The problem was how to have the trunk locked from the outside when the vault was opened the following morning.

Tired from such taxing thought, and without a solution, Burke fell asleep. He had a "dream vision," in which he pictured himself getting in and out of a locked box, yet taking no active part in the proceedings. Suddenly he awoke with the realization that he could enter and emerge from a locked box without having to open it.

He borrowed an old wooden crate from his landlady and from the front cut out two small square holes. Next he drew ropes around the box and stapled them down, further securing the box with two large padlocks, which he sealed with wax. Burke tied his own hands with rope, sat on the box, and, as he later told it, willed himself inside. He was successful, and found himself inside the box with his hands, still tied, protruding from the square holes. He then willed himself outside. Luckily, he was again successful. And so, he claimed, "enter-ology" was born.

The originator of this unusual act was born into a poor family of eight children in Kilkenny, Ireland, on March 4, 1888. When he was nine his mother died of malnutrition and shortly thereafter his father, an alcoholic, left home, never to return. Leaving his brothers and sisters the following year, Burke lived the life of a tramp, with an occasional odd job printing handbills or picking turnips. He had a brief stint with Hanneford's Circus, which included a one-day, hopelessly unsuccessful appearance as a clown. He enjoyed his carefree lifestyle, except in the winter months. On a particularly frigid day in

1904, Burke, stiff with cold, his feet covered with sacking fastened with twine (his boots long since worn through and discarded), lied about his age and enlisted in the British army.

Burke boarded a train bound for his assigned station at Naas. He shared a compartment with an old woman who stared at him for a long time. "Have you joined the army?" she finally said. "Yes, ma'am," Burke answered. "God help us," said the woman, who never spoke again on the entire journey.

Burke took an instant dislike to army life, which for him eventually became unbearable. He deserted and headed to London. Within the year, again desperate for food and shelter, he reenlisted in the army. He was discovered and court-martialed as a deserter and sentenced to 168 days in the "glasshouse," or army prison. Upon his release he was sent to India. He enjoyed that country and his stay there was to have a positive effect on his life, as he learned to play the B-flat clarinet and taught himself to read and write. He also learned the rudiments of comedy and song and dance, occasionally appearing before his fellow soldiers. Burke never went to school a day in his life, and while his accomplishments are in some ways astounding, he had some peculiar notions. For instance, he was convinced that the earth did not rotate, and that it was "flat as pressed turnips."

After World War I, Burke took employment as an elevator operator and began writing songs for music hall acts, achieving some success with novelty numbers like "Remember":

<blockquote>
An old man once sat on his grandfather's knee
His dark hair was crimson as snow
His daughter lay there, sitting down where she stood,
Her face full of worry and woe,
She cried, "Papa, tell me where is my momma?"
And the old man with trembling knees
Wiped a drop of grey hair from his sunburnt cheek
And murmured, as she stood at ease
</blockquote>

CHORUS

<blockquote>
Remember, my darling, you've no mother now
Forget her, dear Mary Ann,
She went for some beer sixty-three years ago
And eloped with the money and can.
When I think of her face all battered and worn
My tears fall like rain on the floor,
And at night when I'm laying,
Asleep I am praying
God send her back to me (pause) . . . no more.
</blockquote>

In 1920, Burke joined the I.R.A. When the "civil war" proved futile, he built a shack in the Dublin mountains and became a hermit. Proud of his freedom and independence, he wrote stories and fished for food. One day, after capturing three trout in a peculiar stick-and-bag trap of his own devising, he "actually heard one fish squeaking with fear." He threw it back in the water and "never again ate any flesh."

When a severe storm destroyed his home and he almost lost his life as a result of exposure and pneumonia, he returned to Dublin and began a career as a nobber (one who bangs on doors and asks for small change in return for singing).

Eventually he returned to England to pursue his writing career. While scratching out a meager living, Burke came across a copy of the *World's Fair*, an English theatrical newspaper, and chanced to see the column "About Magicians," authored by "B. W." (Brunel White). In reading the account of a famous escapologist, Burke reasoned that a man might be more of a theatrical sensation getting *into* things, rather than out of them. Intrigued by this idea, he began a few experiments. Encouraged by his success, he saved some money and built the props which were the basis of his act. Burke later felt the necessity to cloak the origins of his act in psychic mumbo jumbo.

"Being a mystery man," Burke said about his relations with the press, "I handed them a most fantastic story. . . . had I told the same story to a pack of mules, they'd have kicked me to death."

In actuality, Burke seemed a most reluctant performer: a sad-faced, gaunt little man completely out of place in a floor-length green silk cape, which he wore as he descended a stairway between two liveried assistants to begin his act. He labored through his three stunts as his manager provided a constant line of patter and the orchestra played "The Snake Charmer Waltz."

The Liverpool *Gazette* hailed him as "the mystic wonder of the age," and the Birkenhead *Advertiser* pronounced him "a most uncanny phenomenon." The famous impresario Sir Oswald Stoll booked him in London and Burke considered offers to play America at a large salary.

Burke's success was the result of his ingenious approach to illusions, but although he coined the term "enterology," the concept of entering rather than escaping from confinements long preceded him.

The most effective of Burke's predecessors was Bernard Marius ("Le Commandeur") Cazeneuve, one of conjuring's most illustrious figures.

Born in Toulouse in 1838, Cazeneuve distinguished himself as soldier, scientist, inventor, author, and magician of rare accomplishments, modesty excluded, as a quotation from a biographical sketch will illustrate: "An indefatigable scholar, Cazeneuve in journeying

The unlikely star Seamus Burke steps forward to begin his performance.

around the world has seen everything, studied and examined everything deeply, from the fairy-like raising of the Brahmins, the Chinese sorceries, the mysteries of the Egyptians, in fact, *all* subjects. . . ."

On stage Cazeneuve exhibited sleight of hand, lightning calculations, mnemonics (repeating passages of any given page in any history book), second sight, thought transmission, spiritualism, and illusions. According to historians, his outstanding effect was the Double Indian Mail. A Saratoga trunk was shown empty and locked, corded in every direction, and sealed. This was placed in a second trunk, also completely secured. The trunks were put in a small curtained cabinet alongside Mme. Cazeneuve. In less than one minute the curtains were opened

LE COMMANDEUR
CAZENEUVE

and Mme. Cazeneuve was gone. The first trunk was examined and opened, then the second; there, inside a bag, was Mme. Cazeneuve.

On May 19, 1877, Cazeneuve was challenged to a more stringent test by a Boston photographer. W. Eugene Balch, thinking there were trapdoors in the box, suggested fastening strips of paper on the smaller trunk. Cazeneuve agreed to the conditions. Balch and a reporter from the Boston *Post* approached the stage and examined the corded and sealed trunk. They then completely encased the trunk in six large pieces of heavy wrapping paper. Cazeneuve complained that this was not fair, as the challenge had stipulated only paper strips, but he graciously allowed the test to continue. The paper was attached to the trunk with sealing wax and then initialed to preclude any tampering with the experiment. The second trunk was dispensed with, even

The Davenport Brothers, from the biography published in 1869.

though Cazeneuve wanted to use it. In little more than three minutes, Mme. Cazeneuve had vanished from behind the curtain. The committee examined the trunk and found it secured. Inside the trunk, inside the bag, was Mme. Cazeneuve.

Earlier, if less impressive, accounts of enterology appear in the annals of supposed spiritualistic manifestations.

The Davenport Brothers, who began conducting public séances in the 1850's, were the most successful "mediums" and among the most famous figures of their day.

Their cabinet resembled an empty oversized armoire. The brothers, wrists and ankles securely bound with rope, sat inside. When the doors were closed, "spiritual manifestations" took place—musical instruments placed at their feet played or were thrown from the cabinet; unfettered hands appeared at the top of the cabinet—yet, when the doors were immediately opened the Davenports sat serenely and securely bound.

Actually, the Davenports secretly extricated themselves from the ropes, produced the desired effects, and resecured themselves before the cabinet was opened. They were so expert at this deception that they advanced the cause of spiritualism and elicited endorsements of their "psychic" abilities from Dion Boucicault, the playwright, Richard Burton, the explorer, and even from professional magicians.

Since the Davenports claimed psychic powers, one might assume they would conceal their ability to escape and rebind themselves. Strangely, this was not always the case. Upon occasion, they would follow the above-mentioned manifestations by having the cabinet opened and their restraints completely undone at their feet. The doors then closed and quickly opened, and the Davenports were found once again securely tied in place.

Houdini's famous "Metamorphosis" also relied on the principle of reentering restraints. It was first performed with his brother, Theo, in the early 1890's and later with his wife, Bess. Houdini's hands were tied behind his back, and he was placed in a sack and locked into a box which was then tied with cord. His wife pulled a curtain around the box and stepped within that area. In three seconds the curtain was opened. Houdini was on the outside—and in the sealed trunk, bound in the sack, with hands tied behind her back, was Bess.

In the late 1920's psychic investigators were amazed by the exploits of a young Italian "medium" named Nino Pecoraro. In a sitting with Sir Arthur Conan Doyle, the famous spiritualist and creator of Sherlock Holmes, Pecoraro was sealed in a cloth-covered cabinet. His hands were covered with gloves that were sewn onto his shirt. His wrists were then bound with ropes. The cabinet draperies were closed and manifestations began. Voices were heard, tables flew through the air, and when the curtains of the cabinet parted, a "spirit hand" emerged and shook the hand of Sir Arthur.

When Pecoraro was discovered still bound, sitters attributed his feats to some psychic agency. But when a master of rope tying, Houdini, later attended a séance and bound Pecoraro, nothing happened.

After Houdini's death in 1926, Pecoraro promised to produce Houdini's ghost in the séance room. This time it was Joseph Dunninger, the famous magician, who added an expert's touch to the restraints. After a long pause, when no manifestations were forthcoming, a voice with an obvious Italian accent was heard through the curtain in a desperate attempt to impress the sitters. "Hey, Duningeen," the voice said. "This'a Houdeen. How'a you, Duningeen?"

A young Harry and Bess perform their signature piece.

Eventually Pecoraro signed a confession of his fraudulent practices and showed Dunninger his actual techniques. Although Dunninger denounced Pecoraro's fraud, he was absolutely amazed at his ability to rebind himself.

Contortionists have practiced their own form of "enterology" by squeezing into or through small spaces. The December 20, 1950, issue of *Life* magazine featured Del Monte, a full-sized man who managed to pack his body into a plastic cube measuring 19¼ inches on each side.

King Brawn, a vaudevillian whose real name was Brawermann, managed to pass his entire body through a gutted tennis racket. In an act called "The Eye of a Needle," Brawn, wearing white tie and tails,

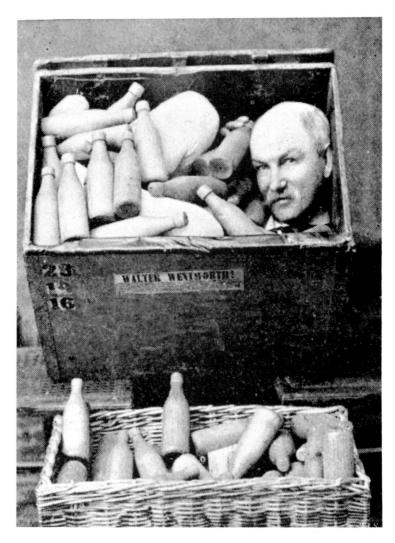

*Walter Wentworth peering out from a crate
which he shared with six dozen bottles.*

exhibited an upright wooden plank which had a cutout keyhole shape measuring 4½″ by 8″. Starting with his hands and arms, he managed to wiggle his entire body slowly through the tiny opening. (Passing his head through the keyhole, he said, was the hardest part of the exercise.) Not content to rest on his laurels with keyhole or racket, he planned to be pulled through a narrow length of pipe ten feet long at the 1939 New York World's Fair. For reasons unknown, the stunt was never attempted.

Before the turn of the century, Walter Wentworth crammed himself into a small crate which contained six dozen bottles. In 1894, Major Zamora, billed as the "triple-jointed dwarf," insinuated himself into a specially crafted bottle of Bass Ale. Audiences witnessed the peculiar wedding of an undersized man squirming into an oversized bottle. It was, however, a full-grown man attempting to put himself into a quart-sized bottle that provoked one of the most bizarre incidents in the annals of the theater and the psychology of human credibility.

On January 11, 1749, a preposterous notice appeared in the London *General Advertiser*. A conjurer, it was announced, would borrow the walking stick of any person present, and upon it play the music of any instrument currently in use. He would identify any masked persons present and for an extra gratuity read the thoughts of any woman in the audience.

He would then have a common quart wine bottle examined by the company. The bottle would be placed on a table in the middle of the stage, where the performer would, in full view of the spectators, enter the bottle.

On the night of the performance, curious spectators filled the theater to capacity in spite of a very high ticket price. When, thirty minutes after the appointed hour, no one appeared to command the stage, the crowd grew impatient, some beginning to suspect a hoax. As the management tried to calm the crowd a voice from the pit cried, "For double the price the conjurer will get into a pint bottle."

This remark ignited the audience and a riot ensued. A lit candle was thrown on stage and as the spectators hurried out, the overflow crowd that had previously been denied entrance rushed into the theater and tore down the house. In the confusion, the strongbox containing the evening's receipts was stolen, pickpockets reaped rich bounty, and a fine sword belonging to the Duke of Cumberland, an embarrassed witness to the proceedings, was lost.

This hoax, generally attributed to the Duke of Montague as a test of human gullibility, generated the immediate sale of satirical prints and pamphlets and spawned theatrical burlesques.

So taken was the public with this event that political cartoons depicting the bottle conjurer were still appearing one hundred years later. (Herman Melville even refers to the event in *Moby Dick*.)

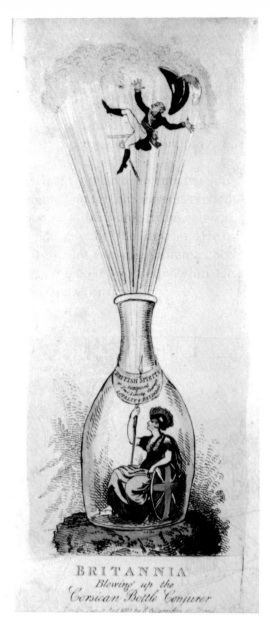

*One of the many nineteenth-century political prints
still depicting the bottle conjurer.*

My favorite squib, an apparent apology from the conjurer himself, appeared a few days after the event. The bottle conjurer stated he did not appear at the theater because earlier in the evening he had, for the sum of five pounds, done a private showing, during which his bottle was corked, with him as prisoner. The bottle had then been put into the pocket of the man who had hired him. After all, he said, he never advertised he would enter two bottles at one time. His sad story continued, "He is still in the gentleman's custody, who uncorks him now and then to feed him and let in some fresh air, but his long

confinement has so dampt his spirits, that instead of singing and dancing, he is perpetually crying and cursing his ill fate."

Perhaps Seamus Burke could envision a similar hell. Once, at the Argyle Theatre, Burke was accosted by a group of drunken sailors as he performed his chair-and-bag finale. One of the sailors insisted upon binding Burke with his own twenty-foot length of tar rope. He did this with such vigor that Burke, who nevertheless managed to complete the stunt successfully, was left severely cut and bruised.

Theater managers compounded Burke's problems by insisting he shorten his act. He refused. At the height of his career he realized his pinnacle of fame was a treacherous one. "It was miles too high for me, and too slippery on the top, with the result that I became dizzy; grabbed at something that wasn't there—to steady myself—fell, and hit the ground like a load of bricks, and not as a wealthy man either, but a nerve-shattered one."

"Down on Mulligan's Farm"
(Comic Song and Crosstalk)
FOR
TWO COMEDIANS (A Toff and a Tramp)

By SEAMUS BURKE.
AUTHOR OF:— "THE BELLES OF CAMOLIN"
(Comedy Sketch And Song) For (Two Dame Comedians).

PRICE - - - - - - - - - - - 1/6

Printed by "The People" Newspapers, Ltd., Wexford

One of Burke's many comedy song-sketches.

Two years after his remarkable debut he left the stage forever. He became assistant secretary to Gracie Fields, the famous British music hall star. After almost a decade in her employ he retired to his beloved Ireland to write his memoirs, *From the Earth to a Star*.

My attempts to reach the enterologist or his family through his publisher, printer, and last-known address have been met only with returned letters stamped, in typically British fashion, GONE AWAY.

Perhaps Burke's enigmatic career and eccentric life were best summed up years before he retired by a Manchester *Guardian* reviewer who said, "If Mr. Burke were to vanish off the face of the earth, one would just shrug one's shoulder and say, 'Well, that's that.' "

INCOMBUSTIBLE MEN
AND FIREPROOF
WOMEN

ARGYLL ROOMS.

THE

FIRE KING

M. CHABERT,

Respectfully announces that, in consequence of the disappointment of numerous parties on Thursday last, the Proprietor of the Rooms has kindly granted the use of them for

Thursday next, OCTOBER 22nd

When Tickets issued for the 15th will be admitted.

FOR THIS OCCASION

A PLATFORM WILL BE ERECTED IN THE CENTRE OF THE ROOM

On which M. CHABERT will repeat his

Extraordinary and almost incredible

PERFORMANCES,

WHICH WERE

HAILED WITH SUCH ENTHUSIASTIC APPLAUSE

ON THURSDAY LAST.

The Gallery will be thrown open: Admittance, 1s. 6d.

M. CHABERT WILL ENTER A

TEMPLE OF FIRE!!!

(TEN FEET HIGH BY SIX BROAD)

Composed of upwards of Five Hundred Cartridges.

M. CHABERT will remain in this immense Body of Flame till one entire Suit of Apparel is consumed on his person, leaving the other uninjured ! ! !

He will remain in an Oven heated to between 500 and 600 degrees of Faht.

To convince the Company of the actual heat of the Oven, M. CHABERT will suspend the Thermometer and the raw Meat from the Ceiling, and will remain outside till the Steak be cooked : he will then enter the Oven with another Steak, and remain in it till that be done. Previously, he will swallow a spoonful of

Pure Florence Oil heated to 340 degrees,

BEING 128 HIGHER THAN BOILING WATER!

HE WILL TAKE 40 GRAINS OF PHOSPHORUS !

The strength of which Poison may be inferred from the fact, that both Fontana and Orfila assert that **FOUR GRAINS OF IT ARE SUFFICIENT TO DESTROY ANY HUMAN BEING.**

He will also inhale

The Vapours of Arsenic, Oil of Vitriol, &c. exposed over a Fire!!!

And will explain to the Company how any one may take Melted Lead, Sealing-wax, &c. &c. &c.

The Doors will be opened at Two o'clock, and the Performance will begin at Three.

Admittance to the Saloon, 3s.—to the Gallery, 1s. 6d.

J. MALLETT, PRINTER, WARDOUR STREET, SOHO.

I n 1818, Chabert, the "Human Salamander," entered a blazing oven with two raw steaks in his hand. He emerged *tartare*—the steaks were cooked to perfection.

The "Really Incombustible Phenomenon," Chabert was one of a peculiar group of men and women who achieved fame and made their living primarily by playing with their food—fire kings who cooked eggs in their bare hands, imbibers of molten lead and prussic acid, spouters of water, consumers of charcoal and burning tar, swallowers of swords, scissors, snakes, and stones.

For most people, playing with one's food is delightful revenge for the rigors of early childhood. For myself the appeal of food is as inexpensive conjuring props. Vanishing raspberries or cherry tomatoes, producing potatoes or cantaloupes, and impaling watermelons with ordinary playing cards kept me, mercifully, from becoming a lawyer.

The thought of blending cards and cooking prompted me to matriculate, albeit briefly, in the Cornell University School of Hotel and Restaurant Management. Whether I hoped to combine the talents of the cooking and the gaming tables, which I then naively believed would uniquely qualify me to manage a Las Vegas casino; or to duplicate the magical pièce de résistance of Sieur Herman Boaz (who in 1795 allowed eight ladies to fix their thoughts on different cards, "the cards so thought of found in, and cut out of, a hot Roasted Leg of Mutton"), is not clear—I was, after all, a callow youth.

In any event, I found myself in the cooking lab of the doyen of the hotel school, a massive and imposing man, all too fond of bellowing "Why do we eat meat?" The professor would then fold his hands and scan the room as if daring some novel retort, so he could pounce on, mix, mash, blend, and puree the would-be heckler.

On that memorable first day of class he instructed us to preheat our ovens and listen attentively to his lecture. Circumspectly watching the others, I quickly learned the secret of igniting the appliance. Having never so much as fried an egg or prompted the ejaculation of my own toast, I was fascinated.

The lecture over, we were told to commence cooking. Our first project was to prepare bacon, by baking it on a rack over a drip tray. Immediately, I opened my oven and grasped the top rack between my thumb and forefinger. For years thereafter the sound of the sizzle, and the brand of the word "Ajax" on my digits, were a reminder of my all too literal acceptance of instruction: the stigmata of blind faith.

What prompted Ivan Ivanitz Chabert to seek solace in the confines of a blazing oven is not known.

He was born on May 10, 1792, in Avignon, France, the son of Joseph and Thérèse Chabert. Little is known of his early life but he supposedly became a soldier in the army of Napoleon, was exiled in Siberia, and escaped to London. He received from his emperor a bronze medal for valor.

The Wonderful Life and Extraordinary Exploits of Monsr. Chabert the Fire King (London, circa 1830), a twelve-page piece of puffery, claims he was a Parisian baker. "It has been said that early in life, when he followed his humble occupation, he would remove the dishes from the oven with his bare hands, feed the fire in the most exposed manner . . . when the heat was the greatest, to the infinite terror of his companions." Since he was a man of genius, fond of scientific pursuits, he began studying practical chemistry, "with the results that the most eminent medical men of both France and England are struck with astonishment at the exhibition of his supernatural powers."

This description implies a curious combination of application and innate ability.

While Napoleon lay despondent on St. Helena, Chabert began his new career. According to the same source, he performed for the royalty of France, Germany, and Austria. The King of France, Louis XVIII, was an admirer and appointed Chabert inspector of the royal kitchens— his job was to enter the ovens and deliver the dishes to waiting attendants.

He commanded attention by rescuing women and children from a blazing house. He provoked amusement by frightening a blacksmith: "Passing by a smith's shop with friends, Chabert entered and took hold of a red-hot bar just removed from the fire. This he placed on the anvil and then he asked the blacksmith to hit the iron. The smith, already struck with astonishment at the fearless conduct of Chabert, thinking him a maniac, or Satan in human shape, ran from the forge, and sought refuge in the next house."

When Chabert went to St. Petersburg, continues the narrative, he so astounded the peasantry that they "looked upon him as an infernal deity and would have prayed to him as the Tartars do to the great and mighty *Chou Cham*."

Chabert eventually came to the attention of scientists in France and in England, where he arrived in 1818. In a letter from Leicester Fields on February 23, Chabert writes to an unidentified worthy: "As I am quite a stranger in London where my claims to patronage are unknown, I have considered it my duty before I submit them to the Public to accrue the attention of those whose talents and pursuits render them competent Judges of their Validity—to this effect I have made bold to request the honor of your presence on Thursday [February 26] as well as that of severall of the most eminent Men of Science in the Kingdom."

The show was an apparent success, with Chabert demonstrating, in various experiments, his fire resistance (although not in an oven) and his capacity to imbibe, without ill effects, boiling oil. The *Times* reported on February 27 that Chabert "did not inhale the vapours of arsenic or sulfuric acid as advertised."

INCOMBUSTIBLE
MEN
AND
FIREPROOF
WOMEN

241

Chabert captured the imagination of the English, and by March was depicted by the artist George Cruikshank with his head colorfully encircled in a crown of flames. Still soliciting the support of scientists, he performed at Oxford University, where he also met with success.

On January 4, 1819, at Kingston Rooms, he appeared with his sister, who also exhibited incombustibility and disdain for poisons. On this and many subsequent occasions, "amateurs of Chemistry" were "requested to bring with them any Materials they may think proper to put the Exhibitor's FIRE PROOF to the test."

If £10 could be raised by subscription, Chabert announced on a playbill, "a beautiful display of FIRE WORKS will play on him until his shirt is burnt off his back." The Chaberts announced their willingness to duplicate their prowess at private engagements. He claimed to be able to speak French, Italian, German, Russian, and Polish, while "Miss Chabert" conversed in "Russian and English, being educated at an English Boarding School."

In June, Chabert's back-burning stunt almost proved fatal, not for the Fire King, but for his audience. At the Theatre Penzance, so much smoke filled the room, and the sulfurous smell became so unbearable, that the attendees were "forced to seek for a purer atmosphere. But as the means of egress did not allow of their doing this as quickly as was necessary, several persons fainted, and a scene of general confusion ensued." Shouts of "Fire!" were raised, and a crowd outside broke through the roof of the building. This averted disaster, allowing the smoke to evaporate and the injured to recover.

By 1820, Chabert's advertisements claimed endorsements from scholars of Winchester College, members of the Royal College of Surgeons, and independent doctors of Portsea and Salisbury, attesting to his talents. For a June appearance at Royal Waterloo Assembly Rooms at 97 Pall Mall, the Fire King, always eager to please, added a special note: "To the Ladies—As some Ladies have expressed a reluctance to see the Exhibition, fearing the Performance must be painful and injurious to Mons. Xavier [the only time I find him so billed], the latter earnestly assures them that such is not the case. The easy and cheerful manner in which he goes through his various operations, will at once assure the spectators of his total insensibility to pain; therefore persons of the most delicate sensibility will not have their feelings hurt, whilst they, at the same time, gratify a natural and laudable curiosity."

While Chabert had the ability to capture the public's attention with apparently new and ever more dangerous effects, his shows consisted basically of the following stunts:

1. Will bear a lighted candle under his feet for several minutes.
2. Will forge a plate of Red Hot Iron with his feet.
3. Will undergo torture by fire as used in the Spanish Inquisition.
4. Will positively drink Boiling Oil.
5. Will drop on his tongue a quantity of Sealing Wax from which any of the Company may take the print of a Seal.
6. Will eat burning Charcoal.
7. Will bathe his Feet in Boiling Lead.
8. Will pour Aqua-Fortis [nitric acid] on Steel Filings and trample on it.
9. Will rub a Red Hot Shovel on his Tongue, Arms, Legs, and on his Hair, until it is so hot that a person cannot bear his hand on it.
10. Will pour Vitriol, Oil, and Arsenic into the Fire, hold his Head in the Flames and inhale the Vapours.
11. Will pour Aqua-Fortis on a piece of Copper in the hollow of his hand.
12. Will put Boiling Lead in his mouth with his Hand.
13. Will eat a torch as if it were a salad.

At 23 New Bond Street in March of 1821 (again sharing the stage with his sister), Chabert deemed it necessary to end the show with the exhibition of "an astonishing Mechanical Piece of Ordinance." This was a cannon combined with "a newly invented mechanical Apparatus" which made the operation of the gun so simple "that it may be performed by a child." "The wonderful precision and extreme exactness which directs every successive Motion of this Masterpiece of Mechanism, having required several Years deep meditation and burning the midnight oil [no doubt on his tongue] the inventor will presume to think himself entitled to the tribute of Public curiosity and to the approbation of Amateurs and Connoiseurs at large."

Apparently, Chabert was eager to be considered a showman, and not just a physical anomaly. To this end he also presented, in 1822, "The celebrated Indian Chief, his Wife and Child in their grand costume . . . who will exhibit feats peculiar to their country."

The chief was responsible for what we are wont to call a "freak accident"; it was reported in a London paper under the heading "Extraordinary Circumstance." While examining one of the Indian's arrows, Chabert grazed his own chin with its tip. A short time later "the whole of his chin and the side of his face turned black and was very much swollen." Realizing the arrow had been coated with poison, observers summoned three doctors, who "were baffled in their efforts in consequence of the very powerful effect of the poison." The Indian

Chabert occupies the position of honor in the frontispiece to Fairburn's
New London Conjuror, *circa 1820.*

stood by with the utmost *sangfroid* and witnessed the skill of medicine,
"when he walked away with as much coolness as he had observed the
operation with . . . and produced some root used in his country to
extract poison from the wound, and he applied some to the master's
face, which rendered immediate relief, the swelling went down and
the discoloration decreased. Had not the remedy been pursued, mor-
tification would have most probably ensued."

The restraint of the London press in not noting the irony of the
Poison Resister's near-death by poison, is admirable but incomprehensible. *Variety*, not to mention *Newsweek*, would have crucified him.

Chabert had for years enjoyed the publicity surrounding his oven-
entry accomplishments without actually performing the stunt in England (his handbills often stated that if a suitable sum could be arranged
by subscription he would wield a leg of mutton and with it undergo
roasting). In June of 1826, either the time or money seemed appropriate
and Chabert entered the oven—once for friends and the press, then
again for the general public.

The scene of the bake-off was White Conduit House in London.
The oven was constructed on four pillars; Chabert, abjuring the use
of trickery, welcomed testing of the "fairness and absolute reality of
the transaction." He even cut an "aperture for respiration and conver-

sation with the Public" during the performance. At noon "three large faggots of wood, which is the quantity generally used by bakers," were placed in the oven. Twelve more faggots were added and set ablaze. At three o'clock he entered the oven with a rumpsteak and a piece of mutton. He stayed until the steak was, in the English fashion, well done. He repeated his experiment with the lamb; then, his ordeal over, he "sat down to partake, with a respectable assembly of friends . . . those viands, the cooking of which he had been so watchfully attending."

According to the *Times*, "this joint was devoured with such avidity by the spectators as leads us to believe, that had Monsieur Chabert himself been sufficiently baked they would have proceeded to a Caribbean banquet."

Performing at his own benefit at the Theatre Belfast in March of 1827, Chabert elevated the stunt of burning his shirt with fireworks into the ominous sounding "Temple of Fire." The "temple" was a framework structure set with five hundred cartridges of fireworks (at a later showing one mathematically minded reporter counted only 129 cartridges), which were fired off and burned the clothes from his body, revealing a second suit of apparel underneath.

Again in London, Chabert featured a program chosen from his previously mentioned repertoire. The oven experiment was described in a playbill for an appearance at No. 275 Strand, but only to be performed if a suitable sum could be raised. Again Chabert announced his willingness to perform privately, but listed only French and Italian as languages spoken. (The press, as we will see, found his English primitive and consequently very amusing.) He graciously concluded his advertisement with the following: "In cases of sudden fire, Mr. CHABERT will be most happy to be called upon, to help any Fellow Creature in Danger; he resides at No. 27 Leicester Square."

The year 1829 was a pivotal one for Chabert. He garnered more attention and publicity than ever before, but with it a notoriety that would hasten his demise in England.

He successfully entertained the Marquis of Hertford and two hundred guests (consisting of Prince Esterhazy, Count Ludoph, members of the English aristocracy, and most of the foreign ambassadors in London) at the lordship's palatial villa, Regent Park. At the fete, Chabert swallowed an ounce of arsenic, thirty or forty grams of phosphorus, and a large quantity of nitric acid. When he offered to consume even more dangerous prussic acid, he was thwarted by the medical men present. This caused one London daily to comment on the conduct of the upper classes: "This temperance is to be admired. If a vulgar mob of two hundred persons could be brought to relish the exhibition of a man taking three rapid poisons, they would see no harm in allowing him to take a fourth; but the tenderness of the aristocracy is more considerate. They were amused by the first, second

INCOMBUSTIBLE
MEN
AND
FIREPROOF
WOMEN

245

and third dose but revolted by the fourth. It is really an example of moderation and high feeling worthy of attention."

Chabert strengthened his reputation by spontaneously replacing, with his bare hands, burning charcoal which had fallen to the ground when a brazier in the mansion accidentally overturned.

Chabert apparently did consume prussic acid in a test widely reported in October of that year. While drinking his now standard poisonous potables he was challenged by a Mr. Cooper, chemist of Exeter, to down a teaspoon of prussic acid. Chabert agreed and left the room, admitting to the public that he would fortify himself by ingesting a secret antidote. Upon his return, he requested the poison be administered to him. No one wanted to take such an ominous responsibility, so he finally took a teaspoon himself from the chemist's vial. Immediately his eyes rolled back in his head and he staggered around the room. There was genuine concern for his life; but he soon recovered to a tumultuous ovation. The vial of acid was tested by medical men, who disagreed on its potency. To settle the argument, it was suggested that a few drops be fed to some animal. A cat was brought from a nearby shop, and over the protests of many, a doctor fed it four drops of acid. The cat died in less than thirty seconds.

Although the medical men signed a paper attesting to the extraordinary events, all present were not satisfied as to the validity of the test. The possibility of deception, either by switching the vial of prussic acid for a non-toxic duplicate or through the collusion of Cooper and Chabert, was suggested.

In the months that followed, Chabert announced a remedy for hydrophobia, "not quite ready, by which he will be able to let a mad dog bite him without suffering any other injury than that which would be inflicted by the bite of a dog not mad."

At a performance in the Argyll Rooms, Chabert was challenged by a rival fire and poison resister, Lewis Lazarus, or rather, by a gentleman called Mr. Pickett representing Lazarus, as Lazarus was deaf and dumb. There was much verbal dueling but little was decided in the disruption, the public eventually asking for Mr. Pickett to take his seat so Chabert could perform. Chabert responded by donning a green baize coat and hood and entering his "temple of fire." For the five minutes during which fireworks were exploded on and around him, he displayed his versatility by singing "Le Vaillant Troubadour."

Nothing more seems to have come from the Lazarus affair, but a challenge from a Mr. J. Smith proved to be a triumph for Chabert. Smith placed an ad in the *Times* in which he accused the Frenchman of chicanery and claimed he would duplicate all of Chabert's stunts.

Chabert quickly accepted the challenge for £50. At the Argyll Rooms on the appointed date Chabert, not seeing his challenger present, "warmed up" the audience by drinking some boiling oil.

Eventually spotting Smith, Chabert brought him forward. He received some phosphorus from Smith and it was examined and guaranteed by Dr. Gordon Smith, a medical professor from London University. To prove that "I do not juggle," Chabert's hands were tied behind his back. (In playbills, he often advertised that he performed "without the least admixture of sleight of Hand Tricks, or contemptible Legerdemain.") He was given, and swallowed, twenty grams of phosphorus. His mouth was examined to prove he had ingested it. He called for the challenger to do the same, but Mr. Smith, pale and frightened, quickly declined the invitation. Smith also declined a seat in Chabert's oven.

Realizing he had lost the bet, Smith explained to the confused crowd that he had never intended to take the poison. He represented, he said, a group of scientific men who did not believe the Frenchman's claims. Smith testified he was now perfectly convinced that Chabert had taken twenty grams of a substance of which three grams would cause death.

The unlikelihood of such conduct again caused the more skeptical of the press to raise the cry of collusion. Chabert denied the accusation and was so taken with the positive *Times* account of the affair that he had it independently published. The pamphlet, printed by Howlett and Brimmer in Soho, was entitled *Narrative of the Unparalleled Feats of the Fire King*.

Chabert, increasingly provoking the ire of the citizenry, found himself embroiled in a philosophical dispute over his antidotes to hydrophobia, rattlesnake bite, and many poisons.

A letter to the *Times* of September 28, 1829, requested that Chabert make his antidote public and "confer a great benefit on society." It was signed "Chirigicus." It prompted a reply from Chabert on the necessity of receiving a suitable reward for his discovery (at one time he specifically requested ten thousand guineas!). Another correspondent, "Chemicophilosopos," argued that such a reward would be a small price to pay to "lessen the catalogue of human misery." Other letters, from doctors worried about the credulity of the public and from eyewitnesses defending Chabert's claims, followed.

A letter from Greenwich Hospital to the editor of the *Times* on October 16 began: "England has long been the hot bed of Quackery. Quacks like oysters soon get fat on this side of the water: even the living skeleton soon felt the revivifying influence of the climate, his fleshless bones glowing anew with marrow. Indian chiefs, dancing dogs, living monkeys and dead mermaids mingle in glorious rivalry for John's [John Bull, i.e., England] enlightened approbation. Otaheitan heads and Hottentot . . . [backsides] are alike inviting to John's insatiable eye of curiosity. But the wonder of wonders is Mons. Chabert, who eats fire with as much *gusto* as other of his countrymen devour frogs."

A cigar-box label featuring the famous scientist Sir David Brewster, who reported the fire tests of Blagden and exposed the methods of many quacks in his Letters on Natural Magic, London, 1832.

ASSEMBLY ROOM,
MERMAID TAVERN
Hackney.

Positively for Three Nights Only!!!
Mr. J. Knight,
Of the late Theatre Royal English Opera House, and Royal Assembly Rooms, Margate,
Ching Lau Lauro,
The Celebrated Chinese Buffo, of the Theatre Royal Drury Lane, who has had the honour of Performing before their present MAJESTIES, at the Pavilion, Brighton,
Mons. CHABERT,
The Celebrated FIRE KING!!
OF THE LATE

ARGYLL ROOMS.

Respectfully informs the Inhabitants of Hackney and its Vicinity that they purpose giving their astonishing Performances at the above Assembly Rooms, on
MONDAY, Dec. 27th,
TUESDAY, Dec. 28th,
AND
WEDNESDAY, Dec. 29th,
PART FIRST.
The Entertainments will Commence with Mr. J. KNIGHT'S Popular
CONVERSAZIONE, entitled
Sketches in Town & Country.
INTRODUCTION.
Age of Improvement. Charles Wright and Macassar Oil. Locks on a Bald-head renovated. The Hyp. Ennui and Blue Devils cured. Cured Incurables. New Lodgings. Landlord great Traveller. Conversation on different things. Query answered in a
Song. 'I fell in Love.'
Introduction to a Birth-day Party. Company described. Mrs. Haversack and Master Haversack, Mr. Felix Fact. Balls and Bears. Auction Mart. Great Bargain. Mrs. Go-to-bed, great Talker. Adventures in Africa 'Only believe half.' Hypocondryism and Nervous debility. 'Not fit to be left alone.' River Nile. When I was in the Army. Never forget the Time. War note of the Drum.
Song. 'Twas in the merry Month of May.
Mr. Gossamer. Habitual risibility. Laugh and Grow Fat. Ox tall soup. Whimsical circumstance. York-shireman building a Mill. Old Maids and Old Bachelors. Matrimony, only Eighty-four.
Song. *Pity the Sorrows of a Poor Old Man.*
Zachary Barnacle peaceful stay at home character. No dancing Bears now, no Lotteries, all our Amusements taken from us. Pompey's Pillar. Vauxhall Hams. Westphalia Boars. The only Old Dornton. Exchange of Umbrellas. Fishing excursion. Patience in a Punt. Cockney Sportsmen.
Song. (by desire) Margate Steam Boats.
FINALE.
PART SECOND.
Ching Lau Lauro's Magical Illusions.
Among the Multiplicity of the extraordinary Fetes of the above Performer, will be introduced the Scientific
Chinese Birds.
So highly Educated as to go through the following Performances:
Play a game at Cards with any of the Company; tell the Hour by a clock or watch; select cards that have been previously marked by the Company and shuffled with the rest of the pack; answer questions put to them with the greatest readiness and facility; with other feats too numerous to be inserted in the bills.

PART THIRD.
Mons. CHABERT,
The Fire King!
Will go through His Wonderful Performance.
M. Chabert will put HOT SEALING WAX and MELTED LEAD ON HIS TONGUE, and instruct any of the Company how to do so without experiencing the slightest ill effects whatever. He will swallow with impunity a desert spoon full of Pure Florence Oil, heated to 340 degrees, being 128 higher than Boiling Water. He will take 10 GRAINS OF PHOSPHORUS, the strength of which Poison may be inferred from the Fact, that both FONTANA and ORFILA assert that FOUR GRAINS of it are sufficient to destroy any Human Being. He will also inhale
Vapours of Arsenic, Oil of Vitriol, &c. exposed over a Fire.
The whole of the Amusements to conclude with CHING LAURO'S
SURPRISING
Feats of Strength, Equilibriums,
Evolutions, &c. &c. never attempted by any other Person.
The SONGS accompanied on the Grand Piano Forte, by a Professional
Gentleman.
Admission.   Front Seats, 2s.   Back 1s.   Children, Half Price.
Doors Open at Seven,   Commence at Half Past.
J. W. PEEL, Printer, 9, New Cut, Lambeth.

Chabert shares the bill with well-known magician Ching Lau Lauro and his Chinese birds.

INCOMBUSTIBLE
MEN
AND
FIREPROOF
WOMEN

249

J. H. H., as the letter-writer identified himself, offered his explanation of the methods used by Chabert. Licking a hot poker, he said, might be done by anyone with sufficient saliva to protect the tongue. This protection was also a retardant to the effect of boiling oil, which, he insisted, was taken in far more minute quantities than advertised. Phosphorus, he claimed, had no ill effects for an hour in the empty stomach of an individual, and a stomach pump was all the antidote anyone would need. As for the oven, J. H. H. mentioned the tests done by Doctors Fordyce and Blagden (also Sir Joseph Banks—these were first mentioned by the London press after Chabert's White Conduit House demonstrations, and subsequently in Hone's *Every Day Book*, where it was remarked that as early as 1674, Tillet's experiments proved that women accustomed to working in ovens could endure temperatures of 280°F for ten minutes). These men of science had shown that humans could survive in air heated to a far higher temperature than boiling water, "Dr. Blagden himself having stayed in a room at 260°F, for twelve minutes." Chabert, he said, claimed his oven was 400°F. But even if this were true, Chabert's oven, he argued, had an aperture at the very back, ostensibly to allow him to speak, but really for the admission of cool air. (Others speculated that Chabert held his thermometer in the red-hot embers to make it read significantly higher than the actual interior temperature.) Chabert, he said, sat "as comfortably situated as if he had been enjoying the luxury of a Lady's fan on a hot summer day." To Chabert's suggestion of a subscription of ten thousand persons at one guinea each to be received before publishing his antidotes, he said: "Was there ever before such an attempt at humbug?" He concluded, "Mons. Chabert claims he has taken large doses of prussic acid. I don't believe a word of it. John, my Friend, take care of your pockets."

Chabert's fame grew. He was the subject of at least three different portrait prints in 1829. In a crudely printed broadside entitled "DEATH/ The FIRE KING/Roasted" (issued by Bishop in Drury Lane, hand-dated November 26, 1829), Chabert's near-death was described, but "we are happy to hear that his Fiery Majesty is in red hot health. . . ."

Perhaps most amusing was a punning poem by an H. W. C. entitled *A Salamander's Apotheosis; or stanzas addressed to Mons. Chabert of the Argyll Rooms* and given in part below:

> No errant-knight in days of yore,
>   Tho' bent on martial toil;
> Like thee was ever known before,
>   Engaged in *red-hot* BROILS!

How vainly would the bigot's ire,
 Around thee blazes make;
Tho' like a *martyr in the fire*,
 Thou'rt bound unto the STEAK!

I see *no cause* but thou should'st cheer
 thy hopes—tho' fortune lingers;
If others chance to interfere,
 No doubt they'll *burn their* FINGERS!

Proud Fashions frown will be surpress'd,
 'Twere vain to call *thee sloven*!
That man must surely be *well dressed*
 who dresses *in an* OVEN!

Thy *warmest* friends encourage thee,
 On holiday and high-day;
I'd GRATE-FUL for a ticket be,
 to pass me in next FRY-DAY!

As the controversy over Chabert (benefactor to mankind or bamboozler of the masses) continued, a small paragraph in a London daily announced, quietly, unceremoniously, the introduction of Thomas Wakely.

Wakely, the editor of the prestigious medical journal *The Lancet*, had thought of the Fire King's oven stunts as mere "curiosity," but on the subject of antidotes for poison he decided to enter the fray. Wakely attended the next performance but Chabert refused arsenic, phosphorus, and prussic acid, claiming a severe cold.

While arrangements were made for another test, Wakely applied to the London magistrate Mr. Halls. What, he wanted to know, would be the legal repercussions of feeding the showman potentially fatal prussic acid? Halls replied that if harm came to Chabert, Wakely could be considered an accessory to injury or death. Chabert, Wakely explained, had asked to take the acid. "Suppose," Mr. Halls said, "that a juggler should say, 'You may cut off my head, for I possess the power of placing it on my shoulders.' Would not the party who took him at his word be guilty of murder?" Wakely confessed to feeling "awkward," but as he had now received more than one hundred letters from his readers, he determined that Chabert's claims should be fairly tested. Halls again cautioned Wakely and the meeting ended.

On February 4, the long-awaited confrontation took place. The Argyll Rooms were filled to overflowing. Mr. Welch, the proprietor of the rooms, took the platform. Mr. Wakely also mounted the stage, heralded by the crowd. Welch said that Chabert would perform his complete repertoire as previously announced, but due to some confu-

INCOMBUSTIBLE
MEN
AND
FIREPROOF
WOMEN

251

sion, he was forced to explain that Chabert never claimed to ingest the prussic acid himself, but rather to administer it to two dogs. Cries of "Shame! Shame! Imposition!" greeted Welch. Wakely pointed out that Chabert had by advertisement agreed to take the acid.

Chabert, barely audible over the crowd's roar, claimed he would do all that was advertised. "De dogs are ready," he said, "but me no say I take prussic acid today myself. You are a clever man, Monsieur Lance," he addressed Wakely, "but it won't do, I am no such fool." The booing and hissing of the audience forced the Fire King to lose "his accustomed composure and . . . he mimicked the yelling of the audience to their no small amusement."

Wakely repeated the challenge: "You have declared you can take prussic acid without injury; are you willing to put your boast to the test?"

"I will do all my bill say. I will kill one dog wid de prussic acid, and another dog dat take it shall not die. What more do you want, Monsieur Lance?"

The audience howled and hooted. Chabert offered to return the admission money. He was greeted with chants of "Cheat!" and "Imposter!" Leaving the platform, he "met with some rough usage and was finally shoved into the street." The Fire King took refuge in an adjoining coal cellar, to which end, one paper noted: "Perhaps the abdication and descent of a Monarch was never more sudden or complete."

A series of attacks and rebuttals appeared in the papers. Chabert claimed he was ill-treated because he was a foreigner. Doctors and men of science labeled him a fraud.

In a peculiar court case, Chabert charged a Mr. Futvoye with jumping through a window and assaulting him in the melee at the Argyll Rooms. Futvoye, in a letter to the *Times* of February 10, stated that Chabert promised to him in front of fifty people to "take any poison brought to him with sufficient notice." He called Chabert "a miserable imposter." Although Futvoye rather eloquently denied Chabert's charges, (while taking every opportunity to label Chabert a cheat) he was nevertheless found guilty and fined £3.

The broadside printers and bedside poets went quickly to work. An anonymous ditty called "The Fire King and the Doctor" captured the general sentiment:

> In marvellous deeds, who was e'er so expert,
> As the mighty phenomenon, Monsieur Chabert?
> To rival his feats it was vain to aspire,
> The phosphorus-eater!—the monarch of fire!

With hot burning coals he would blow out his belly,
And drink boiling oil as you'd toss off a jelly;
And would stop in an oven, he publicly boasted,
Till a large leg of mutton was thoroughly roasted.

For the deadliest poison he car'd not a d—n,
And would take prussic acid by way of a dram,
In short, he possess'd so much chemical knowledge,
That he fairly bamboozled the Physical College.

"Begarr," he exclaim'd, "vere's my equal in science?
As to poison and fire, I can bid dem defiance;
Johnny Bull vants to know how I manage it—'Zounds,
De price of my secret is ten tousand pounds.

"If any ven doubts I can do vat I say,
Let dem come to my benefit—Tursday's de day;
And dem who presume my performance to libel,
I'll convince dat my vords is as true as de Bible."

Cried the Doctor, "I shrewdly suspect you romance it—
If so, you shall soon have a prick of my *Lancet*;
Should you prove an impostor, ere long I shall tackle ye,
And if I don't probe you my name isn't Wakley."

The Thursday arriv'd, and vast multitudes came,
To see the exploits of the Monarch of Flame,
"My performance," he cried, "to all England shall see
Whether Monsieur Chabert's impostor or no."

But the Frenchman drew back, and appeared to demur,
And shew'd manifest symptoms of acting the cur;
"Dat I am von fool," he exclaim'd, "don't you tink it,
And as to your poison I don't mean to drink it.

"You not understand vat I promis'd exactly,
Tho' a shrewd clever fellow, no doubt, Monsieur Vakley,
To poison my dogs my good Sair, you are free,
But vid your dam acid you shan't poison me.

"Begarr it is strange dat you make all dis riot,
An' not let me humbug de public in quiet,
Vy shouldn't you gif a poor Frenchman a chance?
You treat me vid great disrespect, Monsieur Lance."

Sublime was the uproar, and grand was the row,
Poor Chab bolted off without making his hew;
And amid execrations as bitter as dire,
The coal cellar shelter'd the Monarch of Fire.

Then heaven preserve humbug from hostile attacks,
And still send us lots of impostors and quacks!
Chabert, it's all up with you, "Sic gloria transit,"
And luck to bold Wakley, the man of *The Lancet*.

INCOMBUSTIBLE
MEN
AND
FIREPROOF
WOMEN

_____

253

T. Birt, a printer in Seven Dials, issued two broadsides mentioning Chabert. The first was entitled:

Total Destruction of the Argyll-Rooms
BY FIRE
Detection and Exposure of the
FIRE KING!!

It described a fire that broke out in the kitchen of the Argyll Rooms the night of Chabert's benefit.

Birt's second broadside, "Regent Street Hoax," was considerably more amusing. It featured verses, apparently sung, and two spoken segments. It, too, dealt with the gullibility of the English public. The final verse is as follows:

So far-ye-well ye Fire-King,
return to France a-laughing,
To think how you have gull'd the flats,
how the English you've been chaffing;
But the Lancet cut so very sharp,
O lord! how he did hollow—
"Me take de sixty pound to-night,
de poison take to-morrow."

On March 6 at Cox's auction rooms in St. James Street, Chabert finally conducted his prussic acid-and-dogs test under the supervision of a chemist who provided Scheele's acid. A debate, the first of many, arose as to whether Chabert or the chemist should supply the acid. Chabert argued that he had prepared the antidote for his own acid, and above protests, administered three or four minims of it to a "weakly" dog he had provided. The dog agonized for a while but in less than five minutes recovered and ran away.

It was evident from this that Chabert's acid was weaker than he had stated. (Chabert later "admitted he had decomposed the prussic acid—that he mingled his antidote with the poison, and had given it so mingled to various animals without its producing injurious effects on them—that he did not conceive the antidote would ever be of use to society. . . ." Some speculated whether it was prussic acid at all.) Next, grams of his prussic acid were administered to one of the two hardy dogs supplied by a spectator, even though Chabert claimed such a large dose would kill the dog on the spot.

ROYAL COBURG THEATRE,
UNDER THE SOLE MANAGEMENT OF MR. DAVIDGE.

First Appearance of Mons Chabert.—And of Mr. H. Kemble these Three Years.

MONDAY, JUNE 7th, 1830, AND DURING THE WEEK,
Will be presented the highly popular and interesting Melo-Drama of

GILDEROY, THE BONNIE BOY!

Scotch.—Gilderoy, the Bonnie Boy, a Freebooter, Mr. H. KEMBLE, his 1st Appearance these 3 Years.   Walter Logan, a Veteran Highlander, Mr. KING.
Bailie m'Nab'em, Mr. CONQUEST.   Johnnie Howie, a Wealthy Scotch Farmer, Mr. PORTEUS.
Charlie and Willie Robinson,..............Sons of the Jailor of the Tolbooth,..............Miss H. BODEN and Master G. MEYERS.
Andrew Clout'em, ... a Carpenter and Blacksmith, ... Mr. DAVIDGE.
Donald Bean and Niel M'Grimman,..............Chiefs of Gilderoy's Band,..............Messrs. J. GEORGE and SAUNDERS.
Clod and Clump,..............his Servants,..............Messrs. LEWIS and HERBERT.
Jessy,..............Daughter of Walter Logan, and attached to Gilderoy,..............Miss WATSON.
ENGLISH.—Colonel Havoc,..............Commander of the Troops in the Service of the Protector,..............Mr. WORRELL.
Charles Worthy, Captain in the same Service, Mr. FORESTER.   Stephen Fetterall, an Invalid Soldier, Jailor of the Tolbooth, Mr. MORTIMER.
Serjeant Skewer'em,..............of the First Company of Fusiliers,..............Mr. ELLIOTT.
Fitzwalter and Maurice,..............in the Protector's Service,..............Messrs. ELSGOOD and SMYTHERS.

The Proprietor has the honor to announce that, ever anxious to make his Theatre a source of Rational Amusement, he has Engaged,
For this Week only, that most Wonderful and Superhuman Phenomenon, Mons. CHABERT,

THE FIRE KING!

And that, in order completely to eradicate prejudices and false impressions that have been effectually cleared away in other Places where Mons. CHABERT has heretofore exhibited,

Platforms will be erected from the Boxes and Pit to communicate with the Stage, by means of which Medical Gentlemen are invited to a close Inspection of the Exhibition, *and to bring any of the Poisons with them* that Mons. Chabert undertakes to Swallow, and he will use them in preference to his own.

And in consequence of the several contradictions of some of the Public Journals, Mons. CHABERT will, on this occasion, endeavour to convince the Company of the reality of his Talent, and will produce Certificates (which the Company may peruse) of his incomparable Performances at London, Bath, &c. as well as Hamburgh, Altona, Brunswick, Gottingen, and other eminent Continental Towns, acknowledging his Skill in resisting the effects of the most dreadful of all Elements—all devouring FIRE! without the least admixture of Slight-of-hand Tricks, or contemptible Legerdemain; which the celebrated Physiologist, Professor BLUMENBACH, of Gottingen, the highest authority that can be quoted to men of science, has been pleased to certify and attest under his hand and seal; together with Count Groto, the Prussian Ambassador of Hamburgh; M. Aspern, Counsellor of State, Senator; the Director of Police at Altona; and all the Senators, Physicians, Chemists, and Literary Characters of Germany.

For the present, M. CHABERT deems it necessary to publish only the two following CERTIFICATES.

"We, the Members of the Royal Academy of Chirurgery of London, certify of having witnessed the extraordinary experiments of M. CHABERT; we have seen him inhale the most poisonous vapours of Vitriol and Arsenic exposed over a fire, and also saw him swallow portions of Phosphorus and Arsenic, which would prove evidently fatal to any other being. Our most scrutinising attention could not discover any deception whatever; and we are also aware that no human being could withstand the effects of fire and poison.—We are also unable to account for the truly surprising wonders we have seen of M. CHABERT."
Dr. W. Whickham, J. Gordon, M. Machillan, M. Parish, T. Gate, G. Lyford, Mr. Fowler, Mr. Couts, Mr. Wilkinson, T. Porter, T. Davies.

"We, the undersigned, certify that we have seen M. CHABERT take twenty grains of Phosphorus; expose himself during six minutes to the heat of an Oven, heated to 450 degrees Farenheit; expose his palate during several seconds to the flame of a candle."
Thomas King, M.R.C.L. M.D.P. &c. J. Osborn, J. Edmonds, T. Redwood, Lewis Redwood, General J. Chadwin.

Extract from the Morning Chronicle, March 27th, 1830.

M. CHABERT

Various misrepresentations having been circulated respecting the experiments made on Saturday, March 6th, 1830, at the Room, No. 20, St. James's Street, by M. Chabert.

We, the undersigned, having been invited to witness it, do state the following facts:—Two Dogs of an equal strength and size, were selected, when a portion of Prussic Acid (which had been brought by a medical Gentleman) was administered to one of the dogs, which destroyed it; a similar quantity was given to the other Dog, but the antidote being administered too quickly, it was not thought by the medical Gentleman a sufficiently satisfactory experiment; and therefore after some time elapsed, an equal dose of Prussic Acid was again taken out of the same bottle by the same medical Gentleman (Mr. Williams of the London Hospital,) and given to the same Dog, no other being at hand; after the Poison had taken its effect, the signal previously agreed upon being given by Mr. Harrison, one of the medical Professors, M. Chabert administered the antidote, and after a lapse of about five minutes, during which time the Animal seemed expiring, the dog gradually recovered, got well, and walked away, and is now in the possession of the owner, Mr. Bramby Cooper. Mr. Chabert then swallowed 50 grains of Phosphorus in the presence of several scientific Gentlemen, who were fully satisfied of the quality and quantity of the dose stated being fairly taken.—Signed

J. WILLIAMS, London Hospital.
R. M. WILSON, M.P. Regent Street.
C. DURNFORD, Bond Street.
E. COWCHE', Kensington
S. KEAN, Portman Square.
J. KILMACH, Sackville Street.

Extract from the Globe, November 19th, 1829.
Argyll Rooms.

We, the undersigned, certify, having witnessed the extraordinary experiments of M. Chabert, viz. his inhaling the most poisonous vapour of Arsenic, swallowing 21 grains of Phosphorus, and subsequently taking a tea-spoonful of concentrated Prussic Acid, which we brought and administered to him ourselves; at the same time we gave four drops to a Cat which expired in half a minute afterwards. M. Chabert took a table-spoonful of pure Florence Oil, heated to 330 degrees. We saw him enter an oven heated to 500 degrees, (Fahrenheit) the thermometer having been previously hung in the middle of the oven, and a dish of raw meat being done in less than five minutes; no deception could be practised, because we entered very scrupulously into the matter of all his experiments' after a close examination we willingly subjoin our names as follows:

JORDAN COOPER, Exeter.
C. L. J. LORD, Hampstead.
T. MILLAR, Quebec Street, Portman Square.
H. WATTON, Fish Street Hill.
H. HORR, Great Portland Street.
W. JOHNSON, Giffen Street, Bond Street.
J. HOOPER, Old Burlington Street.
J. Edwards, Fleet Market.
S. C. TUCKER, Navy Office.
R. BARRAS, Holborn.
J. HARTLEY, Cannon Street, City.
J. DONNALDSON, 16, Mary-le-bone Street, Golden Square.
&c. &c. &c.

A Letter to the Editor of the Times, in reply to one from Chirurgicus which appeared in that Paper.

I have seen a second Letter in THE TIMES as to my knowledge of an antidote against hydrophobia. Does CHIRURGICUS wish me to publish my secret to the world without a reward, on which myself & family may live? Should CHIRURGICUS desire such an unbounded folly on my part, I feel assured, Sir, that you are more liberal, & I shall be much obliged by your informing that Gentleman, that it is my intention to publish the whole of my secrets, as to antidotes against every species of poison,—the bite of the rattle snake, mad dog, &c. on the following plan—a book will be opened at a respectable banking house, where subscriptions will be received, and prior to my claiming any part, I will expose myself to a committee of professional gentlemen and others, who shall call on me to take any poison they think fit, which I will do, and be informed of every ingredient necessary to compose the antidote. Should I fail to prove the efficacy of my antidotes, my claim to the money will cease, and the whole will be returned to the Subscribers: should I succeed fully in proving their powers, the certificate of the committee shall vest in me a right, after the delivery of the masks, to draw on the Banker for the sum subscribed. If CHIRURGICUS will allow me the pleasure of doing him or his friends a service gratuitously, which he seems to desire, tell him that if he labours under the painful effects of tooth-ache, and will call on me at the Argyll Rooms, accompanied by his suffering friends, I will, within the space of two minutes, relieve both him and them, without extracting a tooth or putting them to the least possible pain.
X. CHABERT.

Routine of Performance.—M. Chabert respectfully announces that he will put HOT SEALING WAX and MELTED LEAD ON HIS TONGUE, and instruct any of the Company how to do so without experiencing the slightest ill effects whatever.

Pure Florence Oil heated to 340 degrees, being 128 higher than Boiling Water. He will take 10 Grains of Phosphorus. The Strength of which Poison may be inferred from the Fact, that both FONTANA and ORFILA assert that FOUR GRAINS of it are sufficient to Destroy any Human Being;—He will also inhale Vapours of Arsenic, Oil of Vitriol, &c. exposed over a Fire!
And at the end of the Faithless Friend, he will conclude his Wonderful Performances by entering a

Temple of Fire, 10 feet high by 6 broad, composed of upwards of 500 Cartridges!

M. CHABERT will remain in this immense Body of Flame till one entire Suit of Apparel is consumed on his Person, leaving the other uninjured !

To conclude with a Serio-Comic Melo-Drama, the Plot and principal Incidents, taken from a highly popular Spectacle of the late celebrated Mr. Cross, but which, in some few respects, is now attempted to be rendered more accordant to the prevailing Public Taste, Entitled, The

Faithless Friend, or a British Seaman's Fidelity.

Captain Augustus Arundel,.......... Mr. BLANCHARD.   Ben Billows, ... his faithful and attached Boatswain, ... Mr. H. KEMBLE.
Lord Edmund Fitzwalter,.............. the Faithless Friend, ... Mr. SERLE.
Lord de Howard, Mr. WORRELL,   Maurice, his Agent, mr. KING,   Lance Lave, Mr. SCARBRO.   Foam, Mr. J. GEORGE.
Hugh Jackington, Mr. PORTEUS.   Gregory Griphard, Mr. HENNING.
Strongbow, ... an Outlaw of the Desolate Pass, ... Mr. ELSGOOD,   Israel Manoah, ... a Travelling Jew, ... Mr. MORTIMER.
Lady Julia, Daughter to Lord de Howard, Miss WATSON.   Edith, her Attendant, Mrs. LEWIS.
The Widow Wantly,...... Mrs. WESTON.   Jane, ... Mrs. MORRIS,   Rose Wantly, ... betrothed to Ben, ... Mrs. DAVIDGE.

The extensive and brilliant Paraphanalia of the Scenery, Dresses, Decorations and appropriate Embellishments, being nearly completed of the Grand Historical Drama of
Darnley, the Knight of Burgundy; or, The Field of the CLOTH of GOLD!
Mr. DAVIDGE can safely announce it for MONDAY Next, the 14th Instant, when it will be positively produced.

A verbose Fire King tells his tale, 1830.

INCOMBUSTIBLE
MEN
AND
FIREPROOF
WOMEN

255

The dog did die, but only after ten excruciating minutes. A like amount was then given to the second dog. Chabert immediately gave the antidote—so quickly that many thought he'd snatched the poison out of the dog's mouth. The dog, "though he appeared frightened, did not exhibit any symptoms by which it could be supposed that the poison had affected its nervous system." Chabert proudly solicited the applause of the crowd, claiming to have been completely successful. He was "met with a disdainful laugh" and forced to try the experiment again, this time giving the dog time to completely swallow the toxic substance. Another animal could not be found, so the same dog was used again.

The dog, as might be expected, was reluctant to open its mouth. Eventually, it was fed ten minims of Chabert's acid, and the dose was allowed to take effect. Its lower extremities were paralyzed before the antidote was administered. After an agonizing half hour (which included the application of ammonia to the animal's nose as it lay insensible), the dog recovered.

The audience responded with "a tumult of applause." Though the newspaper reports were again mixed, many scientific men present were impressed with the results. The experiment, however, did little to exalt Chabert's name in London.

On February 15, 1830, "The proprietors of *Sadler's Wells Theatre*, ever anxious to cater to the amusement of their Patrons, beg to announce the first representation of a splendid Melo-Drama, and a laughable Extravaganza founded upon a RECENT FACT, Which will introduce to the Friends the celebrated adventure of the FIRE KING." *The Fire King, or the Frenchman Puzzled* was written, produced, and directed by Mr. Campbell, who also starred as "Monsieur Poison, the Fire King." Other characters were "Frisk 'em," "Nibble," "Wide awake," and a group of doctors called "Thin, Seedy, Stout, and Needy." Also listed on the playbill were two dogs, "Mssrs. BARK and BITE." The final scene of the one-acter took place in "a correct Model of the OVEN used by the Fire King."

As a blurb in one of the papers put it, "M. Chabert, who recently met with such a warm reception at the Argyll Rooms, is destined to undergo another roasting this evening at Sadler's Wells where his majesty is to be introduced as the butt of a local extravaganza. . . ."

The success of the play led the management of Sadler's Wells to engage Chabert himself for one night, May 12. The audience was invited to mount the stage during his performance and told (with the usual artistic license) that "this celebrated individual . . . not only defeated the calumnies and reports which were issued to his prejudice but on the contrary having proved every assertion he had made to the entire satisfaction of the PUBLIC and the Medical World."

This performance met with such success that the Frenchman was rehired. Medical men were invited to the shows, which consisted of demonstrations from his usual repertoire, ending with the "Temple of Fire." No mention was made of prussic acid.

Chabert appeared in the provinces and London until the end of the year. From reading the bills and advertisements of the events one would assume that the controversy with Wakely and the events at the Argyll Rooms had never taken place. They were dismissed and forgotten like a bad meal.

It can be seen from the preceding appearances that Chabert worked frequently in England following the Argyll debacle, and was not, as other writers have suggested, driven immediately from the country because his inhumane treatment of animals repulsed the English public.

Shortly before leaving England, the Fire King was mentioned in a curious article in the *Mechanics Weekly Journal*: "A machine to be built by Mr. Rogers, coach maker of Plymouth, under the direction of M. Chabert and which in the course of ten days will be launched to travel to London in three hours less time than the mail." Chabert finally departed England in 1831 and never returned.

CHABERT IN AMERICA

The Fire King made his debut in New York's Clinton Hall on October 14, 1831. He swallowed pure Florence Oil at 340° F, ingested twenty grams of phosphorus, and inhaled the vapors of arsenic, oil of vitriol, and so on.

In November, at the New York Museum, he featured both the "Temple of Fire" and the cooking of steaks in an oven heated to 400° F. "He will, as usual," he promised, "learn the company many amusing experiments." In February of the following year, billed as "Professor of Chemistry and Pyronechic Arts," he drank heated oil, molten lead, and sealing wax, and in the Philadelphia Ballroom asked doctors to try and poison him.

He offered for sale "TAPUYAS ELIXIR for the instantaneous cure of the tooth ache." In a bill advertising the tooth product, Chabert claimed to have learned the special formula from long study of Tapuyas savages of the Brazils. The elixir, he claimed, was also "certain and powerful" to combat scurvy. The product could not be considered genuine, he added, without "T.W.X.C." or "Xavier Chabert" signed on the wrapper. He provided a "liberal allowance to Druggists and Captains of Ships."

While Chabert braved fire and fixed teeth, W. C. Houghton, the "American Fire King," challenged the Frenchman at the Arch Street

Theater in Philadelphia, where he announced "several fiery feats pronounced by MONS. CHABERT as an IMPOSSIBILITY." He also confronted his rival in Baltimore, where at the Athenaeum he outlasted Chabert's run by a week.

INCOMBUSTIBLE
MEN
AND
FIREPROOF
WOMEN

257

Houghton performed on the East Coast and excited the press for a few months, though he shared some of the difficulties of his predecessor. The Boston *Advertiser* of June 15, 1832, reported that in South Carolina Houghton fed two cats prussic acid, but that even the one given the supposed antidote died. On March 19 the *Advertiser* carried a note saying "twelve gentlemen of Baltimore swear they saw Houghton kill a cat with one drop of prussic acid. He then made a dog take fifty drops and took fifteen himself, applying an antidote in each case."

Houghton managed a notice as a competitor of Chabert's even in far-off England, whose public, it seems, had not lost their curiosity about the Frenchman. The English papers also carried an erroneous report of Chabert's death by ingesting phosphorus.

Whether he was hurt by the short-lived competition of Houghton, suffered ruin from his disastrous tour of the States, or was simply tired of traveling and showcasing his odd talents, Chabert soon retired from performing.

It was reported in London on February 15, 1833, that Chabert had opened a drugstore in the United States. This he did in New York City.

An outbreak of cholera provoked Chabert to advertise his great success in combating that disease. Of 528 cases, he proudly claimed, he lost only 4 by death. His technique was a cathartic and a nostrum. He proclaimed his treatment "neither Charlatanism or Quackery but the truth." He invited physicians and members of the Board of Health to "come and see." At the time he resided at 34 Reed Street.

"He made and sold," states Houdini, "an alleged specific for the White Plague, thus enabling his detractors to couple his name with the word Quack."

Chabert had shops at, variously, 322 and 344 Broadway. From this latter address in 1836 he published a *Medical Notice* listing himself as J. X. Chabert, M.D. He was, at the time, residing at 310 Broadway. This slim volume listed cures and testimonials for a remarkable number of diseases. A brief sampling included: rheumatism, gout, dropsy, pulmonary consumption, piles, scrofula, immoderate flow of the menses, ringworm, chilblain, fall of the womb, palsy, corns, diarrhea, cancer, leprosy, and St. Vitus' Dance.

Graduating from his oven to a sudden listing as "member of the College of Physicians at New Albany, Indiana, late Head Physician to Mahomed Ali Pacha, Viceroy of Tripoli," perhaps he may have been an inspiration for Walford Bodie.

He was still an object of attention in England. In 1836 it was reported in a London paper that Chabert was about to be married to "a very rich widow. It is believed he had a wife and family in England."

In New York, with his "Fire King's Drug Store" now on Grand Street, calling himself at various times doctor, professor, celebrated Fire King, maker of Chinese Lotion, and curer of consumption, he was a familiar figure. He was often seen on Broadway, first decked out in a four-horse carriage, later switching to a fashionable tandem coach.

Chabert died on August 29, 1859 of pulmonary consumption. His obituary in the New York *Herald* claimed he was a "fast liver." The Irish woman he married (the apparent subject of the London article), presumed to be very rich, was not, and he left this earth with "little of the world's goods."

He was buried in Cypress Hills Cemetery.

Chabert was only one of a long list of fire and poison resisters who astounded audiences for hundreds of years. But few stirred the public's imagination with as much passion, and none, with the exception of Robert Powell, the eighteenth-century fire-king, captured it for as long. The length of Chabert's career is even more astonishing, given that in his era each month seemed to bring some new freak of nature or mechanical masterpiece to excite the masses.

Directly preceding Chabert in England was Signora Josephine Girardelli, who arrived from the Continent in 1814 with claims of royal patronage. Described as a Venetian lady between thirty and forty years of age, she was billed, oddly, as "The Great Phenomena of Nature." She made her debut in London in August.

Appearing at Mr. Laxton's Rooms, 23 New Bond Street, the Signora put boiling lead in her mouth (on which she happily showed the imprint of her teeth). She walked barefoot on a red-hot iron bar and passed the bar over various parts of her body. She washed in aquafortis and put boiling oil in her mouth, exhibiting every day at 12, 2, 4, and 6 o'clock for a fee of three shillings.

She quickly became a topic of conversation and appeared as the subject of prints published by Fores, Smeeton, and Kirby; the latter included a short biography of her in his *Wonderful and Eccentric Museum or Magazine of Memorable Characters*. (Kirby spells her name "Giraldelli"— obviously an error.) Kirby says, after describing her act, "that the whole is a trick cannot be doubted; but the vulgar gape and stare, and are fully prepossessed that the fair heroine is by nature gifted with this extraordinary repellent [to fire]." Kirby realizes that the "secret of the art doesn't seem to rest with her . . . as . . . several of this salamander tribe have appeared and may now be seen traveling from town to

INCOMBUSTIBLE
MEN
AND
FIREPROOF
WOMEN

259

A subdued Signora before her ordeal by fire, 1813.

town." Among them he mentions the Frenchman "Chaban" (obviously
Chabert), who, he claims, in addition to his aforementioned stunts,
"standing in the midst of a tar-barrel . . . remained therein till the
whole was consumed to ashes around him." The Signora performed
at Bartholomew Fair, and at the Theatre Portsmouth, under the
direction of well-known impresario John Richardson. Houdini states
that she toured England with the troupe of Signor Germondi, who
exhibited trained dogs.

An undated bill for the Signora's performance at Larkin's Great
Room, Grafton Street, announced, at reduced prices, "the last week of
the Fire-Proof Lady's Performance in this Kingdom." Promising upcoming engagements in America (which never, in fact, materialized),
she augmented her English appearance with an enlarged repertoire,
including torture by fire, the passing of lighted candles under her
arms, dropping sealing wax on her tongue, and cooking an egg "fit for
eating" while holding boiling oil in her hands.

The wonderful caricature of Girardelli shown in the color section of this book features the Signora in two stunts heretofore associated with Chabert. In one, she stands "unhurt amidst a blaze of Fire Works." The other pictures her emerging from an oven. I have never seen another reference to her performing these feats. One can deduce either that she introduced them before Chabert or, more likely, that the artist used the license long associated with his craft and that the print (unfortunately, unsigned and undated) was made after Chabert's initial performance of these stunts at a time when the Signora was still fondly remembered by the multitudes.

In *Demonologia; or Natural Knowledge Revealed* (London, 1827) the stunts performed by Chabert and Girardelli are recorded in the repertoire of an American female fire-queen called Miss Rogers.

A Mr. Carlton, "Professor of Chemistry, on his route to Scotland," duplicated most of the Signora's stunts in Mr. Blackett's Front Room, Three Tuns, Old Flesh Market, Newcastle, in December 1818. In addition, Carlton promised "to explain the Deceptive Part of the Performance, as practised by Fire-Proof Ladies and Gentlemen, and the Whole of the Performance, when there is sufficient Company. Mr. C. begs to say, that he has not come to perform in opposition to MADAME GIRARDELLI, but to gratify the Inhabitants of this Town with a satisfactory Explanation of what has so long been asserted as a supernatural Gift and baffled the Skill of many eminent Professors of Chemistry.

"Mr. C. proposes to instruct any of the Company to do as much as Madame Girardelli, or any Fire-Proof Lady or Gentleman in the World."

Neither the Signora nor the exposer were much heard of again.

Accounts of resistance to the effects of fire are recorded in many ancient cultures. Fire was a mystery; it was feared, even worshiped. One who could manipulate this terrible element was worthy of respect. Invincibility to flame led to power.

As seen in *Antigone*, ordeals by fire were common. Soldiers agreed to hold a red-hot iron or walk through burning coals to prove their innocence. At Etruria, Pliny tells us, the Herpi jumped through burning coals and were therefore accorded special privileges by the Roman senate. Priestesses of the Temple of Diana at Castabala did the same to "command public veneration."

Around 150 B.C., a Syrian named Eunus pretended communication with the gods by breathing fire and flames. For his deception he concealed in his mouth a nut shell pierced at both ends and filled with a burning substance. Many other methods to obtain the same effect have since been contrived.

Naphtha (which bursts into flame as it comes near fire) was used in ancient assassinations. Creusa, daughter of Creon, was given a fine dress soaked in naphtha by Medea. As Creusa approached a temple altar, she was consumed by flames. Alexander the Great, says Plutarch, was intrigued by the secret use of naphtha.

In the fourth century, Simplicius, Bishop of Autun, placed burning coals on his body without harm to demonstrate religious purity.

A *Book of Secrets* which contained recipes for fire resistance appeared in the thirteenth century; it was attributed to Albertus Magnus and published in English for the first time in 1550. It recommended:

IF THOU WILT BEAR FIRE IN THY HAND,
THAT IT MAY NOT HURT THEE.

Take lime dissolved with hot water of beans and a little magrencules [perhaps buttercup] and a little of Great Mallows or Hollyhock, and mix it well with it. After, anoint the palm of thy hand with it, and let it be dried; put in fire and it shall not hurt.

When thou wilt that thou seem all inflamed, or set on fire from thy head unto thy feet and not be hurt.

INCOMBUSTIBLE
MEN
AND
FIREPROOF
WOMEN

261

The well-known print of Ms. Girardelli from Kirby's Wonderful and Eccentric Museum.

This was accomplished with a combination of hollyhock and egg whites applied to the body, after which was rubbed alum and then brimstone beaten into powder.

Hugh Plat's *The Jewel House of Art and Nature* (London, 1653) tells "how any may safely put his finger or hand into molten lead without danger of burning." Zoroaster was said to confound his calumniators by shaking a shower of molten brass over his entire body. Plat saw a chemist named Hance perform this feat "for a pot of the best Beer in a garden in Southwark about 10 or 12 years since." (No fool, this Hance.) Plat recorded the formula for the ointment with which the chemist anointed himself.

Also in *The Jewel House* is: "How any man may hold a hot iron Bar in his hand without burning his flesh." This stunt, too, relied on a paste. It was made from applying "powder of horn burnt to ashes" upon a molten glue in which the hand was dipped. This was repeated to make a thick crust. How the ointments, assuming they worked at all, were concealed from the spectators who witnessed the stunts is not discussed.

Varying formulae for the same effects are found in conjuring books and books of secrets well into the nineteenth century. Frequently the author would try to make the account topical by referring to the personalities of the day, as in J. Victor's *Magic Recreations . . . Containing the Explanation of the Indestructible Man Residing in an Oven till a Joint of Meat Is Cooked* (Bristol, circa 1850) or in the following quote from Ingleby's *Whole Art of Legerdemain* (London, 1815):

TO WALK ON A HOT IRON BAR

Take half-an-ounce of camphor, dissolve it in two ounces of aqua-vitae, add to it one of quicksilver, one ounce of liquid storax, which is the droppings of myrrh, and hinders the camphor from firing; take also two ounces of hermatis, which is a red stone to be had at the druggists; and when you buy it let them beat it to powder in their great mortar, for being very hard it cannot well be beat in a small one; put this to the above-mentioned composition, and when you intend to walk on the bar, anoint well your feet with it and you may walk on it without danger or the least inconvenience.

N.B. By the explanation of this trick . . . the reader will become acquainted with the deception of the Wonderful Lady, now exhibiting. [Signora Girardelli]

In Nathaniel Wanley's *The Wonders of the Little World; or A General History of Man* (London, 1678) is mentioned a Negress at Pisa who easily handled hot coals. Wanley also mentions Martinus Ceccho, from Montelupo. Ceccho was well known in Pisa for his ability to put boiling

Illustrations of walking on hot iron bars and eating fire,
from the first edition of The Whole Art of Legerdemain,
or Hocus Pocus in Perfection by Henry Dean, London, 1722.

lead in his mouth, allow candles to be placed under his tongue, and handle red-hot coals, which he would place in his teeth until extinguished
and then "thrust them as a suppository, in his fundament," the latter
a stunt mercifully missing from the repertoires of other performers.

In Sir Henry Wotton's *Reliquiae Wottoniae* (London, 1685) is a
letter to Sir Edmund Bacon. It describes the performance, for twopence,
of an Englishman recently arrived in London from the West Indies,
"where he has learned to eat fire as familiarly as I ever saw cakes, even
whole glowing brands, which he will crush with his teeth and swallow."
(As the letter was dated June 3, 1633, Houdini, in *Miracle Mongers and
their Methods*, supposed this to be the first public performance of a fire-
eater in England.) The author of *Hocus Pocus Junior* (London, 1634)
describes a man he saw "eat half a dozen quick charcoal," which may
have preceded Wotton's description.

Some thirty years later, there appeared an Englishman who would
set the standards for generations of fire resisters. His name was
Richardson, and he excited the interest of scientists and the aristocracy,
gaining fame in France before doing so in his native country. His work
was chronicled in the *Journal des Scavans* in 1667 and again in 1680.
He was mentioned in other Continental accounts, and by John Evelyn,
who saw him at Lycester House (the site of the present Leicester

SUM SOLUS

ROBERT POWELL, the Fire eater, Drawn from the Life whilſt
he was exhibiting at Guildford in the Year 1780 He exhibited in
publick from the Year 1718 to the above mentioned Year. as may be
collected from his Advertiſements during that Period.
Published July 29th 1790 by J. Caulfield N.º 13 Castle Street Leicester fields.

Square) in October 1672. Richardson drank flaming melted pitch in
combination with wax and sulfur. He placed a red-hot iron bar between
his feet, bent down, and picked it up, using only his teeth. He melted
a beer glass and ate it. He devoured brimstone. He put a live coal on
his tongue, atop which he placed a raw oyster, and stoking the coal
with a bellows until it flamed and sparked, let the oyster remain until
it was "quite boil'd." (Illustrations of such stunts appear in seventeenth-
century conjuring books such as J. M.'s *Sports and Pastimes* and Simon
Witgeest's *Natuurlyk Toover-boek*, and early eighteenth-century editions
of Henry Dean's *Whole Art of Legerdemain*.)

Richardson suffered an exposure at the hands of his servant, who
made public recipes for the performer's secret preparations. The recipe
used by Richardson, it was reported by the French physics professor,
Dr. Panthot, was to rub his hands, mouth, tongue, etc., with pure

INCOMBUSTIBLE
MEN
AND
FIREPROOF
WOMEN

265

spirits of sulfur, which "burns and cauterizes the epidermis . . . until it becomes hard as leather." The swallowing of wax, resin, brimstone, etc., was eased by the ingestion of oil and warm water until the fiery substances could be regurgitated after the show. Such exposures, usually motivated by jealousy or the promise of financial reward, are all too common in the annals of conjurers and showmen, from earliest times to the present day.

The James Paris du Plessis manuscript mentioned previously contains an account and illustration of a fire-eater called De Heightre-hight (sometimes Heiterkeit). (A similar account appears in Malcolm's *Anecdotes and Customs, on London of the Eighteenth Century*.) He was born in the Valley of Annivi, between the Swiss and Italian Alps. In January 1718, Parisians saw a show at the Duke of Marlborough's Head, near Fleet Street, very similar to Richardson's performance years earlier (although De Heightre-hight broiled beef, not oysters, on his tongue). The Swiss performer exhibited his skills before Louis XIV of France, the Emperor of Germany, the Doge of Venice, and most of the princes of Italy. Called a wizard, he was twice brought before the Inquisition in Italy to officially determine his incombustibility. He was saved from this ordeal first at Piedmont by the intervention of the Duchess Royal Regent of Savoy, and later at Bologna by the Marquis of Bentivoglia.

Voltaire, in his *Commonplace Book*, reports on the performance of a "fire king" at Lyon. The mountebank and his female companion performed the usual tests, and walked barefoot on red-hot iron. This, they confessed to Voltaire, was made possible by a solution made of "oil and iced alum," a recipe which differed significantly from any others described. As for dropping sealing wax on the tongue, they explained, the only trick was the courage to do it.

The most famous of eighteenth-century fire resisters was undoubtedly Robert Powell, who had a long and significant career. He claimed an impressive list of distinguished patrons, including the Duke of Cumberland, the Duke of Gloucester, Sir Hans Sloane, and several members of the Royal Society, who presented Powell with a purse of gold and a large silver medal on May 4, 1751 ("which the curious may see by applying to him").

Affixed to a later bill of Powell's was the following sad note:

> Mr. Powell was on Wednesday the 19th of April robbed of a large Silver Medal, a Silver Trumpet, a Gold Lace'd Waistcoat containing Ten Guineas and about Thirty Shillings in Silver, in the Pocket, by a Young Man about 18 years of age, dressed in a green Coat and Waistcoat, and had sandy Hair, at a House in Windsor, where he lodged. A person or persons that can give Information of the Offender so that he may be brought to Justice shall receive Four Guineas Reward.

Powell melted a "quantity of rosin, pitch, beeswax, sealing wax, brimstone, alum and lead" and ate "the same combustibles with a spoon as if it were porringer of broth (which he calls his dish of soup)." His repertoire varied little from Richardson's and ironically, the exposé from the *Journal des Scavans* was reissued to explain Powell's stunts as part of an amusing letter to *Gentlemen's Magazine* of February 1755, signed Philopyrphagis Asburniensus. Part of this letter was again published in 1815 in an attempt to expose Signora Girardelli.

Notwithstanding, Powell enjoyed a remarkably long career. In addition to his fire stunts he also pulled teeth and performed amputations "so easily as scarce to be felt." And he preceded Chabert as a vendor of nostrums: "He sells a chemical liquid which discharges inflammation, scalds and burns in a short time, and is necessary to be kept in all Families."

In the years after Chabert's infamy, fire and poison resisters rarely claimed the attention of scientists and nobility. Their stunts did, however, become firmly entrenched in the repertoires of street buskers and carnival performers, and can be found in such places at the present time.

Over the years many unusual acts presented themselves to a bemused public. A few of them seem worthy of particular notice.

Jean Chacon, "L'homme Incombustible Espagnol," appeared in France in 1806. He ran red-hot iron over his tongue, hands, arms, and head (without his hair catching on fire). His feet were the major appendages of exhibition. He stood over lit candles for fifteen minutes, washed his pedal extremities in both molten lead and sulfuric acid, and did English dances on four red-hot pieces of iron.

Signore Lionetto, another "Incombustible Spaniard," aroused the curiosity of Lewis Seminti, Chief Professor of Chemistry at the Royal University of Naples. In 1808, Seminti noted that the Spaniard only entered ovens of his own specific design. Seminti also gave recipes for retarding the effects of fire and performed many of the Spaniard's effects himself. He applied a red-hot iron to his tongue after rubbing the tongue with a hard soap and an alum-based paste topped with fine powdered sugar. When he applied burning oil to his tongue, a hissing sound alarmed spectators, but caused the professor no pain. He waited for the oil to cool and then swallowed it.

In 1809, D. W. E. Müller wrote in German an exposé entitled in translation *The Unburnable Man, Herr Roger, How does he do it?* In a fairly substantial thirty-six-page pamphlet, Müller surveyed the exposure of Richardson and the tests of Sir Joseph Banks in an attempt to debunk another popular Spanish fire king and poison resister, Herr Roger.

On May 1, 1817, John Brooks sent a letter to Thomas Dibdin, then with the Royal Circus. A peculiar character for employment, Brooks wrote, "I do not want anything for my Performing for I have

A contemporary Dutch engraving of Herr Roger standing with his leg in a
candle flame, a smoldering shovel on his arm, and a red-hot iron bar in his mouth.

got a Business that will Sirport me. I only want to pass a Way 2 or 3
Hours in the Evening." To induce Dibdin to hire him he stated
unequivocally, "i Can Sing a good Song and i Can Eat Boiling Hot
Lead—and Rub my naked Arms with a Red hot sheet of iron, and do
Different other things."

In 1828 a French medical journal, *La Clinique*, took note of
Martinez, the French salamander. He was a Havana-born man of 43,
robust and healthy, but his "Creole-like features" were evidently
somewhat marred by the bursting of a thermometer which was impru-
dently carried too near his person. Martinez was successful at under-
going the oven ordeal at very high temperatures.

In 1841, J. A. B. Chylinski featured "Chemico-Physical and
Gymnastic Representations in Four Characters, viz., the Athletic Man,
the Modern Hercules, the Fire King, and the Polish Salamander."
Among his varied experiments, Mr. Chylinski "will suffer a 300 lb.
weight to be broken on his head by a heavy sledge hammer." After
which he "will hold his head in a blazing charcoal fire." He was Polish.

At almost the same time, Madame Kowalsky, the "Polish Enchant-
ress," was charming audiences in the United States. In Philadelphia in
1849 she featured " 'the astonishing supper,' in which Madame produced from her mouth the most brilliant fireworks of various colors,
which were changed at the will of the audience."

The illustration from a printer's proof featuring Rivalli in Hartlepool, England, 1869.

American audiences had witnessed fire acts at least eighty years earlier, when Mr. Baly ate red-hot coals out of a chafing dish. In 1770, Shaghnussy devoured "several combustibles in a Blaze with as much ease as ladies drinking teas." Taking the analogy a bit further, Leitsendorfer promised, at a show in St. Louis in 1814, to "place a burning coal on his feet, throwing it up and taking it in his mouth and eating it with as much facility as our young gentlemen and ladies would eat sugar plimbs." At 40 Nassau Street in New York, Day Francis "verily and in good sooth . . . danced a *pas seul* on red hot iron. . . ."

INCOMBUSTIBLE
MEN
AND
FIREPROOF
WOMEN

269

Richard Potter, the first American-born magician to achieve success in his native country, also resisted fire. In a long, colorful, and versatile career, Potter was occasionally billed as an "Anti-Combustible Man Salamander." He passed his hands and feet through flames and handled a red-hot iron bar, which he would bend "into various shapes with naked feet as a smith would an anvil."

In 1857, a heated court battle raged between Christo Buono Core, the Fire King then performing at Cremorne Gardens in London, and

A Camel cigarette ad featuring Chabert. One would not suggest
performing the stunt based on this explanation.

Francisco Fillipino, the Emperor of Fire. While they were ostensibly enjoying the pleasure of each other's company over strawberries and rum, Buono Core "perfidiously mixed prussic acid with the drink, from the effects of which the 'Emperor' greatly suffered." After a number of hearings, the Fire King, claiming the accusation was the fabrication of his jealous rival, was acquitted.

Well into the nineteenth century, the public's fascination with fire effects continued. Fire resisters, who traditionally appeared on the bills of magicians or ventriloquists, even found their way to the séance room. In the heyday of spiritualism, mediums sometimes claimed to be fireproof to impress their gullible sitters. In a classic book of the genre, *Revelations of a Spirit Medium* (published in 1891 and immediately sought and burned by mediums to prevent their secrets from being revealed), the anonymous author gave recipes for incombustibility.

The celebrated Daniel Dunglas Home, perhaps the most renowned of all mediums, was known to handle live coals. He impressed the world-famous, though gullible, scientist Sir William Crookes. In a

INCOMBUSTIBLE
MEN
AND
FIREPROOF
WOMEN

271

séance on May 9, 1871, Crookes saw Home go to the fireplace and "stirring the hot coals about with his hand, [he] took out a red hot piece nearly as big as an orange and putting it on his right hand, covered it over with his left hand, so as to almost completely enclose it, and blew into the small furnace thus extemporized until the lump of charcoal was nearly white-hot; and then drawing my attention to the lambent flame which was flickering over the coal and licking round his fingers; he fell on his knees, looked up in a reverend manner, held up the coal in front and said, 'Is not God good? Are not his laws wonderful?' "

The effect of such a dramatic and seemingly impromptu stunt on an already believing admirer can easily be imagined.

As the novelty of fire-eating and -handling wore off, those performers not versatile enough to combine their talents into more diversified shows took to the streets. In 1861 Henry Mayhew, in Volume 3 of *London Labour and the London Poor*, described one such salamander. After a fascinating and detailed account of a fire king learning his trade and preparing for his demonstrations, we find the poor fellow has been reduced to catching rats with his teeth to earn enough money to survive.

Occasionally a new or cleverly marketed stunt was enough to earn some status and success. Eugene Rivalli, the Prince of Fire, captured the public's imagination with his Cage of Fire. This was an open-front variant of the oven which was made famous by Chabert. Born John Watkins, he took the name Rivalli to capitalize on the appeal of Continental salamanders. He frequently topped the bills in music hall shows and was favorably reviewed by the press. He had a long career, and died on February 16, 1900.

In 1903 a Russian playbill for the Circus Noni-Bedini announced "Mr. Kluganek the Unburning Man and Conqueror of the Fire Elements." In the surrounding arena he entered the raging cage of fire and emerged unharmed. Underneath the identical cut of Rivalli at the Victoria Music Hall was the copy, "Mr. Kluganek is the inventor and only performer of this trick."

By the turn of the century, the tricks of the fire kings had been largely made public and were sold by magicians and specialty shops. Barnello, the "Human Volcano," a well-known fire performer, became a leading purveyor of such equipment. He was born Edward Barnwell in Decatur, Illinois, on September 8, 1857, and first presented his fire act in San Francisco in 1879. His book, *The Red Demons or Mysteries of Fire*, included the sketchily explained secrets for sixty-four different stunts, including the fire cage.

Our fascination with this most terrible of the elements continues. Fire-eaters are still featured in circus sideshows and carnival performances. The fire ordeals of the ancients have given way to the positive

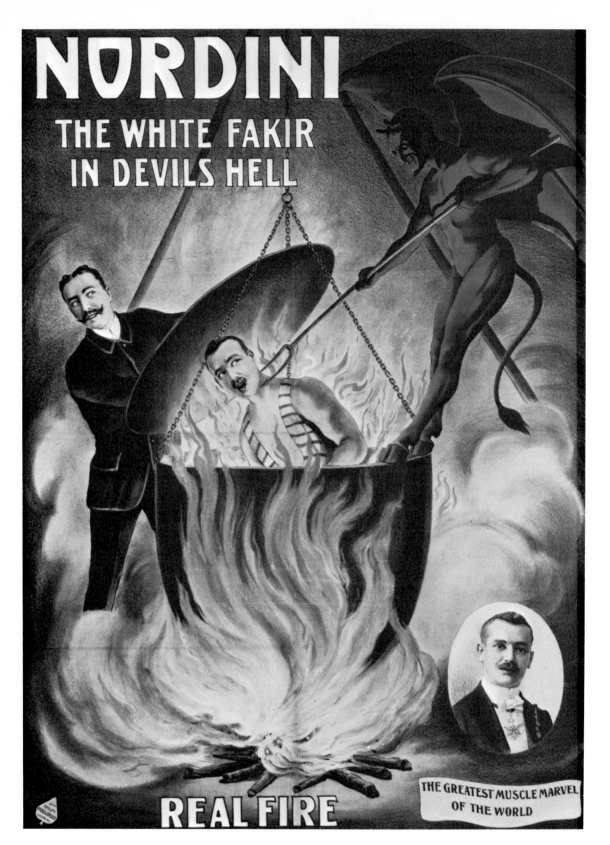

Nordini, yet another fire king, in a flaming caldron, 1909.

thinkers of the present. As this is written, groups of Americans walk over red-hot coals in an attempt to prove their "assertiveness."

In spite of the obvious dangers, fire acts are among the longest-running in show business. Rather than giving the standard disclaimer ("Kids, don't try to perform the effects described in this chapter, as they are done by professionals who have dedicated their lives . . ."), I will leave would-be salamanders with some sage advice from that most practical of wizards, Houdini, who said: "Do not bite a piece of red-hot iron unless you have a good set of teeth."

INCOMBUSTIBLE
MEN
AND
FIREPROOF
WOMEN

273

STONES, SWORDS,
SNAKES, AND
OTHER ENTRÉES

An original hand-colored drawing of an Oriental sword-swallower.

STONES,
SWORDS,
SNAKES,
AND
OTHER
ENTRÉES

ondon in the 1780's offered attractions designed to educate, amaze, amuse, and arouse its citizenry.

One could choose from balloon ascensions to elevate the body, philosophic discourses to elevate the mind, and a "celestial bed" to elevate the loins, hence increasing the likelihood of fertility, at Dr. Graham's Temple of Health and Hymen in the Strand.

Showmen battled one another for the privilege of exhibiting moving picture machines, sagacious sows, and automaton tarantulas.

Into this climate of appreciativeness and acceptance stepped the major attraction of 1788: a man who, while he captured the public's imagination, did not reveal his name. In an age of "emperors," "kings," and "princes of prestidigitation," professors of "proetics," "stynacrophy," and "caprimancy," "philosophical fireworks," and "man-salamanders," he used no catchy billing.

He was called the Stone Eater. One needed no other information, although admittedly he was billed as the "Extraordinary Stone Eater," "The Original Stone Eater," and "The Only One in the World." If you wanted to see a fellow gulp gravel and pop pebbles, here was your man.

STONE EATER. The Public are most respectfully informed, that the Exhibition in future will be This and Every Day, from Twelve to Three; and on account of the numberless applications, after the Exhibition has been closed every evening, from Seven to Nine, at No. 10, Cockspur-street, Charing-Cross. Admittance Half-a-Crown.

☞ The Stone Eater hopes Ladies and Gentlemen will indulge him by a few minutes attendance, as the many visits he receives in a day, render a short delay unavoidable.

Newspaper advertisement from 1788.

For an appearance at Denew's Auction Rooms it was announced (in the *Morning Post* of March 7, 1788) that "science, like the air, rides over the face of the Universe, and Nature cannot deviate from her accustomed rules with her observations and scrutiny. Nature, as if to shew her superiority, and mock her rival has lately formed a pair of HUMAN JAWS, with power to crack Stones, and a Stomach to digest them, having fixed at the same time, health and gaiety in the countenance—the emblems of her victory and triumph."

Further grasping the tenor of the times, the Stone Eater's handbill for March 22, 1788, explained: "At the Moment when Philosophers are most distinguished and revered for their Knowledge, and consulted as Oracles who can interpret all Causes from Effects, and explain the Unchangeable Laws of Nature . . . Comes this same Nature, and by a Single Act o'erturns their Systems in the astonishing Faculty of a Man who Eats and Digests STONES and FLINTS.

"Since the above assertion has staggered the Belief of all who have not had Ocular Demonstrations, the Curious are invited to witness the Fact. In the presence of any Spectator, he Eats the hardest FLINTS that may be offered him; Cracks them with his Teeth like Nuts; Gnaws, Crunches, and Reduces them to the smallest Pieces; at the same Time, by striking him on the Stomach, the STONES resound as in a Sack."

He demonstrated every day from 11:00 A.M. to 4:00 P.M. at the Great Room in the Globe Tavern.

The Stone Eater was taken to task by a letter writer to the *Morning Herald*, who apparently found the advertisement (p. 279) too conservative: "It is not enough to be a prodigy and curious," he admonished. "You must tell the world you are so." With proper advertising, the writer suggested, the metal muncher would be assured of deserved success.

For the next few months the Stone Eater performed at various London venues. Perhaps his quick departures from these sites were hastened by his lack of promotional skills. At Mr. Hatch's, Trunk-Maker, 404 Strand, and at Mr. Beckett's, Trunk-Maker, No. 31 Haymarket, he offered virtually the same program and advertised with the same bill. The puzzling relationship between stone-eater and trunk-maker notwithstanding, our all-consuming artist announced the ingestion of "pebbles, flints, tobacco, pipes, and mineral excrescences."

"The present is allowed to be an age of Wonders and Improvements in the Arts. The idea of Man's flying in the air, twenty years ago before the discovery of the Use of Balloons, would have been laughed at by the most credulous. Nor does the History of Nature afford so extraordinary a relation as that of a Man's EATING and subsisting on Pebbles . . . but so it is, and the Ladies and Gentlemen of this Metropolis . . . have now an opportunity of seeing the most Wonderful Phenomenon of the Age, who GRINDS and SWALLOWS STONES, etc.; with as much ease as a person would crack a nut and masticate the kernel."

Clearly seeming to grasp the importance of scientific credibility, our masticator referred the curious to Dr. John Hunter and Sir Joseph Banks, who could bear witness to his "surprizing performance," and to Dr. Munro, who wrote of the Stone Eater in his *Medical Commentary* in 1772.

As the Stone Eater demanded more attention, he was, like most celebrities, expected to provide a personal history (whether real or fabricated not being the issue). Accordingly, in the *Morning Herald* of May 30, 1788, the story of his shipwreck and salvation appeared. He was the only survivor, it said, of a boat disaster that had occurred off

THE ORIGINAL
STONE EATER

The only one in the World,

Is arrived and means to perform this and every
Day (Sunday excepted) at Mr. Hatch's,

Trunk Maker, 404, Strand, opposite Adelphi.

STONE EATING
AND
STONE SWALLOWING

and after the Stones are swallowed may be
heard to clink in
his Belly the same as in a Pocket.

The present is allowed to be the age of Wonders and Improvements in the Arts.—The
idea of a Man's flying in the Air, twenty
years ago before the discovery of the Use of
Balloons, would have been laughed at by the
most credulous! Nor does the History of
Nature afford so extraordinary a Relation as
that of a Man's EATING and subsisting on
PEBBLE FLINTS, TOBACCO PIPES, and Mineral Excrescences: but so it is, and the
Ladies and Gentlemen of this Metropolis and its vicinity have now an opportunity of witnessing this extraordinary Fact,
by seeing the most Wonderful Phenomenon
of the Age, who GRINDS and SWALLOWS
STONES, &c. with as much ease as a Person
would crack a nut, and masticate the kernel.

This Extraordinary STONE EATER
appears not to suffer the least Inconvenience
from so pondrous, and to all other persons
in the World, so indigestible a Meal, which
he repeats from twelve at noon till seven.

*** Any Lady or Gentleman may bring
Black Flints or Pebbles with them.

N.B. His Merit is fully demonstrated by Dr.
Monro, in his ' *Medical Commentary,*'
1772, and several other Gentlemen of
the Faculty. Likewise Dr. John Hunter and Sir Joseph Banks can witness
the Surprising Performance of this most
Extraordinary STONE EATER.
Admittance Two Shillings and Sixpence.
† A private Performance for five Guineas,
on a short Notice.

A nineteenth-century reproduction
of the Stone Eater's playbill from 1788.

the coast of Norway in 1761. "A lonely rock received him and that became his asylum and habitation." Thirteen years later he was rescued by a Captain Alleonore, having survived the entire time on a diet of stones. "Should any person yet doubt the above story [oh, damnable incredulity!] they are invited to be themselves witnesses of the fact; for although he has changed his situation, he has not altered his food, to this day, in his private life."

On July 7, appearing at No. 10 Cockspur Street, Charing Cross, he offered a £50 reward for "a small Spaniel Brown Bitch, short legs, long hair, and carries her tail well." The notice implies both solvency and compassion. Yet on the same day another paper contained the contradictory note: "The Stone-Eater is now confined in Newgate whither he has been led at the suit of a person in whose house he lodged. It has been commended to Mr. Ackerman to have him surely watched lest he should eat his way through the walls of the prison."

Such attention elicited both satire and imitation. Siderophagus, or Eater of Iron, appeared at the Great Auction Rooms in Piccadilly and devoured iron "in any shape, including pins, needles, wires and nutcrackers." Spectators were requested to "bring a Bunch of Keys, a *Bolt*, or a *Poker* which he digests with as much ease as if they were gingerbread." A scheduling conflict sadly prevented his exhibition continuing for more than a few nights: he was also engaged by a firm to smooth their cannon by biting off the rough pieces.

Siderophagus' wife, Sarah Salamander, was "remarkable all over Europe for drinking aquafortis . . . she swallows the liquor without any wry face or contortions as if it were small-beer." And if one preferred a less formal, more sociable atmosphere, Sarah "will hob or nob with any person [while] in a bumper of Aqua Fortis or Oil of Vitriol."

A Spanish stone-eater appeared in a comic droll in 1788 and at the Richmond Theatre in 1790. "That stone eaters are not uncommon," said a London paper on July 10, 1788, "may be inferred from there being now one exhibiting at Cheltenham: who is eating for a livelihood—with uncommon applause."

After Mr. Palmer's Pantomime at the Royalty Theatre on July 16, 1788, "A New *Stone-Eater*, formerly a Trumpet in the Band, was introduced, and swallowed nearly a dish of pebbles." He may have been the Spaniard previously mentioned. The Pantomime of the Gnome featured a comic "Stone-Eaters Song" written by the then incredibly popular J. O'Keefe.

Yet another irate letter written to the *Morning Herald* defended the original swallower: "The individual, who has for some time past been content to eat Stones for a subsistence, could not avoid being the subject of theatrical notice: they have represented him and his mode of living on their stage—they have by this means certainly trespassed on a natural, if not legal right; and while they are so desirous of not

STONES,
SWORDS,
SNAKES,
AND
OTHER
ENTRÉES

281

having their property invaded, it very ill becomes them to invade the right of a poor humble individual to obtain a living by so inoffensive a method . . . they have by making his representation a stage exhibition, not only excluded him from the right of performing his own original amusement but also subjected him to the penalties of the said acts, should he dare again to Eat Stones . . . Thus may they usurp the right of exhibiting every species of genius, and punish the original vendors for daring to continue to reap the praises and profits of their own talents and industry."

The intrepid Stone Eater survived this onslaught until at least October 15, 1790 ("now exhibiting his masticating powers in York, and as a most appropriate place, has chosen *Stone Hall* for the scene of exhibition"). He was even immortalized in machinery, as an automaton duplicating his act was built and exhibited at Merlin's Mechanical Museum in London. We bid him adieu by quoting Mr. O'Keefe's ditty (keeping in mind, however, that Charles Hogan said, "The history of drama has seldom witnessed so total an eclipse of popularity as subsequently and deservedly befell O'Keefe."):

STONE-EATER'S SONG
In the new Pantomime of the Gnome

I.

Make room for a jolly Stone-Eater,
    For Stones of all kinds I can crunch;
A nice bit of Marble is sweeter
    To me than a Turtle or Haunch.
A Street that's well pav'd is my larder—
    A Stone you will say is hard meat,
But, neighbors, I think 'tis much harder,
    Where *I* can get nothing to eat!
        With my crackledy mash, ha! ha!
And a jolly Stone-Eater am I.

II.

London Bridge shall just serve for a luncheon—
    Don't fear—I won't make it a job:
The Monument next I will munch on,
    For fear it should fall on my nob:
Ye *Strand* folks, as I am a sinner,
    Two nuisances I will eat up;

Temple-Bar will make me a good dinner,
    Because on St. *Clement's* I'll sup!
    With my, &c.

III.

I think, if my mind does not alter,
    The *Spaniards* some trouble I'll save—
I'll eat up the Rock of *Gibraltar*,
    And still if my stomach should crave,
I'll eat up *Pitt's* Diamond at Paris,
    I'm told 'tis the rarest of Stones—
If Monsieur inclin'd then for war is,
    At *Cherbourg* I'll eat up the Cones.
    With my, &c.

IV.

The Ostrich, Sir, I can beat hollow,
    Tho' smartly he gobbles horse shoes;
For cut out in stone, and I'll swallow
    An Ostrich for *Michaelmas* Goose!
Tho' with Stones I came here to be treated,
    whilst Liberty Britons enjoy,
The Rock where the Goddess is seated,
    May no-Stone-Eater ever destroy.
      With his crackledy mash, ha! ha!
And a jolly Stone-Eater am I.

Our principal Stone Eater was not, of course, the originator of his act. Within weeks of his initial London appearance, the papers listed accounts of earlier stone-eaters, the most prominent of whom was Francis Battalia.

Battalia was observed by John Bulwer, a seventeenth-century physician who was a pioneer in the use of sign language for the deaf. In his *Anthropometamorphosis: Man Transform'd; or the Artificiall Changling* (London, 1653), Bulwer recorded his meeting with this stone-eater, who he estimated to be about thirty years old. Battalia, he said, put three or four stones in a spoon, swallowed them down, and enjoyed a beer chaser. "He devours about halfe a pecke of these stones every day: and when he chinks upon his stomach, or shakes his body, you may heare the stones rattle as if they were in a sack, all of which in twenty-foure houres are resolved, and once in three weeks he voides a great quantity of sand by seige, after which digestion of them, he hath a fresh appetite to these stones as we have to our victuals." According to Bulwer, Battalia took nothing else, except beer and tobacco, but was nonetheless a "swarthy little fellow active and strong enough to have been a souldier in Ireland." This worked to Battalia's advantage as he was able to sell his rations and live on gravel while pocketing the profit.

If such an existence could stretch the credulity of the most devout believers, lend an ear to Bulwer's explanation of this phenomenon: Battalia, he states, "was borne with two stones in one hand and one in the other; who as soon as he was borne having the breast offered unto

Print of Battalia after the engraving by Hollar, published in Arnett's The Lives and Portraits of Remarkable Characters, *London, 1819.*

him, refused to suck"; when he also refused any other nourishment a doctor was summoned and told of the peculiarity of the baby's birth. The physician advised that the child be given small pebbles in liquid, which he happily devoured, and for thirty years he ate almost nothing else.

Battalia was immortalized in an engraving by Hollar done in 1641. His portrait was redrawn in the eighteenth century and he was a featured figure in the literature of "wonderful characters" well into the nineteenth century.

Bulwer likened Battalia to three earlier eaters: A man witnessed by "Lusitanus at Ferrara who did eate hides, potsheards, or broken glass, and concoct and digest them in so much that all men called him the Ostrich . . ."; a "beggar boy spoken of by Platerus" who for a fee would swallow stones as big as walnuts; and a Castillian mentioned by Abraham de Porta Leonis who was also a "gourmet o'gravel."

In Nathaniel Wanley's *The Wonders of the Little World* there is an account of a Silesian who at Prague in 1006 "for a small reward" swallowed thirty-six white stones weighing about three pounds (the smallest of them being the size of a pigeon's egg) with no ill effects.

In 1746 Reeves Williams, a Welsh laborer called the "Man-Ostrich," performed locally, swallowing pieces of iron, stones, and coins, with no harmful results. *Gentlemen's Magazine* for 1769 mentions a stone-eater in an article on digestion: this "true lithophagus or stone eater" was brought to Avignon in May 1760. He ate pebbles only after they were ground and made into a paste, but he also ate flints an inch and a half long and a half inch thick. Father Paulian, in his *Dictionnaire Physique*, found this same stone-eater's teeth to be very strong and his saliva highly corrosive. Parisian doctors, he noted, found almost no serum in the man's blood, which two hours after drawing became "as fragile as coral."

This stone-eater was found on a northern island by a Dutch crew on Good Friday, 1757. He was taught to eat raw meat, but would not touch bread. Unable to pronounce but a few sounds, he slept twelve hours a day and smoked tobacco almost constantly while awake. He was taught to make the sign of the cross and was baptized in the Church of St. Come in Paris. "The respect he shows to ecclesiastics, and his ready disposition to please them," says Father Paulian, "afforded me the opportunity of satisfying myself as to these particulars; and I am fully convinced that he is no cheat."

In the seventeenth century, "Thomas Gobsill, a lean man aged 26 or 27 years, being for three years extremely tortured with wind, was advised to swallow round white pebbles." This, according to the well-known physician Sir Charles Hall, he did to the point of extreme discomfort and pain for most of his life. The procedure, it should be circumspectly noted, did cure his flatulence.

STONES,
SWORDS,
SNAKES,
AND
OTHER
ENTRÉES

———

285

While stones may have been the most bland repast of performing artists, they were by no means the most unusual. It was not uncommon to find the swallowing of silverware listed on eighteenth- and early nineteenth-century conjurers' playbills. Highman Palatine's performance of the stunt prompted the following verse in 1802:

> Highman! I've long admir'd thy sallow face.
> Smiling above thy coat with tarnish'd lace;
> Swallowing knives, forks, and spoons, as they were meat,
> Thereby to get thy daily bread to eat.
> Thy harmless tricks and juggles gain'd thee praise,
> And strong digestion caus'd thee lengths of days.
> But life thou could'st not further carry on—
> In thine own words—"Presto!" cried Death—"Begone!"

While I have always felt that the performance of magic was one of the few wholesome professions, that the enjoyment it causes and the thought it provokes are worthy of the highest approbation, I must confess concern over possibly deleterious side effects—witness the case of John Cummings.

Cummings, an American sailor, saw a conjurer near Havre-de-Grace amuse a crowd by *pretending* to swallow knives. Mr. Cummings, exhibiting what is wont to be labeled Yankee bravado, told his shipmates that he could swallow knives as well as any Frenchman. Encouraged by a rowdy group prepared to take him at his word, and fortified by grog, Cummings produced his pocket knife and chasing it with a potable slid it past his throat into his stomach—accomplishing in reality the illusion achieved by the conjuring Frenchman. The unsatisfied throng asked if the stunt could be repeated, to which our intrepid sailor requested, "All the knives aboard ship." Whether it was a ship understocked in cutlery, or a suddenly sobering seaman, the demonstration ended after three more knives had been ingested.

In the next two days, three of the four knives were seen again as the result of natural process; one, however, lodged permanently in his stomach, with no apparent inconvenience.

Some six years later, in Boston, Cummings was induced (by what means is not clear) to repeat the banquet of his youth. That evening he swallowed six small knives and the following day added another eight. Cummings was taken with incredible pain but, according to Wilson and Caulfield's account, "between that time and the 29th of the following month, he got rid of the whole of his cargo."

On December 4 at Spithead, challenged and insatiable, he downed five knives. The following day he added nine more, some of which were larger than usual, and a final four knives, which Cummings, then no doubt arithmetically disabled by drink, failed to count.

His folly soon proved fatal. From December 6 until his death in March of 1809, "in a state of extreme emaciation" due to the cumulative effect of his exotic dinners, Cummings survived only in a most uncomfortable state, no doubt mulling over his deception at the hands of a conjurer who merely pretended to swallow. An autopsy revealed fourteen blades still in his stomach, but the immediate cause of death was the backspring of one knife which lodged in his bowel.

About fifteen years later the case of "a juggler of inferior ability," called variously William or C. A. Demster, was reported. While performing in a public house at Botchergate, Carlisle, Demster accidentally swallowed a table knife "rather more than nine inches long"; in the process of removing the blade from his throat, it "accidently slipped his hold, and the knife passed into his stomach."

The Chester *Courant* stated that Demster immediately left Carlisle to see the famous surgeon Sir Astley Cooper in London. The extreme discomfort of the rocky coach ride prevented the completion of the journey. He died en route in Middlewich. Doctors who examined the body thought Demster might have survived had he lain still at Carlisle instead of undertaking his bumpy trip.

In spite of its obvious hazards, sword swallowing survived as an attraction, popular to the present day. One theory for its longevity is that, with few exceptions, it is an exhibition devoid of trickery. The performer does exactly what he claims to do—swallows and retrieves swords. The act was popular enough in the nineteenth century to elicit the following entry from Albert A. Hopkins in *Magic: Stage Illusions and Scientific Diversions* (New York, 1897):

> These experiments are nearly always the same. The individual comes out dressed in a brilliant costume. At one side of him are flags of different nationalities surrounding a panoply of sabers, swords, and yatagans, and at the other a stack of guns provided with bayonets. Taking a flat saber whose blade and hilt have been cut of the same sheet of metal, the blade being from fifty-five to sixty centimeters in length, he introduces its extremity into his throat, taps the hilt gently, and the blade at length entirely disappears. He then repeats the experiment at a single gulp. Subsequently, after swallowing and disgorging two of these same swords, he causes one to penetrate up to its guard, a second not quite so far, a third a little less still, and a fourth up to about half its length. . . .
>
> Pressing now on the hilts, he swallows the four blades at a gulp and then he takes them out leisurely, one by one. The effect is quite surprising. After swallowing several different swords and sabers, he takes an old musket armed with

STONES,
SWORDS,
SNAKES,
AND
OTHER
ENTRÉES

287

*Ramo Samee, the famous Oriental juggler and magician,
swallowed a sword two feet long.*

a triangular bayonet, and swallows the latter, the gun remaining vertical over his head. Finally he borrows a large saber from a dragoon who is present for the purpose and causes two-thirds of it to disappear. As a trick, on being encored, the sword swallower borrows a cane from a person in the audience and swallows it almost entirely.

Ramo Samee, who was featured with the first group of Indian jugglers to appear in London early in the nineteenth century, swallowed a sword two feet in length. Later in his career, he repeated the stunt with the sword set on fire.

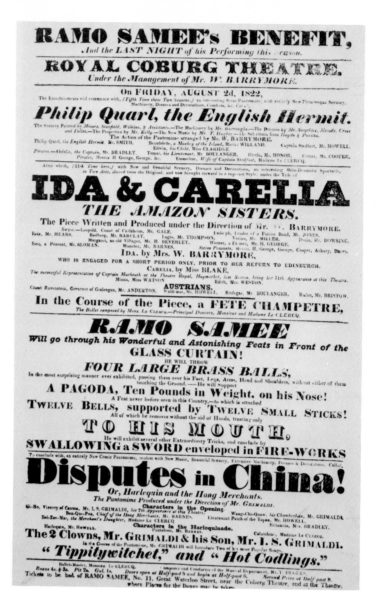

Ramo Samee's sword enveloped in flames.

Cliquot, a French-Canadian who gained prominence in London
years later, was more original and daring than the run-of-the-mill
performer. In an article by Framley Steelcroft in an 1896 *Strand
Magazine*, a short biography of Cliquot is given. As a child, Cliquot ran
away from home in his native Quebec and joined a circus that was en
route to South America. Witnessing a performer swallow a machete in
Buenos Aires and unable to pay for lodging, he began his own
experiments.

The key to this art is the ability to overcome the natural gag reflex
caused by the touching of the pharynx, which reacts violently to any
obstacle which might impede respiration. Cliquot's early attempts were

made with a thin piece of copper wire. After conquering this initial obstacle, he mastered cavalry swords, bayonet blades (which would be recoiled down the esophagus as the attached rifle was fired), and a borrowed pocket watch, which could be heard ticking in his stomach.

An original trick of Cliquot's was to swallow a bayonet sword weighted with a crossbar and two eighteen-pound dumbbells. The entire apparatus weighed seventy-six pounds. He also swallowed a sixteen-candlepower electric light bulb (which was connected to an eight-volt battery onstage). Once, a skeptical doctor in New York, anxious to discover chicanery, impulsively withdrew fourteen nine-inch bayonet blades, all of which protruded from the performer's mouth. The injuries caused by this action necessitated a long and painful period of recovery.

Although Cliquot was proficient enough to offer a £500 reward if he failed to swallow any swords, his real deception came in his stage persona. According to H. J. Holmes, in *The Royal Magazine*, the

STONES,
SWORDS,
SNAKES,
AND
OTHER
ENTRÉES

289

Cliquot swallows a twenty-two-inch cavalry saber.

supposed French-Canadian was in fact Fred McLane, who came from a comfortable Chicago family.

Cliquot claimed to teach his art to Delno Fritz, who was a popular act in circus sideshows and British music halls. Houdini states that "Fritz was not only an excellent sword-swallower, but a good showman as well," and somewhat puzzlingly adds that "he was a clean man with a clean reputation." Fritz's pupil was the great woman sword-swallower,

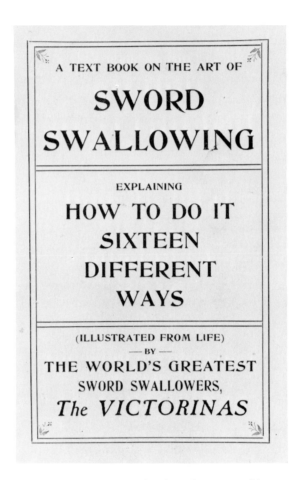

A TEXT BOOK ON THE ART OF

SWORD
SWALLOWING

EXPLAINING

HOW TO DO IT
SIXTEEN
DIFFERENT
WAYS

(ILLUSTRATED FROM LIFE)
— BY —
THE WORLD'S GREATEST
SWORD SWALLOWERS,
The *VICTORINAS*

The cover of the Victorinas' ponderous pamphlet.

Edith Clifford. Houdini states that Mlle. Clifford was born in England in 1884 and began swallowing swords at the age of fifteen. He did not, nor will I, question her motivation. She joined the Barnum & Bailey Circus in Vienna in 1901 and worked with the show for many years. Mlle. Clifford tackled blades of eighteen to twenty inches with "no trouble whatever" and on occasion swallowed a twenty-six-inch sword. Houdini states that of women sword-swallowers she was "perhaps the most generously endowed." When the magician witnessed her in 1919 she had added some original conceptions to her act. She devoured an elongated (to five times normal length) razor blade, a pair of giant scissors, and a two-and-a-half-inch-wide saw "with ugly-looking teeth."

Her pièce de résistance was to place the tip of a twenty-three-and-a-half-inch-long bayonet in her mouth. This was affixed to the breech of a cannon, which fired a ten-gauge shell, the recoil from which drove the bayonet down her throat. (She is pictured in the color photo section. Her husband, whose sole function appears to be handing his wife the objects she will devour, is generously given equal billing.)

Also featured on a splendid Donaldson litho is Miss Victorina (see color photo section), who along with her husband swallowed swords and performed magic. They also authored one of the few volumes dealing exclusively with their art: *A text book on the Art of* SWORD SWALLOWING, *explaining* HOW TO DO IT SIXTEEN DIFFERENT WAYS. Lest some vision of a tonsil-testing *War and Peace* stir the reader's imagination, one should mention that it is a three-by-four-inch pamphlet of sixteen leaves, including covers, blanks, and ten photographs.

Joe Van Victorina briefly performed as Vanoran, and also as Kar-Mi, an Indian prince in tune with the powers of the spirit world. He presented some genuinely mystifying magic illusions in addition to the sword-swallowing stunts he demonstrated with his wife.

Mysteries of the Orient notwithstanding, it was really thick, dark makeup and a long robe and turban that created the character of Kar-Mi. Joe Van Victorina was *also* created. They were all really Joseph B. Hallworth, a native American born in 1872. His sword-swallowing wife was really Kitty Fisher.

HOW TO DO IT SIXTEEN DIFFERENT WAYS was not written to create competition, but rather to confound and amuse the public, who might purchase the work at the Victorinas' exhibitions. A brief synopsis of the sixteen explanations follows:

1. Learn to swallow swords by hypnosis. "Van," as the author refers to himself, relates the sad story of his friend "Punkrot Smith," who "had a mouth like a catfish and a neck like a crane." Through hypnosis Smith became an outstanding student until he accepted a wager to swallow an umbrella in Showbegan, Maine. He was successful until the "new-fangled press-the-string-and-it-flies-up sort of a rain catcher" opened unexpectedly. "It was a sad funeral," said Van, "and I was broke up for weeks afterward, for Punk had been my most apt pupil and I have not the slightest doubt that had he lived he would have proved a marvel."

2. Learn from a professional; start by swallowing a sterling silver chain.

3. Use a peacock feather dipped in oil to tickle the throat, which helps you become familiar with the sensation.

4. Secretly swallow a rubber tube before the performance—when the sword is later swallowed, it will be encased in the tube.

5. A similar method but using a metal scabbard.

6. The Chinese way, by first eating opium to dull the sense of touch so the sword will not be felt; this "should never be tried by any other than those of the Mongol race."

7. An herb solution "used by the Llamas of Thibet" to combat the retching reaction.

8. "Placing an article down the throat regardless of consequences and acquiring further ease of habit by force of will." ("From three to five years' practice in this manner will usually prove sufficient.")

9. A sword with a detachable handle—the handle is placed in the mouth but the blade goes down the performer's sleeve.

10. A sword with a telescoping blade, which retracts into the handle.

11. A blade constructed of clock-spring metal, which coils up in the mouth.

12. [A personal favorite] An imitation sword made out of licorice covered with tin foil or aluminum paint. The licorice sword is swallowed and a real one produced from behind the back, giving "the impression the sword has passed entirely through you."

13. A method to dilate or enlarge the throat by use of apparatus constructed from wire. This allows for easy access in swallowing the sword.

14. Dilation by drinking huge quantities of water, which opens the throat and allows for the introduction of the blade.

15. "Hire somebody to do it for you, as it may save you much annoyance, and though more expensive is very satisfactory in the long run."

16. The Javanese way: "As it is impossible to give you a correct translation of the original text without destroying the delicate humor and pathos of the original author," Van shows sup-

posedly Javanese symbols, concluding: "As the great Tana Shisavino himself says in the fourth line of his incomparable demonstration:

STONES,
SWORDS,
SNAKES,
AND
OTHER
ENTRÉES

293

$$ \text{⚇ ⟊⟦ ⤬⟋ ⼋⼂ ⼑⟍ ⼁⼣⼀ ⽂⟒⨯⼊⼡ ⽀⽀⟊}$$
$$ \text{⼋⼣ ⼈⼋⼂⼡ ⼋⼳⼊⼂ ⼂⼂ ⟅⼀⧸ ⼂⼀ ⼂⼀ ⼂⧸}$$
$$ \text{⼂⼨⼽ ⼑ ⼂⼂⼋ ⼣⼣⼚ ⼂⼂⼣⼂⼗}$$
$$ \text{⼂⼤ ⽂⼂⼳⼳ ⼋⼗⼡⟊ ⼑⼂⼂ ⼋⼂ ⼗⼗ ⼂⟌⼋⼂}$$

which is without question a statement none can contradict."

Before departing the circus of oral entertainment, a brief survey of the sideshow is in order. It may be difficult for readers to assume that the stone-, knife-, and sword-swallowers previously discussed are major attractions, but compared with those who follow . . .

Healthy appetites have often met with approval. Excesses in this area have evoked astonishment and been recorded since ancient times. Olympic athletes were often prodigious eaters. Astydamus the Milesian was invited to a banquet for nine people and ate the food for the entire company. Milo, the legendary Crotonian wrestler, bore an ox on his shoulders, carried it for a furlong, and then devoured it ("sounds," said a friend, "like my first honeymoon").

Lest vegetarians think they are above such displays, consider the case of Claudius Albinus. This Roman emperor was reported to down for breakfast "as many apples as no man would believe, five hundred Greek figs, ten melons, twenty pounds of grapes, one hundred gnat-snappers, and four hundred oysters." Lipsius said of him, "God keep such a plague from the earth, at least from our garden."

Nicholas Wood, the Great Eater of Kent, immortalized by John Taylor the Water Poet, was known to eat an entire sheep, thirty dozen pigeons, or eighty-four rabbits at a single sitting. Once he ate sixty pounds of cherries followed by a whole hog, and for dessert three pecks of Damson plums.

A fellow called John Dale bet he could satiate Wood with whole-some food costing only two shillings. The wager agreed to, Dale provided six pots of ale and twelve loaves of bread, which he soaked in the potable. As Wood began to eat the loaves, fumes caused him to fall asleep and lose the bet.

A far worse fate befell a Danish stage player of considerable corpulence with the appetite of ten men. When the king was told that this great eater could act no better than other, thinner men, he was hanged "as a devourer of the labourer's food, and a public annoyance."

Such eating was an exercise in indulgence rather than creativity. To please a paying audience, a certain theatricality was required.

Dufour, a Frenchman who made his debut in 1783 and who was a subject in Martin's *Natürliche Magie* in 1792, added comedy—according to Houdini, a fellow not applauded for a sophisticated sense of humor—to the act of eating:

"His last appearance in Paris was most remarkable. The dinner began with a soup of asps in simmering oil. On each side was a dish of vegetables, one containing thistles and burdocks, and the other fuming acid. Often side dishes of turtles, rats, bats, and moles were garnished with live coals. For the fish course he ate a dish of snakes in boiling tar and pitch. His roast was a screech owl in a sauce of glowing brimstone. The salad proved to be spiderwebs full of small explosive squibs, a plate of butterfly wings and manna worms, a dish of toads surrounded with flies, crickets, grasshoppers, church beetles, spiders, and caterpillars. He washed all this down with flaming brandy and for dessert ate the four large candles standing on the table, both of the hanging side lamps with their contents, and finally the large center lamp, oil, wick, and all. This leaving the room in darkness, Dufour's face shone out in a mash of living flames.

"A dog had come in with a farmer, who was probably a confederate, and now began to bark. Since Dufour could not quiet him, he seized him, bit off his head and swallowed it, throwing the body aside. Then ensued a comic scene between Dufour and the farmer, the latter demanding that his dog be brought to life, which threw the audience into paroxysms of laughter. Then suddenly, candles reappeared and seemed to light themselves. Dufour made a series of hocus-pocus passes over the dog's body, then the head suddenly appeared in its proper place, and the dog, with a joyous yelp, ran to his master."

As wildly comic as this may have been, Dufour capped it with an even more amusing stunt. He would tear a cat "from limb to limb and eat the carcass," then after suitable byplay extract it whole again from his mouth.

The barbarous inclination of such an act has not been restricted to the dim past. In our own century, and until very recently, carnivals and sideshows featured the "geek." Presented as a wild man, a sort of missing link not truly human, the geek would eat snakes and mice and bite the heads off live chickens and drink their blood. As with Dufour's dog, the act was often faked, relying on trickery for its effects. Occasionally a conjurer could entice a *real* or "glomming" geek, as legitimate counterparts were called, to do the act—usually by providing drink or drugs to the performer.

Distasteful as this may be, the concept of the geek has entered reality, fiction, and mythology. William Lindsey Gresham (who was familiar with the worlds of circus and magic, and who wrote an excellent biography of Houdini) authored *Nightmare Alley* (New York and Toronto, 1946). It was a novel of carnival life which began and ended with a startling look at how a geek was created. Tyrone Power starred in the movie version and was most convincing in his portrayal of a once powerful performer who ends his career as a geek. Craig Nova's novel *The Geek* (New York, 1975) further explores our fascination with a freak who is made rather than born, a freak, in the words of Leslie Fiedler, who was "invented to satisfy psychic needs bred by infantile traumas and unquiet ancestral memories."

It is difficult to imagine a sophisticated and pleasant performance which features the swallowing of live animals, but such, we are told, was the presentation of Mac Norton, the Human Aquarium. Mac

*An older Mac Norton
still plies his trade.*

Norton swallowed live goldfish and frogs as a featured attraction in many Continental music halls shortly after the turn of the century. He later joined the famous Circus Busch in Vienna, where on one occasion he shared the bill with Houdini. Mac Norton was really Louis Claude Delair, a dignified Frenchman who performed in full tails and who took his nom de plume from a bodyguard to Mary Queen of Scots. As an appetizer for his fish dinner, Mac Norton performed the ever-popular act of water spouting. He downed thirty or forty glasses of beer or water in rapid succession. This he spewed from his mouth in a high-arching shower into a receptacle some twenty feet away. (Houdini noted that Mac Norton got rid of excess brew by discreetly spitting

SOLVS SICVT SOL

FAMA
VOLAT

An eighteenth-century engraving patterned after
Hollar's seventeenth-century original.

into yet another container as he turned his back on his audience to reach for new glasses of beer; see poster in color section).

Water spouting, as an act unto itself, dates at least as far back as the seventeenth century, when one Blaise Manfre (or Manfrede), a native of Malta, made the act famous in Europe. He drank large quantities of water, then spouted multiple streams, and even appeared to change the liquids which came from his mouth, producing wine, beer, oil, milk, and various scented waters. He was the subject of a print by Hollar done in 1651. Jean Royer of Lyon was reputed to spout for a greater length of time than Manfre (specifically, as long as it would take to recite the fifty-first psalm or the time required to walk two hundred paces). Both Royer and Manfre were briefly imprisoned as witches by the Inquisition.

Floram Marchand of Tours learned the act from Manfre, and was the subject of an exposure at the hands of his managers, who had brought him to perform in England. Thomas Peddle and Thomas Cosbie's *The Falacie of the Great Water-Drinker Discovered* (London, 1650)

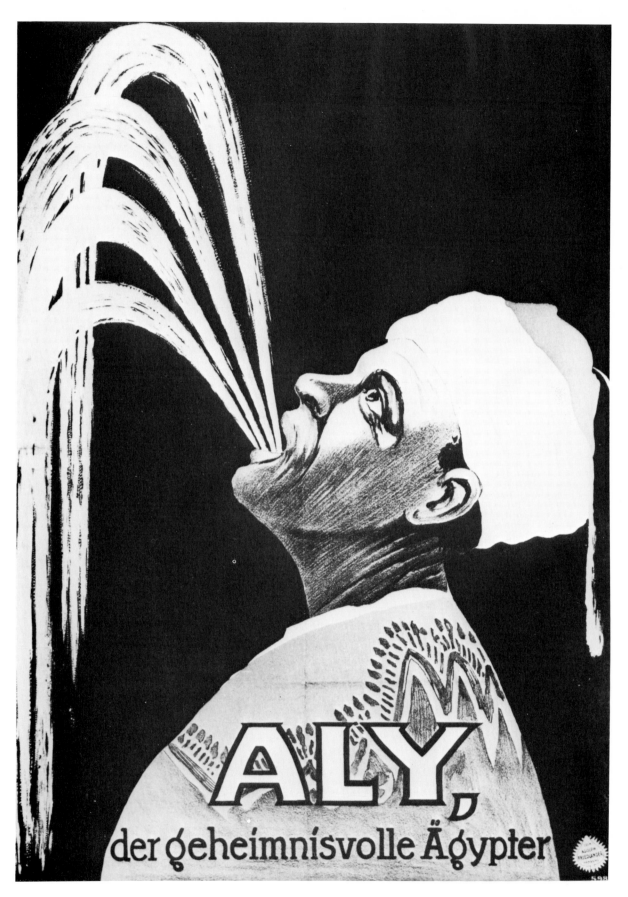

A striking Friedlander lithograph of the still popular ancient spouting act, 1913.

A Bedouin troop eats snakes, fire, and anything else that crosses its path.

was an eight-page elucidation of the act "for which many eminent gentlemen who have offered great sums of money to have the Misterie discovered . . . [It] is exposed herein for a pittance."

The performances of these men required a combination of natural skills and conjuring principles to accomplish their effects, which were told and retold in books about unusual characters for centuries to follow.

Mac Norton used no deception in his spouting but rather featured the stunt in an attempt to prove his theory that he possessed three stomachs, like a cow. After spewing the water and washing his hands in the spray, the Human Aquarium swallowed six live goldfish and a dozen frogs. He then produced, one at a time, between his lips, each fish and frog, head first. "All alive and keeking," he would exclaim, and walk off to resounding applause.

The well-known impresario Willie Hammerstein once booked Mac Norton to appear at the Victoria Theatre in New York but, according to Houdini, the Society for the Prevention of Cruelty to Animals refused to sanction the performance. Although Mac Norton did not play in America, he was brought to England in 1949 under the auspices of British showman Pete Collins, thus capping a career of some fifty years during which time, he said, he never lost a single pet.

More recent exponents of water spouting include Hans Rohrl, "der lebene Hydrant," or living hydrant, who, with his wife, Mary, assisting, performed in the 1920's. In the German magazine *Das Programm* (June 5, 1921), Rohrl advertised his twelve-minute act, which consisted of spouting water a distance of four-and-a-half meters with a spray two meters wide. Seeking only first-class houses, Rohrl issued a warning against all imitators, inviting legal action to copyists. He also noted that he would provide wonderful lithographs to theater owners. The two different posters I have seen of his act are most interesting. One (color plate 15) features him in fireman's garb quelching flames.

It was a variation of this stunt (it is difficult to establish priority) which was the most well-known feat of the Turk Hadji-Ali, who also swallowed and regurgitated stones and nuts. Ali drank a large quantity of water and then downed a quantity of kerosene. Moving to the corner of the stage, Ali would spout the gasoline, which would then burst into flames. Ali would now issue a second geyser, this time of water, and with perfect aim quelch the conflagration.

A brief clip of Hadji-Ali performing this stunt (probably shot in the 1930's) can be seen in the documentary film *Gizmo*, which still appears on various cable networks.

Harry Morton, who billed himself as both a human hydrant and a human aquarium, also worked in Germany in the 1920's. His act featured the swallowing of enormous quantities of beer on stage. In a six-minute spot, he swallowed one hundred glasses; in twelve minutes, no doubt in some near ecstatic frenzy, he downed three hundred mugs.

The tradition of unusual appetites continues to this day with Michael Lotito of Grenoble, France. Calling himself Mons. Mange Tout ("Eats Everything"), Lotito, according to the *Guinness Book of World Records*, has since 1966 eaten (in small pieces) a supermarket cart, seven entire bicycles, and, on an otherwise festive holiday in Caracas, a Cessna airplane.

LE PÉTOMANE:
The End

Joseph Pujol in performance.

A tall, dignified, crew-cut, mustachioed man slowly mounted the stage. He wore a bright red tailcoat with a red silk collar, a white butterfly tie, black shoes and socks, and elegant black satin breeches. He leaned forward, clutching a pair of white gloves, turned his back to the audience, and issued a series of sonorous, but odorless, notes from his body's most secret orifice.

Even the worldly Parisians who witnessed his debut at the gardens of the famous Moulin Rouge in 1892 were astonished. Within a few moments their consternation gave way to laughter. The laughter turned to tears of joy. According to contemporary reports, women especially were beside themselves: "Many fainted and fell down and had to be resuscitated."

Joseph Pujol, a modest baker from Marseille, earned a footnote in popular entertainment history as "Le Pétomane" (the fartomaniac), "The Only One Who Pays No Authors' Royalties." Today his fame rests largely on a wonderful little biography published in 1967 and a cult following in the sordid Hollywood world where this author hangs one of his hats. In fact, during the long course of writing this book, when its subject became known, I was frequently asked at show-business gatherings, "Oh, I suppose you're including Le Pétomane?" Or, "How about that guy who cuts the cheese?" For years, rumors of a film about his life filtered through the Hollywood grapevine (a foreign film biography about Pujol has even been produced). As a kind of inside joke, Mayor LePétomane is the name of the character played by Mel Brooks in his classic of cinematic crepitation, *Blazing Saddles*.

While I am not normally influenced by cocktail party pressures, I am aware of the fascinating dichotomy that left our subject a cult hero in part of the world and unknown in most of it. It's the last chapter, I thought. Although an Anglophile, I am clearly not an impassioned fan of scatological humor. But I am, I feel, an admirer and chronicler of *unusual* acts. Here was the most unusual of the unusual. A challenge which could not be refused . . .

Joseph Pujol, according to a memoir by his eldest son, Louis, was born in Marseille on June 1, 1857, at his parents' home, 13 rue des Incurables—a providential address. As a youngster he experienced a peculiar phenomenon while bathing. When he was submerged, not breathing through nose or mouth, water entered his body. Frightened at first, he was taken to a doctor who advised that he discontinue swimming. Years later, while serving in the army, he recalled the earlier incident and found he could control the intake of water in his body by contracting his abdominal muscles. He could also control the release of the water. He began to demonstrate a unique brand of water spouting which would have left Blaise Manfre, Floram Marchand, and other masters of the more traditional art speechless. This sphincter-spouting alone could have qualified him for stardom, but Pujol soon learned to control air as he had done water. With practice he found he could "modulate sound from the smallest and almost inaudible to the sharpest and most prolonged, simply according to the contraction of his muscles . . . and there was no smell."

For several years Pujol amused his friends without the aid of liquor or lampshades. Eventually, he was persuaded to perform on stage, which he did in his hometown. The first performance, according to Louis, was coolly received. Soon, however, the audience overcame their initial aversion to his act and he became a great success. First in Marseille, then at Toulon, Bordeaux, and Clermont-Ferrand, his fame grew. In 1892 he was bold enough to audition for his "dream engage-ment" at the Moulin Rouge. Monsieur Oller, a fearless theater manager, engaged him.

Pujol's "turn," which commanded attention and acclaim, consisted of a wide variety of effects.

After a spoken introduction during which Pujol explained that he had the ability to break wind at will, but fortunately did not produce the noxious fumes which usually accompany such activity, he proceeded to do a series of imitations of occupational farts—those of a bricklayer, a nun, etc. These were followed with impressions of two yards of calico being torn, the sound of a cannon, and the noise of thunder. Later in his career Pujol added a piece called "The Chanticleer" with words (by himself) and music, which provided a background to his barnyard mimicry:

Old cock of the village—my name's Chanticleer
My plumage is tattered—my voice very clear.
Now tonight, my dear public, I'd like to present
Some friends from the barnyard, each one an event.
I'd like to start up—with an eight-day old pup. (Here followed
    his impeccable imitation.)
Now dogs of all kinds I can do by the score
We next hear the watchdog—his tail caught in the door. (imitation)
Patau, his old father, wants to help him be freed
But alas and alack, why! he's still on the lead. (imitation)
The all-seeing blackbird is out of his cage
Mocking and laughing them all into rage. (imitation)
The blackbird declares that there's clearly a plot
To kill Chanticleer—and the owl laughs a lot. (imitation)
They chatter and chortle, discuss and surmise
Awaiting the Cock who makes the sun rise. (imitation)
Next comes the duck who is stretching his wings
His quack makes you laugh but just wait till he sings. (imitation)
Here comes the bees with a hum and a swish
Waiting their turn to get into the dish. (imitation)

Now a hen laying eggs makes a terrible racket
From the sounds that we hear, it's not one—it's a packet. (imitation)
Chanticleer, in his turn and to prove his devotion,
Warbles away to calm down his emotion. (imitation)
Tomcat in his basket wakes up when it's night
And makes love to his lady until it is light. (imitation)
Down by the pond at the side of the road
Sits the raucous-voiced, ugly, repellent old toad. (imitation)
In a neighbouring thicket a nightingale sings
Though we hear him much less as autumn takes wings. (imitation)
In December it's cold and down comes the snow
Covering the ground like a tomb in one go.
The poor and the needy—does anyone care?
Have all lost their homes and are out in the air.
But Christmas Eve comes! Alas! for the beasts
Cruel farmers will slaughter them all for their feasts.
That well fattened pig—his sad end is nigh
Destiny calls—he'll be part of a pie. (imitation)
Dear Public, if now that I've given you cause,
Reward Chanticleer with your welcome applause.
If you come back tomorrow, I'll always be proud
To keep you amused with my song small and loud . . .

Perhaps it was the only one-man dialogue in history.

Pujol would then briefly leave the stage and return with a yard-long rubber tube emerging from his body like a tail. Into the far end of the tube he placed a cigarette, which would then be drawn and blown as if manipulated by mouth and lungs. He soon replaced the cigarette with a small flute on which he played "Au clair de la lune" via his own peculiar embouchure. He removed the flute and blew out gas jets in the footlights of the stage, and occasionally extinguished a candle at a distance of one foot without hose or indeed any apparatus.

For private engagements Pujol appeared in swimming trunks from which a large hole had been cut, to prove his act was done without chicanery.

A careful newspaper critic, in an account published prior to Pujol's Paris debut, noted that the performer's "séance ended with an attempt to run through the gamut of sounds. In reality he produced only four notes, the do, mi, sol, and do of the octave. I cannot guarantee," he prudently added, "that each of these notes was tonally true."

Le Pétomane became a sensation in Paris; he outgrossed the leading artists of the day on stage, or anyplace else they might have met. Where Sarah Bernhardt commanded eight thousand francs per engagement, Pujol netted twenty thousand in a single afternoon. He was parodied and imitated. At the height of his success, disputes with

Pujol extinguishes a candle, his pièce de résistance.

Oller, the manager of the Moulin Rouge, led to Pujol's leaving that establishment (and eventually finding himself in court for violation of his contract). In retaliation Oller hired, and publicized prominently, a woman "Pétomane." When Pujol realized his competition augmented her nether regions with mechanical apparatus (a bellows-like contraption) to produce the sounds he came to naturally, he instituted a counter suit. The fraudulent farter, Angèle Thiébeau, started a suit against the paper *L'art Lyrique et la Music Hall* for defamation of character. The paper's exposé, claimed Thiébeau, had damaged her reputation and ability to earn a living when her only sin had been employing a gadget. Her lawyer claimed "the majority of physical feats produced in public places owe their effectiveness not only to the skill of their authors but also to apparatus and to tricks designed for illusion." Nevertheless, Thiébeau lost the case. Vindicated, Pujol withdrew his own court action.

In fact, a *legitimate* lady "Pétomane" gained a following in the French countryside. She was called La Mère Alexandre. She dressed like Pujol and exhibited extremely clever patter with her performances. She imitated the farts of the mason, the notary, and the nun, but her pièce de résistance was her impression of the bombardment of Port Arthur. At Bordeaux, Mère Alexandre pitched her act in the manner of carnival performers to attract a crowd. She promised that her performance was done without trickery or odor, that it was in "good taste even for women, girls and infants," and was "instructive and fun-provoking for tiniest infants to men with white hair." Mère Alexandre was so confident of her ability to please, she did not charge customers entering her show. If you're happy, she said, just pay when leaving.

Perhaps even more remarkable is a current-day specialty act who owes her inspiration to Le Pétomane. The performer, a stripper who uses the sobriquet of Honeysuckle Divine, has mastered the extinguishing of a candle flame from two paces and the playing of "Jingle Bells" using an orifice not even possessed by Pujol. Or, for that matter, by any man.

An anonymous nineteenth-century illustration satirizes the act of Le Pétomane.

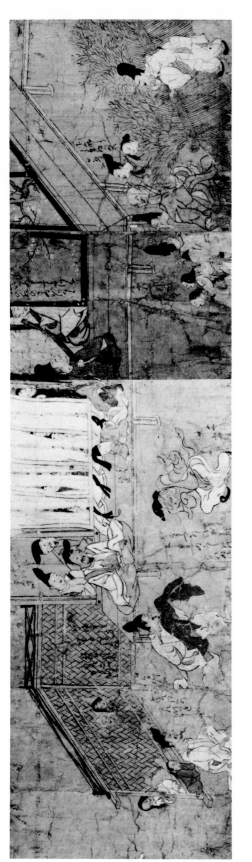

Hidetake's performance garners an enthusiastic audience and the gift of an expensive crimson robe. From "Fukutomi Zoshi."

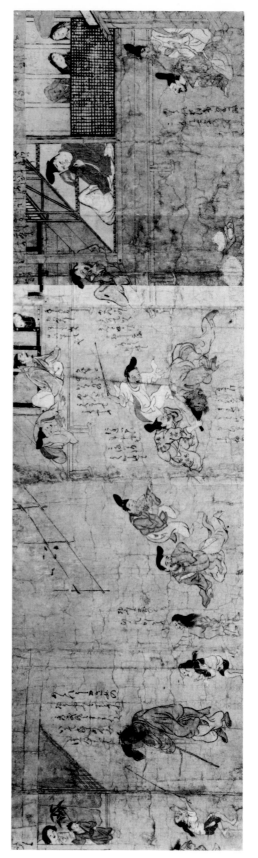

Fukutomi's exhibition results in a beating. From "Fukutomi Zoshi."

E. Grenet-Dancourt, the author of numerous comic monologues for the French stage, wrote the most popular satire of Pujol. Called "Le Ventomane" (Paris, 1893), it was a one-person sketch acted by a character who claimed to have been an enthusiastic witness at a Pétomane-like wind-chiming. The protagonist attempts to emulate the "master." After futile attempts on his own, he elicits his idol's aid with the proper tutelage, and practices faithfully twelve hours a day for six months. The neophyte, still concerned with his technique—"a little thin in volume . . . but of quality . . . so I am no longer an amateur"—ventures the formal stage. He assumes the position and with intense concentration attempts to perform, but "his face clouds over with the look of a man who has just suffered a terrible accident," and he runs, horror-stricken, from the stage.

Curiously, this scenario bears a striking resemblance to a fifteenth-century Japanese narrative picture scroll called "Fukutomi Zoshi" (the "Scroll of Fukutomi"): A poor old man called Hidetake prays to a Shinto deity and then has a dream. A fortuneteller interprets the dream to mean that Hidetake will "become rich aided by an unexpected voice within himself." The old man soon learns to dance to the sound of his own musical accompaniment. Hidetake's remarkable performance garners for him the patronage and reward of the nobility, whose gifts of damask, brocade, and gold make him a prophetically fulfilled, wealthy man. Fukutomi, the old neighbor of the newly successful performer, is envious of Hidetake. Urged by his wife, Fukutomi becomes his pupil. Before Fukutomi's first performance Hidetake gives his student "morning glory seeds which, unbeknown to Fukutomi, induce diarrhea." The ensuing debacle can be imagined by readers of even limited imagination. Fukutomi returns to his wife bearing blood and bruises rather than coins and robes. The story ends with the enraged wife attacking Hidetake and biting him. This work is considered one of the "best of the [Japanese] folk tale scrolls" and an "important cultural property."

Japanese literature is rich with tales of farting, an act which is devoid of some of the social taboos found in the West, but still subject to prejudice. For anyone uncomfortable with the subject matter, I highly recommend the piece by Furai Sanjin (Hiraga Gennai) first published in 1774. Gennai's treatise *On Farting* is a lucid evocation of the cultural and social importance of an eighteenth-century musical farter.

The subject of Gennai's thesis was one of the most famous of all Japanese "misemono" showmen, Kirifuri-hanasaki-otoko, the "mist-descending flower-blossoming man." "Misemono" were spectacles or exhibits, usually of variety entertainments, freaks, or unusual inventions, which enjoyed their greatest popularity during the Edo Period in Japan (1603–1868). The entertainments in large part paralleled similar exhibitions in the West.

The most famous location for such attractions was the Ryogoku Bridge in Edo. It was there in 1774 that Kirifuri performed. A "placard was set up with a picture of a funny little man, buttocks thrust forward, surrounded by . . . legends." The legends announced a partial repertoire of the performer, whose act consisted of the "farting scale," the "rosary routine," the "yoshiwara fanfare," the "kanoko curtain-raiser drum pattern," the "Nō drum duet," the imitation of specific ballad styles, the barking of dogs, the crowing of cocks, and the simulation of a major exhibition of fireworks.

Kirifuri was described as a man "slightly plump and of pale complexion." He wore a "soft blue unlined robe over a red crepe undergarment." Like Le Pétomane, he introduced his act with a short monologue but seemed to favor a more literal interpretation in his imitations as exemplified by his water mill routine, "which he performed while doing cartwheels, contriving the effect of water pushing down from one side and turning him over and over." This was of course accompanied by the appropriate sound effects.

Kirifuri, too, was accused of trickery and hidden gimmicks, but Gennai defended his natural ability. Further on, he passionately stated: "This prodigy of flatulence is unprecedented in the 2,436 years of this hoary land of Japan . . . Not only are these accomplishments unique in Japan, never has their like been heard from China, Korea, India, not even from the various states of Oranda [Holland]. What Art! What Farts!"

To those modernists who lift their noses at such spectacle, or who begrudgingly accept it as a sign of the barbarianism or silliness of bygone eras, the following must come as a shock: Japan has a current "Pétomane." Perhaps inspired by the reverence of Gennai, or the deep-rooted traditions of the art in his country, this unnamed but not unheralded champion emerged from obscurity to a more powerful venue than even the Moulin Rouge—he appeared on television. Joe Grace, a reporter for the Mainichi *Daily News*, described an act on the program *Two P.M. Show* which produced a "tuneful, incredible repertoire" of crepitating sounds. The Asahi *Daily News* stated that on a television show, the performer claimed he "could break wind 3,800 times in succession. He took off his pants and lay on the studio floor in his underwear while the M.C. placed the microphone in a strategic position." Later the performer had the studio orchestra accompany him in a song. Perhaps realizing there were precedents which would affect his claim to originality, he encored with a stunt which, to this author at least, could be considered unique: "He applied a blowgun to his posterior and accurately fired darts into a target ten feet away."

The indignation which followed the performance seemed greater in America than in Japan. In a Detroit *Free Press* column of June 21, 1980, entitled "The U.S. May Be No. 2 in TV Vulgarity," writer Jim

Fitzgerald said that American commercials for laxatives and feminine hygiene products, and *The Gong Show* and *The Dating Game*, took a back seat to the offensive Orientals. "Once you learn what's on Japanese TV you'll feel better about the American brand," he said. "You may also feel better about Toyotas and Pearl Harbor. It's hard to stay mad at a nation of people doomed to suffer under the yoke of imperial vulgarity."

In spite of the outrage which invariably accompanies the expulsion of wind, historically an eclectic and impressive group of westerners have added their thoughts to the literature of flatulence. Aristophanes, Chaucer, Rabelais, Villon, Swift, Ben Franklin, and Mark Twain all explored, in print, their observations on the topic. My inquiries into their work, and other scholarly material likely to shed light on unusual performances in the field, have not been accomplished without considerable hardship. A case in point: I have written much of this work in a cubicle provided for me at the William Andrews Clark Jr., Memorial Library, a splendid rare-book repository on beautiful grounds, physically separate from, although part of, the University of California at Los Angeles. I daresay I may have been unable to complete the project at all if not for the help of the splendid staff and the use of the facilities. Nevertheless, I detected a subtle change the day I excitedly requested a work entitled *The Benefit of Farting Explain'd*. The Clark specializes in English literature from 1640 to 1750. As the work in question appeared both separately and in Swift's *Miscellanies* (Dublin, 1722), and was often reprinted in the eighteenth century, it seemed to me likely to be among their holdings. Indeed, in a few minutes I was handed the object of my desire, accompanied by a disdainful look and raising of the eyebrow I had distinctly *not* requested. I felt that whatever reputation I had achieved as a serious student of the arts—admittedly already sullied by inquiries into the exploits of armless violinists, dwarf fan painters, and geeks—had now received its death blow.

Giggles and pointing (I began to notice) now accompanied my wanderings through the labyrinthine stacks of rare books. Worse, I sensed staff and readers alike shying away from me at the card catalogue and in the lounge. Undaunted, resolute, I carefully watched my diet and pressed on.

My intrepidity was rewarded with yet another resounding reference to musical effluvium: *The Benefit of Farting Explain'd, or the Fundament-All Cause of the Distempers incident to the Fair Sex Enquired Into. Proving a Posteriori most of the Dis-Ordures In-tail'd upon them, are owing to Flatulencies not seasonably vented. Wrote in Spanish by Don Fartinando Puff-indorst Professor of Bumbast at the University of Crackow and translated into English at the Request, and for the Use of the Lady Damp-fart of Her-Fart-Shire by Obediah Fizzle, Groom of the Stool to the Princess of Arsimini in Sardinia*. This was published, according to the title page, which provides the paragraph just cited, at Long-fart (*Longford* in *Ireland*), printed by *Simon Bumbubbard*, at the Sign of the Wind Mill opposite Tawattling Street, MDCCXXII.

The punning pamphlet contains, on page 12, a reference to a book, *Laugh, and be Fat*, by a celebrated Dr. *Blow*, who in "his Treatise on the Fundament-alls of Musick asserts that the first discovery of Harmony was owing to an Observation of Persons of different sizes sounding different notes in Musick." The good doctor recommended placing the players of his human "Bum-Fiddle" in size order, like a set of bells or organ pipes, to provide a more diverting entertainment than that usually associated with the Tea Table scandal.

French literature of the period produced works of similar interest. An "Essay on the Physical Theory and Method of Farting" entitled *L'art de péter* (Westphalie, 1751) contains a farting contest between champions of the warring armies of Prince Airfart and the Queen of the Amazons. The Amazon participant wins "by releasing one which spilled out and flowed graciously, accompanied by melodious and wondrous sounds without odor."

Joseph Pujol was probably uninterested in academic expostulation on his art. He remained a man of the streets. He seemed unaware of the references, classical or otherwise, to the history of his art, and unaffected by the fame and fortune he received. Indeed, it was his association with humble acquaintances of his earlier life which got him in trouble with the law. In the suit brought against him by Oller of the Moulin Rouge, Pujol was charged with violating the terms of his contract by performing at a gingerbread stand in the market. This he did, without pay, to help a girl, an old friend, who owned the modest business.

Although Pujol lost the suit, he gained his freedom. He built a remarkable traveling fairground show, "Théâtre Pompadour," which toured and performed for many years featuring his children and other performers doing playlets, "poses plastiques," and serpentine dances before Pujol's headlining act. He was heralded in Algeria and Egypt. Though Pujol was a great success in Belgium, the Belgian king, Leopold II, felt it necessary to travel to France, incognito, to watch him perform privately. In Spain, local officials were outraged by Pujol's act and wanted to renege on a lucrative contract. According to his son Louis, Papa, trooper that he was, appeared as a clown and collected his money.

Only World War I put an end to his long career. Disheartened by the hardships of the conflict and the injuries suffered by his sons, Pujol never again performed publicly. He went back to his former profession and ran bakeries and a biscuit factory. Although examined by astonished French doctors who marveled at his unusual abdominal control, he was urged by his family to turn down a large sum of money

Pujol in front of his "Théâtre Pompadour."

in exchange for the donation of his body to the French Faculty of
Medicine after his death. He passed away in 1945 at the age of 88.

The derisive comments which accompanied his exhibition never
affected Pujol, who felt his peculiar talents were a gift. Perhaps he
would have been comforted by the words of St. Augustine, who in the
fifth century exhibited a worldliness not usually associated with those
of his calling. In his *City of God*, in an argument in support of free will,
Augustine noted: "Certain human beings have natural endowments
quite different than others and remarkable for their very rarity . . .
Some people produce at will, without any stench, such rhythmical
sounds from their fundament that they appear to be making music
even from that quarter."

For the Curious...

While no attempt has been made at a definitive bibliography of all the works consulted in preparation for this project, the author hopes that these notes will list the major sources and aid others doing similar research. In addition, they afford the opportunity of adding material too obscure for the book proper (how, you are asking, can this be?) and to single out the help of many people who graciously provided the author with materials and information.

I have avoided the use of "*sic*," which I find grating to the eye and ear. It may be assumed that the quaint and curious spelling and grammar preserved within quotation marks were the intentions of the original author. In an age when the performers themselves signed their own names with different spellings (i.e., Mathew, Matthew, Matthias, Buckinger, Buchinger, etc.), who am I to seek conformity?

1. HARRY KAHNE: THE MULTIPLE MENTAL MARVEL

Numerous reviews of Kahne's shows appear in English and American variety and conjuring periodicals. Particularly helpful were long write-ups in *World's Fair* (London), May 21, 1938, and *Abracadabra* (London) in the 1950's.

There is a popular biography of Kahne by Penn Sherrie in the October 1925 issue of the *Strand Magazine*. Ads for Kahne, under the direction of Lew Golder, appear in National Vaudeville Artists' Annuals of the 1920's. Other biographical material, including Kahne's death date (which contradicts his age in the *Strand* article), is provided through correspondence between Kahne's widow, Marguerite, and Charles Miller. Mr. Miller wrote of Kahne and another similar mental marvel, John Stone, in the November 1968 issue of *Genii, the Conjurer's Magazine*. He related some interesting technical details of Kahne's performance: There was a night club version of the act, all of which could be packed into a standard size automobile. It used two slates (one was two-thirds the size of a car door, the other about the size of a *Life* magazine) and a chalkboard marked into squares. For larger shows he frequently wrote with soap on glass to ensure visibility. Later in life, after suffering a stroke, Kahne did a version of the act writing with only one hand and was seen on Art Baker's *You Asked For It*.

His inspiration for the spot may have been a Japanese worker named Tameo Kajiyama, who did similar stunts on the Pantages Vaudeville Circuit. The "Jap Mirako" act of writing upside down and backward was described and explained in a monograph written by juggler-magician Vin Carey.

Hubert Leslie appeared at St. George's Hall in London in the 1920's in the "Multiple Simultaneous Celebration Act." He authored *Artful Art and Breathless Brain Waves* (Sussex, privately published, 1954).

Kahne's own seventy-page treatise never appeared in book form and was provided through the courtesy of Jay Marshall of Chicago, who owns the original manuscript. Marquis MacDonald published Kahne's exercises as a manuscript entitled *Multiply Your Mind Powers* and says the Kahne manuscript was sold as a correspondence course.

Thea Alba's tour with Pete Collins is described in his book *No People Like Show People* (London, 1957). She is also mentioned in Kurt Moller Madsen's *Markedsgogl og cirkuslojer* (Copenhagen, 1970) and in *Das Programm* (Berlin,

1902–1935), the organ of the Internationale Artisten-Loge, which was presided over by her sponsor, Henry de Vry.

The variety theater has abounded in acts similar to, but perhaps less cleverly prepared and presented than, those of Kahne and Alba. The techniques of such phenomena are now under investigation by scientists, as in the case of Andrew Levine, a philosophy professor at the University of Wisconsin. According to the July 1980 *Scientific American*, "As someone speaks to him, even quite rapidly, he can almost simultaneously utter the same sequence of words with the sounds of each word reversed." Remarkably, when words have the same spelling but different meanings, Levine's backward pronunciation is altered, based on the context of the sentence.

2. PORCINE PROPHETS AND PIG-FACED LADIES

Brief but lively discussions of learned pigs are to be found in the works of Milbourne Christopher (*Panorama of Magic*, New York, 1962; *ESP, Seers and Psychics*, New York, 1970; *Illustrated History of Magic*, New York, 1973) and Edwin Dawes (*The Great Illusionists*, London, 1979). Richard Altick's *Shows of London* (Cambridge, Mass., 1978) provides fascinating material on pigs and indeed on any subject he addresses, many of which are important to this study.

A scholarly and most entertaining account of learned pigs and the Romantics is in a paper by Professor G. E. Bentley, Jr., of the University of Toronto, entitled *The Freaks of Learning* (1980). The Abbot of Baigne is mentioned in *Wanley's World of Wonders*, 4th ed. (London, 1806) and cited by Bentley. Additional material is in *The Dictionary Historical and Critical of Mr. Peter Bayle*, 2nd ed. (London, 1734–1738).

Thomas Frost's *The Old Showmen and the Old London Fairs* and *Lives of the Conjurers* (both London, 1874) provide nineteenth-century accounts of trained pigs, as does Lord George Sanger's autobiography, *70 Years a Showman* (London, 1908). The pig at Astley's is mentioned in the *Memoirs of J. Decastro, Comedian* (London, 1824).

The scrapbooks of the Reverend Daniel Lysons at the British Library are a source of marvelous material on varied attractions and exhibitions. The newspaper reports from London and the provinces, unless otherwise noted, were collected by Lysons. The American material is to be found in G. C. Odell, *Annals of the New York Stage* (New York, 1927–1949), Pecor, *The Magician and the American Stage* (Washington, D.C., 1977), and Moulton, *Houdini's History of Magic in Boston* (Glenwood, Ill., 1983).

Material on Nicholas Hoare is largely from playbills at the Humanities Research Center, University of Texas at Austin and the author's collection, as well as in the works of Thomas Frost. *The story of the learned pig as dictated to an officer of the Royal Navy* is in the Folger Shakespeare Library. I am grateful to Betsy Walsh for helping me obtain a copy of it.

The story of Fred Leslie and his pigs is told by Bert Chipman in *Hey Rube* (Los Angeles, 1933).

The 1640 edition of the Tannakin Skinker story is at the British Library and is also collected in the Ashbee reprints. Eugen Hollaender's *Wunder, Wundergeburt und Wundergestalt in Einblattdrucken des Fuenfzehnten bis Achtsehnten Jahr-*

hunterts (Stuttgart, 1921) contains the German broadside of 1717. The Paris manuscript at the British Library is discussed in detail in the Matthew Buchinger chapter. Material on Morland is in the *Dictionary of National Biography* and Wilson and Caulfield's *The Book of Wonderful Characters* (London, 1869).

Broadsides of the pig-faced lady which provide much information are in the collection of the author or Peter Jackson, who graciously made them available. In discussing caricatures in this work, the author frequently made use of *The Catalogue of Political and Personal Satires Preserved in the Department of Prints and Drawings in the British Museum*, by Frederick G. Stevens and M. D. George (London, 1870–1954).

The Bartholomew Fair figures are cited by Frost and Altick. The waxwork show is described in a 1901 issue of the *Showman Magazine*; the Sanger story is from *70 Years a Showman*.

3. ATTENUATION AS ART: WILLARD, THE MAN WHO GROWS

Clarence Willard is frequently mentioned and reviewed in the conjuring and variety periodicals of his day. His portrait graces the cover of the November 1957 issue of the magic journal *M.U.M.* This issue contains a short biography of Willard by Leslie Guest.

The *World Magazine* of June 3, 1923, contains an interesting article related by Willard to Ernest Brennecke. In his later life Willard was frequently featured in newspapers in his native Oakland. His obituary appeared in the Oakland *Tribune*, August 2, 1962.

Twenty Years of Spoof and Bluff by Carlton (Arthur Phillips) was published by Herbert Jenkins (London, 1920).

Orville Stamm's act is amusingly related by Fred Allen in *Much Ado About Me* (Boston and Toronto, 1956).

4. MORE THAN THE SUM OF THEIR PARTS: MATTHEW BUCHINGER, SARAH BIFFIN, AND OTHER ANOMALIES OF NATURE . . .

I have been fortunate in obtaining numerous cuttings, prints, and even original works of art of many of the subjects in this chapter.

The standard scholarly work on the subject of freaks, often consulted here, is Hollaender's *Wunder, Wundergeburt und Wundergestalt* . . . (Stuttgart, 1921).

Buchinger, Biffin, Valerius, and others appeared for many years as the subjects of brief biographical sketches in works such as Caulfield's, Kirby's, etc., usually with the same misinformation repeated without change. The standard magic histories mention Buchinger but add little material. Dawes, *The Great Illusionists* (London, 1973), and Phillip H. Highfill, Jr., et al., *A Biographical Dictionary of Actors, Actresses, Musicians, Dancers, Managers & Other Stage Personnel in London, 1660–1800* (Carbondale and Edwardsville, Ill., 1973 ongoing), which provide more detailed accounts, are welcome exceptions and are highly recommended. Dawes draws the parallel between Buchinger and modern-day showmen.

The calligraphic request of 1708 is preserved in the city library of Bamberg, which also retains an original Buchinger calendar drawn with highly ornamental borders and dated 1709. The Nuremberg Council, which recorded its notes on the Buchinger petition on December 24, 1708, admitted to being favorably influenced because Buchinger's wife was pregnant. The council notes of January 31, 1709, show a favorable impression made by Buchinger's generosity in boarding an imbecilic child called Hieronymus Frank, whose condition was attributed to a bite on his head. This material appears in Walter Brod's article "Der Schreibmeister Matthais Buchinger" in the *Mainfrankishes Jahrbuck fur Geschichte und Kunst* (Wurzburg, 1985). It was brought to my attention by Volker Huber.

I'm grateful to Nicolas Barker at the British Library for a spectral dating of an original Buchinger drawing, in ink on vellum, in my collection. The date established, May 10, 1739, proves that the little man was alive and most steady of hand at that late date. An earlier manuscript containing samples of at least a dozen different calligraphic styles states that eight of Buchinger's fourteen children were alive in 1731. One grandchild is said to have become the best lutenist in England.

The British Library was also the source of other original material, the Paris du Plessis manuscript and the Tillemans–Cox Macro correspondence. Samples of Buchinger's work are also in the Henry E. Huntington Library in San Marino, the William Andrews Clark Memorial Library in Los Angeles, the Germaniches National Museum, Nuremberg, and the collection of Peter Jackson. The Nicola manuscript was among the remarkable collection of materials purchased by the Library Company of Philadelphia at the auction of the estate of Pierre Eugene Du Simitière in 1785. The Geneva-born Du Simitière was the first museum proprietor in the United States, inviting observers to the "American Museum," which was on view in his Philadelphia residence from 1782. He died in October 1784.

The only known copy of the first edition of *The Whole Art of Legerdemain; or, Hocus Pocus in Perfection. By which any Person of the meanest Capacity may perform the whole Art without a Teacher, as performed by the best Artists in the World, To which are added, Several Tricks of Cups and Balls, &c. As performed by the little Man without Hands or Feet. Also the wonderful art of Fire-eating* (Wolverhampton, circa 1737) is in the Mulholland Library. Raymond Toole Stott, the bibliographer of circus and conjuring material, told noted collector Leslie Cole that he believed this edition to be the rarest important book of magic extant. There are at least three subsequent editions, which run into the 1750's.

I am currently trying to prepare a detailed iconography of Buchinger's work. It should be noted, for instance, that the engraving of Buchinger surrounded by thirteen vignettes appears in at least five different variants done by two different engravers, and with explanatory text in two languages.

An album of Valerius' with original specimens of his writing is in the collection of Peter Hackhofer in West Germany. He graciously allowed me to study it when I visited him there. Hackhofer also supplied an important article on the careers of Buchinger and Grigg written by Stephan Ottermann. It provides excellent new information on Grigg used in this chapter and lists early German references, the most noteworthy of which are Konrad Ludwig Walther's *Thesaurus medico-chirurgicarum observationum curiosarum* (Leipzig, 1715) and *Sammlung von Natur- und Medicin- wie auch hierzu gehörigen Kunst- und Literaturgeschichten* (Breslau, 1719). The article will appear in Hackhofer's magazine *Der Taschenspieler*. Interestingly, Grigg is incorrectly referred to as Brigg in most English language descriptions, no doubt due to the confusion of the ornate seventeenth-century German letter "G," which resembles the English "B."

The biography of Miss Biffin is largely put together from cuttings, letters, and playbills (sadly, rarely dated) in my collection. The letter about Biffin's proposed trip to America is from the Harvard Theatre Collection. The Unthan letter is reproduced in *Fahrend Volk* by Signor Saltarino (pseud. W. H. Otto; Leipzig, 1895), which is a wonderful account of abnormal and curious entertainers. Material is also to be found in Frost's *The Old Showmen and the Old London Fairs* (London, 1874) and Henry Morley's *Bartholomew Fair* (London, 1859).

Walter Gibson, the prolific author and authority on magic (and, as Maxwell Grant, the creator of "The Shadow"), told me the strange story of Johnny Eck and the sawing illusion; Rajah Raboid, he said, was the magician who presented the act. Tod Browning, who used Eck in *Freaks*, also wrote and directed *The Unknown* (1927), which starred Lon Chaney as a circus performer who pretended to be armless (his limbs were strapped to the sides of his body) to do an impressive sideshow act. Chaney actually taught himself to wash, eat, and throw knives with his feet for this role.

The magician Harry Leat, in a pamphlet entitled *Tragic Magic* (London, 1925), suggested an illusion called "The Lunar Rays" in which a scientist assembled, piece by piece, a mechanical man. The robot suddenly became imbued with its own power and attacked the scientist, who, in a horrible battle, ripped the limbs from his creation. The effect required a double amputee with one arm and one leg. "Unfortunately," Leat noted shortly after World War I, "the chief factor in the sketch is only too easily obtained; yet there is no reason why he should not have a good time for his labour is light." To my knowledge, this stunt was never performed. (For a much less bizarre and highly skilled act on the scientist-robot theme try to see "Al Carthy," currently working at the Club Eve in Paris).

Johnny Eck, recently interviewed in Richard Lamparski's series *Whatever Became of . . . ?* (1985), gave his birthdate as August 11, 1927, twenty minutes after his full-sized brother Robert was born. He spoke glowingly of Tod Browning and the film *Freaks* (for which he was paid $35.00) but added that he did not get along with Peter the Skeleton Man. After the movie, Eck noted, "All of the freaks started wearing sunglasses and acting funny . . . in other words, they went Hollywood." Living in a dangerous part of Baltimore, Eck was recently asked what he would do if he were a full-sized man for one day. He said: "I'd get my brother's baseball bat and beat the hell out of that son of a bitch next door who makes our lives so miserable."

5. BLIND TOM

Endorsements, testimonials, and a basic biography of Tom Bethune appear in at least three editions of *The Marvelous Musical Prodigy, Blind Tom, the Negro Boy Pianist, whose performances at the Great St. James and Egyptian Halls, London, and Salle Hertz, Paris, have created such a profound sensation. Anecdotes, songs, sketches of the life, testimonials of musicians and savans, and opinions of the American and English press of "Blind Tom"* published during his long career. Accounts of Tom appear in Pratt's *American Music and Musicians*, Hutton's *Curiosities of the American Stage* (New York, 1891), and the February 10, 1866, issue of *Harper's Weekly*. Amalie Tutein's memoir appears in *Etude* magazine of February 1918 and is the source of the Robert Heller story. Strangely, Heller (pseudonym of William A. Palmer) does not mention Tom in his own autobiography. Houdini refers to Tom in *A Magician Among the Spirits* (New York and London, 1924). Tom is the subject of numerous contemporary newspaper accounts, and his 1861 New York appearance is mentioned in T. Allston Brown's *A History of the New York Stage* (New York, 1903, volume I). Tom's later New York engagements are noted in G. C. Odell's *Annals of the New York Stage* (New York, 1927–1949, volume VIII).

Dai Vernon, the great sleight-of-hand magician now in his nineties, saw Tom play at the Russel Theatre in Ottawa, Canada, around the turn of the century. Vernon corroborated for me the stories of Tom's remarkable ability and animal nature. His performance was accompanied by grunting, horrible facial contortions, and an inability to control his bladder onstage, but he perfectly duplicated, including mistakes, any selection played by a member of the audience. Vernon's vivid recollection of a show seen more than eighty years ago attests to its lasting impact.

Tom's court battles are detailed in an important scholarly monograph, *Free at Last: Legal Aspects Concerning the Career of Blind Tom Bethune, 1849–1908* (1976). The author, Arthur R. LaBrew, also gives much important information on Tom's performing career. Among the fascinating technical details he notes are that it would be possible to play only the introduction (not the entire concerto) of Beethoven's "Third" while standing with one's back to the keyboard. LaBrew also includes a listing of Tom's musical compositions.

A man in his twenties, Leslie Lemke of Pewaukee, Wisconsin, is a modern-day prodigy. He can play piano in jazz, classical, rock—or any style—and duplicate music after hearing it played only once. He sings in a deep, rich voice, in English, German, Italian, and Chinese. Mr. Lemke was recently seen by millions of television viewers on CBS' *60 Minutes*. Mr. Lemke, who was featured in a segment on idiot savants, is retarded, blind, and afflicted with cerebral palsy.

6. MAX MALINI: THE LAST OF THE MOUNTEBANKS

Malini's press coverage was so remarkable that newspaper accounts and reviews of his performances appear in almost all the major magic collections already cited in this book.

Most helpful were the personal scrapbooks, letters, and programs of Malini, which I was able to examine through the kindness of his son, Oziar. A captivating storyteller who often accompanied his father on his tours, Oziar regaled me with wonderful anecdotes. Particularly pleasing were the stories of Max's compassion, kindness, and generosity in his personal relationships.

Interesting published accounts by Dai Vernon (*Malini and his Magic*, edited by Lewis Ganson, London, 1962), S. Leo Horowitz (*The Sphinx*, December 1939), and P. T. Selbit (*The Wizard*, November 1905) are all laudatory in their praise of Malini. Shigeo Takagi, the wonderful Japanese magician, told me about watching Malini perform in Tokyo when Takagi was a small boy.

Eddie McGuire, a magician and one-time manager of Malini, wrote a long account of his performance in a letter to T. Nelson Downs on July 15, 1926. McGuire also contributed articles about Malini's magic to the January and June 1964 issues of the *Linking Ring* magazine.

Additional material in the non-magical press appears in J. B. Booth's *Old Pink 'un Days* (London, 1925), George Altree's *Footlight Memories* (London, 1932), *Datas: the Memory Man*, by Himself (London, 1932), and Charles Drage's *Two-Gun Cohen* (London, 1954).

In number 101 of his long and fascinating series in the *Magic Circular* magazine, Edwin Dawes relates the story of Malini's appearance on an all-star bill in memory of Charles Morton, "The Father of the Music Halls." In *Malini and his Magic*, Faucett Ross tells of a similar American event with Paul Whiteman, Frank Fay, and Will Rogers in which Malini was to be paid an enormous fee only if he was the hit of the star-studded show. He was.

Malini authored "How I Mystified King Edward" in *Pearson's Weekly*, January 25, 1906. "The New Yorker Who Fooled the King" was the title of a story of the same event in the *World Magazine* of January 14. Malini was the subject of a 1904 article in the *Penny Magazine* which featured photographs of his performance, one of which appears as the cover of an anonymous book of card tricks, undated but published at about the same time.

So secretive was Malini, so apparently impromptu was his magic, that Charles Miller may have been the only person to ever see Malini rehearse his effects. Miller watched him execute his sleight-of-hand technique with the door ajar in a Los Angeles hotel room in the 1930's. Even his son, Oziar, has no clear recollection of seeing his father practice. Miller also illustrated Malini's playful side with this story: Malini noticed a wealthy woman who had idly kicked her shoes off under the table while eating dinner in an elegant restaurant. Unseen by the woman, Malini crawled under the table and took the shoes. Moments later a waiter presented the woman with a silver domed platter which she uncovered, revealing her own footwear.

Malini's remarkable personality and skill have given rise to such elaborate stories that it is almost impossible to document them fully. The exaggeration of magical effects into impossible incidents is a technique which can be cultivated by an exceptional magician. No one orchestrated such incidents like Malini.

7. DATAS: THE MAN WHO KNEW TOO MUCH

Our subject authored *Datas: The Memory Man* (London, 1932) and *Memory by "Datas," a Simple System of Memory Training* (London, 1910). The memoirs, though clearly not documented, give interesting anecdotes of his life and career. Magician Walter Jeans was (according to the late Ken Brooke) once involved in the management of Datas' career. It was suggested by Jeans and others that the Memory Man's fondness for strong potables kept him from even more singular accomplishments in his career.

The Crocombe interview is from an unidentified magazine hand-dated April 1928. A short biographical sketch of Datas appears in volume III of *Boys of Our Empire* (London, 1903). An obituary from the *World's Fair* (London, September 1, 1956) mentions that as a child of five Datas was carried on the back of the famous rope walker Blondin as he crossed from the towers of the Crystal Palace. An article by Datas entitled "What Memory Did for Me" appeared serially in *Pearson's Weekly*, November 7 to December 26, 1936. He is also mentioned in Herman Darewski's *Musical Memories* (London, 1937).

Fred Barlow's *Mental Prodigies* contains a sketch of Datas and a later "Memory Man," Leslie Welch. Born on December 29, 1907, Welch performed his act on radio and television as well as in live performance. He also used his superior memory as part of his steady employment as the manager of a sports periodical.

Other memory acts who played vaudeville or music halls included "Memora," who was booked by William Morris in 1909 (*Edward's Monthly*, May 1909), and the "Infant Salambo," who appeared at St. George's Hall in 1901 (*Showman Magazine*, October 18, 1901). Elre Cecilia Salambo debuted as a seven-year-old in the act of her parents (Salambo & Ollivette's New Wonders Company), which featured conjuring, mathematical calculations, fire manipulations, and demonstrations of electricity. Elre, who was taught an original system of memory by her father, claimed to have a repertoire of ten thousand answers to questions of "a historical and general nature." The magazine reporter was so impressed as to call her one of the "wonders of the world" and "absolutely the most clever and best informed child of her age the world has ever known."

8. EQUINE AMUSEMENTS

A series of articles which I wrote for *Arabian Horse World Magazine* (commencing in July 1982) forms the basis of this popular look at equestrian entertainment.

Many references to Banks and Marocco may be found in Raymond Toole Stott's *Circus and Allied Arts: A World Bibliography* (4 vols., Derby, 1958–1971. A fifth volume was completed before Stott's death and it is hoped by all lovers of the circus that it will eventually be published) and Arthur Freeman's *Elizabeth's Misfits* (New York and London, 1978). Freeman's excellent account is the first to identify "William" as Banks' first name. I was able to examine the rare 1595 *Maroccus Extaticus or, Bankes Bay Horse in a Trance* at the Huntington Library in San Marino, California. It is the source of this quote: "Truly there was never horse in this world answered man with more reason, nor ever man in this world reasoned more sensibly with a horse, than this man and this horse. . . ."

Karl Krall's famous account of the Elberfield horses is *Denkende Tiere Beiträge zur Tierseelenkunde auf Grund Eigner Versuche* (Leipzig, 1912). Accounts of Lady Wonder and other mind reading horses may be found in Christopher's *ESP, Seers and Psychics* (New York, 1970). "The Clever Hans Phenomenon: Communication with Horses, Whales, Apes & People" is the subject of volume

364 of *The Annals of the New York Academy of Sciences*. Another more recent claimant of psychic power was Serrano, billed as the world's "best educated horse," owned and exhibited in the 1940's by Clint Brush, a southern California lima bean farmer.

I am grateful to Charles and Regina Reynolds, who provided information on the horse effects of Dante and Thurston, some of which is to be found in their *One Hundred Years of Magic Posters* (New York, 1973).

Reliable material on early circus riders can be found in Stuart Thayer's *Annals of the Early American Circus, 1793–1829* (Manchester, Mich., 1976). Arthur Saxon's excellent books *Enter Foot and Horse: A History of Hippodrama in England and France* (New Haven and London, 1968) and *The Life and Art of Andrew Ducrow & the Romantic Age of the English Circus* (Hamden, Conn., 1978) were most helpful, as was their author, with various questions I posed to him. Early playbills and the book *2,000 Years of Juggling* by Karl-Heinz-Ziethen (Paris, 1981) provided additional material on unusual acts on horseback. The story of the Little Military Learned Horse is told in Decastro's biography cited earlier.

Cuttings of Wildman and a handwritten account from the *Dictionary of the Wonders of Nature* are to be found at the Humanities Research Center, University of Texas at Austin. The poem appears in John Timbs, *English Eccentrics* (London, 1866). *The Universal Magazine*, September and October 1766, contains a description of Wildman, as does Campardon's *Les Spectacles de la Foire* (Paris, 1877) and the Reverend I. Platt's *The Book of Curiosities or Wonders of the Great World* (London, 1822).

The sister of circus founder Philip Astley performed a similar act with as many as three swarms of bees. This is noted by Highfill, et al., in *A Biographical Dictionary of Actors, Actresses, Musicians, Dancers, Managers, & Other Stage Personnel in London, 1660–1800*, and Arthur Saxon, who speculates that Wildman may have taught her the secret.

An earlier "King of the Bees" was witnessed by Brué, a Frenchman visiting Senegal, Africa, in the seventeenth century. "Let his secret consist in what it may, this much is certain; that they followed him wherever he went as sheep do their shepard. His whole body and particularly his cap, was so covered with them that they appeared like a swarm just settled. When he departed they went along with him; for besides those on his body, he was surrounded by thousands which always attended on him." This quote and the story of the German imposter are cited in Beckmann's *History of Inventions and Discoveries* (London, 1797). The account of caging the queen is from *The Real Conjuror* (London, 1822).

Raymond Toole Stott devotes a section of his bibliography to Adah Isaacs Menken, who inspired numerous accounts, often unreliable. Her boxer husband was John Heenan, "The Benicia Boy"; her spiritualist suitor was William Henry Harrison Davenport of the famous Davenport Brothers. (Incidentally, Stott exhibited the "amazing equine calculators Reggie and Secundo" when he was the impresario of his own "Ray Stott's Circus.")

Posters and additional material on many late nineteenth- and early twentieth-century riders are housed at the Circus World Museum, Baraboo, Wisconsin, where Bob Parkinson was most helpful to me during my visit.

A playbill of the Blondin Horse is in the collection of materials assembled by magician Henry Evans Evanion, housed in the British Library. The Blondin Horse is mentioned by Fox in *A Pictorial History of Performing Horses* (Seattle, 1960), which also reproduces the bill of Freyer's Pony Circus. An interesting biography of Doc Carver is Raymond Thorp's *Spirit Gun of the West* (Glendale, Ca., 1957), although it contains little material on diving horses.

The story of the Sybarites is told in Joseph Strutt's *Glig, Gamena, Angel-Deod, or, the Sports and Pastimes of the People of England* (London, 1801).

9. GENIUS OR CHARLATAN?: WALFORD BODIE, M.D.

An obvious starting point for these notes would seem to be a bibliography of works produced by Bodie himself. Unfortunately, as with so many of the subjects of this book, even this basic task is far from simple. The late James Findlay, well-known magic historian and collector, listed only one item by Bodie (and one each by his son and wife) in his *Scottish Conjuring Bibliography* (Shaklin, Great Britain, 1951). In fact, the doctor wrote: *The Bodie Book* (London, 1905, and various other editions), which provides information on Bodie's personal philosophy; *Stage Stories* (London, 1908), the source of the Billington and Diamond Ring stories; and *Harley the Hypnotist* (London, 1910). These are Bodie's major books. He also authored these pamphlets: *Thousands Buried Alive* (Macduff, n.d.), which is the exact text of *Hypnotism* (recorded by Findlay, but without the addition of five pages of testimonials); *Dr. Bodie's Valuable Prescriptions* (Macduff, n.d.), a listing of recipes for the cure of nasal catarrh, tapeworm, piles, etc., plus recommendations from satisfied customers; and *How to Become a Hypnotist* (Macduff, n.d.), which contains methods for trance induction of dogs, cats, rabbits, and hens, and (a personal favorite) "How to Mesmerize Water: Take a glass of water (distilled preferred), hold it firmly in the left hand, make a few passes with the points of the fingers almost touching the water. The glass being a perfect insulator and the water being a splendid conductor, it soon gets charged with MESMERIC AURA which proceeds from points of the fingers, by the suggestion of the mesmerist he can make the water act as an anaesthetic, an aperient, or an astringent, and it will act as such when given to the medium."

While I have obtained and examined the above-mentioned titles, the Christmas issue, 1919, of *The Performer* magazine contains an advertisement for additional works by the doctor which I have never seen: *Electricity and All About It, Hypnotic Suggestion, The Cause and Cure of Paralysis*, and the provocative *The Mouth, Its Beauty and Importance*. Bodie also contributed articles to conjuring and theatrical periodicals.

In order to give the flavor of Bodie's speech and style, I have quoted liberally from his works. I have been fortunate to obtain the Findlay scrapbook on Bodie, which contains numerous cuttings, photographs, letters, etc., relating to the conjurer. Additional materials have been supplied by Gordon Bruce and Stuart MacMillan in Scotland and Patrick Page, Peter Lane, and John Fisher in England, to whom I am most grateful. The University of Texas at Austin has the correspondence from Bodie to Houdini pertaining to the gift of the electric chair. These letters give further insight into the conflicts in Bodie's life and are quoted with permission.

One of the most remarkable aspects of Bodie's strong stage persona is that once seen he was rarely forgotten. Three well-known conjurers, Bruce Posgate, Eric Lewis, and Billy McComb, each regaled me with eyewitness accounts of seeing the doctor in their youth. Not only magicians but the general public found him unforgettable. Elliot Williams, the Scottish actor, collected hundreds of anecdotes about Bodie. He wrote articles about and planned a major biography of Bodie, but, sadly, died before its completion. It should be mentioned that these tales, particularly from rural Scotsmen, were often elaborated beyond the actual effects which Bodie performed. Bodie was the subject of a BBC radio show which elicited numerous written responses from an enthusiastic audience, who still remembered him vividly.

Material on Bodie and Chaplin can be found in Edwin Hoyt's *Sir Charlie* (London, 1977) and Theodore Huff's *Charlie Chaplin* (New York, 1951); the latter is the source of the quote on page 137. As a sixteen-year-old, Chaplin sat next to, and was outraged by the actions of, Bodie at the funeral of the great actor Sir Henry Irving. Remarkably, however, he may have done his imitations of Bodie without having ever seen the doctor's act. The photos of Bodie and Chaplin appear in the autobiography, *Chaplin* (New York, 1964), published by Simon & Schuster, who allowed us to use the photograph on page 136.

Numerous electric acts existed in the Bodie era, inspired largely by his success: the Salambos, Volta, C. E. Jenkins, Dr. Herman, Bill Lenton, Resisto, Resista (a woman), and a slew of other girls calling themselves Miss Electra or Miss Electricia, etc. Many learned their craft from mail-order houses like G. W. Allen's, which sold instructions for "The girl who tames electricity act."

The Bodie court battles were widely reported in the British press. See *Lloyds Weekly*, *The Sketch*, and *The People*, each of November 7, 1909, for accounts of the Irving trial, and *Lloyds*, November 14, for material on the Glasgow riots. Edwin Dawes writes most interestingly of Bodie in *The Great Illusionists* and reproduces the Bodie lithograph, the text of which is quoted here on page 146.

The doctor was also the inspiration for the character of McKyle, the Electric Wizard, in Peter Barnes' play (London and New York, 1969) and subsequent movie *The Ruling Class*, directed by Peter Medak. In a remarkable scene, the Christ-like Peter O'Toole duels verbally with the Doctor of Electricity as thousands of volts sizzle through the air.

10. BORN TO A DRIER DEATH THAN DIVING: SAMUEL GILBERT SCOTT AND OTHER DAREDEVILS

The bulk of material for this chapter appears in cuttings and playbills in the author's collection. A full-length portrait print of Scott, his head covered with a handkerchief, preparing for a dive, is in the Harvard Theatre Collection. Additional undated clippings are to be found at the Humanities Research Center, University of Texas at Austin. *The Picture Magazine* of January 1895 also contains material on the diver.

The sixteenth-century "slide for life" is chronicled by Arthur Freeman in *Elizabeth's Misfits* (New York and London, 1978). Numerous instances of daredevils losing their life in such stunts are extant. For example, Robert Odlum was the first man to jump off the Brooklyn Bridge. He died in the attempt on May 19, 1885. One hundred years later (July 5, 1985) Roy Fransen, a veteran stuntman, performed his "Dive of Death" from a sixty-foot tower into a small pool as part of the British Airways Open Day at Concord Centre, Crandford, England. As was his custom, Fransen's clothes and the edge of the pool were set on fire as he commenced his dive. Apparently, the wind shifted and the sixty-eight-year-old man was moved slightly off course. He hit the side of the pool and died shortly thereafter of multiple injuries.

The death of the Great Peters was reported in obituaries in the St. Louis *Post Dispatch* and the *Star Times* on October 23, 1943.

11. A FEW WORDS ABOUT DEATH AND SHOW BIZ: WASHINGTON IRVING BISHOP, J. RANDALL BROWN, AND THE ORIGINS OF MODERN MIND READING

Particularly helpful in compiling the material for this chapter were files of correspondence, largely unpublished, in major collections. The Library of Congress houses scrapbooks of the mind reader C. A. George Newmann, which contain much material on early muscle readers and a fascinating group of letters from Newmann to Joseph Rinn. The Humanities Research Center of the University of Texas at Austin contains letters from Eleanor Fletcher Bishop to Houdini, as does the Mulholland Library in Los Angeles.

These letters to Houdini, which provide the most important single source of insight into Eleanor's plight after her son's death, were initially so bizarre as to seem almost amusing. Continued perusal, however, revealed the desperate rantings of a frightfully paranoid and psychotic woman who had likely been driven mad by misfortune, both real and imagined.

Houdini, reading of her plight in the New York *Dramatic Mirror*, offered assistance. Their initial correspondence resulted in the two-part article Houdini wrote about Bishop in his *Conjurer's Monthly*, July and August 1908. Eleanor insisted that she be allowed to read the articles before publication.

In letter after letter, she referred to her son as Commander Washington Irving Bishop, 32° Mason, Elk, Knight Templar, and Philanthropist. "Please only write & publish *praiseworthy things* about my *darling*—let all law suits *vanish* into *oblivion*," she urged in a letter of July 11, 1908. As for J. Randall Brown, she wrote, "Be *sure* and *cut* out all about *Mr. Brown* as it is *false he never* taught my son—he tried to learn some of my son's *power* and I wrote him a *severe letter* & told him I would have him arrested if he did not recant his *false statements relative* to my son—Brown was only my sons *valet*." No doubt in an attempt to rebut the knowledge that Brown performed his mind reading before Bishop ever took to the stage, she added, "My son showed his wonderful power at 2½ years old—and at 5 years Commodore Cornelius Vanderbilt would while visiting us bind my childs eyes & ask him to write what stock he should buy and my *little child* would write while blindfolded what *stock to buy*— but it would be written backward, & you would have to hold it before a mirror to read it correctly."

As the letters and pleas for money became more frequent, Eleanor painted a scarcely-to-be-believed picture of horror coupled with hopes of receiving untold millions of dollars to which Houdini would become heir. On May 1, 1916, she wrote, "Please save me from a paupers grave . . . pardon pencil as I am almost blind and cannot use ink." On April 10, 1917, she revealed, "We are entrapped in this hospital which is a den of horror and will die here of cruelty and starvation." Her horrifying scenario continued in another letter: "3 AM, Beloved Brother and Sister in the name of God lend me some money to hire empty rooms and remove from here before we are poisoned by rat bites . . . we are starved on dry bread and bitter coffee." Racked by "groans of the dying, screams of the mad woman—constant crying of babies. . . . We get a spoonful of mush, a little watered milk. The Doctors have every luxury, also the nurses but the patients starve."

On July 19, 1917, she wrote: "Do for God's sake send me some money so I can settle my business and make you a millionaire." When Eleanor died five months later Houdini had long since refrained from answering her. Nevertheless he was named as the beneficiary of a thirty-million-dollar estate. Like most of the numerous court proceedings of Eleanor and her son, Washington Irving Bishop, this claim, too, was never settled.

The scrapbook of Charles Montague, an invaluable research tool, was made available to me by Milbourne Christopher before his untimely death. Christopher's books contain excellent material on Bishop.

I have made great use of contemporary newspaper articles which, in the case of these colorful characters, for once seem abundant. I am grateful for cuttings provided by Frank Koval, Father Cyprian, and Dennis Laub.

The Augustus Thomas article in the *Saturday Evening Post* is from April 1, 1922, and is the source of the Barrett Boys story. Enjoyable but largely unsubstantiated accounts of Bishop are Maurice Zolotow's article in *Detective Magazine*, Summer 1951, and Walter B. Gibson's article in the May 1957 *Mystery Digest*. An excellent article by Bob Lund appears in the July 1958 issue of *M.U.M.*

George Francis Train is a character worthy of further study. His name pops up frequently in New York papers of the period, championing varied causes (like the crusades of Victoria Woodhull). In 1893 he ran on stage to assist Maud Lancaster in a mind reading demonstration but, according to *The New York Times* of December 13, he "kept hopping about the stage to avoid Miss Lancaster's touch," proclaiming, "I have not been touched or come into contact with either man or woman for twenty years."

Anna (originally Annie) Eva Fay is also worthy of more attention. In spite of her exposure at the hands of Bishop, she successfully performed well into the 1920's and died in 1927. Fay and Bishop, thinly veiled, appear as medium Evalena Grey and manager W. Sterling Bischoff in Alan Pinkerton's *The Spiritualist and the Detectives* (New York, 1877). Corroboration of Bishop as Fay's manager appears in advertisements from *The New York Times* of January 16 and 20 and February 10 and 17, 1876.

Dr. Beard coined the term "muscle reading" in the first technical work on the subject in the *Archives of Electrology and Neurology*, November 1874. Other articles by him appeared in the Detroit *Lancet*, 1875, and *Popular Science*

Monthly, February 1877, and he wrote a monograph, *The Study of Trance, Muscle Reading, and Allied Nervous Phenomena in Europe and America, with a letter on the moral character of trance subjects and a defense of Dr. Charcot* (New York, 1882). Romane's article in *Nature*, June 23, 1881, paralleled exposures of Bishop without knowledge of Beard's earlier work on Brown. Sugden in the 1882–83 *Proceedings of the British Society of Psychic Research* provides similar results when examining Cumberland. See also accounts by W. F. Barrett in volumes 10 and 11 and A. E. Outerbridge in volume 11 of the same journal. Dessoir's findings appear in the *Journal of the Society for Psychical Research*, 1886–87, and in Jastrow's work *Fact and Fable in Psychology* (Boston, 1900).

G. M. Stratton's findings on Rubini are listed in the *Psychological Record*, 1921, and in *The New York Times*, March 4, 1927. A good account of mind reading technique, written by Newmann, appears in *Elliott's Last Legacy*, Harry Houdini, editor (New York, 1923).

J. N. Maskelyne is a major figure in magic history and is particularly well represented in *Maskelyne and Cooke. Egyptian Hall, London, 1873–1904*, by George Jenness (Enfield, Middlesex, 1967). Bishop's fine to Maskelyne was reduced from £10,000 to £500 in a later court decision but still never paid.

Information on Bishop's San Francisco engagements may be found in an entertaining though not well-documented volume by his one-time manager, M. B. Leavitt, *Fifty Years in Theatrical Management, 1859–1909* (New York, 1912).

Material on the acts investigated by Harry Price appears in his *Confessions of a Ghost Hunter* (London, 1936) and Johnstone and Tyndall are mentioned in the Newmann scrapbooks and in various newspaper cuttings. Kuda Bux is the subject of voluminous newspaper and book accounts including Price's *A Report on Two Experimental Fire-Walks* (London, 1936).

Hanussen is the author of *Das Gedanhenlessen/Telepathie* (Vienna, 1920) and appears as a subject in numerous German articles.

Arthur Hammer's act is described in Violet McNeal's *Four White Horses and a Brass Band* (Garden City, N.Y., 1947), and an amusing article on Lev Schneider appears in the Los Angeles *Times* (September 4, 1981).

Tebb, Vollum, and Hawden are the authors of *Premature Burial, How It May Be Prevented* 2nd ed. (London, 1905).

12. LAROCHE: THE SISYPHUS OF THE CIRCUS WORLD

A chapter in A. H. Kober's *Star Turns* (New York, 1929) first piqued my interest in the "Bola Misteriosa" many years ago. Bob Bramson, the great juggler, was able to provide me with valuable information about his grandfather LaRoche and his mother, Gertrude, who also did the act. (Bramson tried it, he said, only once.) A controversy still exists as to whether or not LaRoche emerged from the top of the spiral as featured in his posters. Bramson says that he did but that Gertrude was not able to push open the sphere at the top of her ascent. Circus historian Jacques Garnier states that LaRoche fired a pistol and waved flags from inside the ball at the height of his ascent but only appeared when the ball descended to the ground. Excellent articles by Garnier, listing many people who performed the act, appeared in the conjuring journal, *L'Escamoteur*, September–October 1961 and November–December 1962, and in *Le Cirque dans l'Universe*, number 41.

Lepere is the subject of an article in *La Nature* (Paris, May 18, 1889) and is mentioned in Albert A. Hopkins' *Magic: Stage Illusions and Scientific Diversions* (New York, 1897) and Saltarino's *Fahrend Volk* (Leipzig, 1895).

References to Ethardo appear in Raymond Toole Stott's circus bibliography. The Buislay bill is in the Harvard Theatre Collection. "Minting the Marvel" is the subject of an article in the January 3, 1902, issue of the *Showman Magazine* (London). He performed at Madison Square Garden on a spiral weighing almost six tons. Leonce, who was a multi-talented equilibrist, performed in a variety of acts in the decades prior to the turn of the century. Leonatti also did a spiral ascension bicycle act.

Even the toy of "La Boule Mysterieuse" was controversial. An ingenious toy maker named Gasselin claimed to have invented it after witnessing LaRoche on the Barnum & Bailey tour of Paris. He said his design was copied by the well-known manufacturer Fernand Martin, who created the toy in tin in 1906. A strong spring allowed the ball to climb a sixty-centimeter spiral; the ball then opened, revealing the performer holding French and American flags; and a string enabled the ball to descend the track. It is described and pictured in Mary Hillier's *Automata and Mechanical Toys* (London, 1976) and in *Le Cirque et Le Jouet* (Paris, 1984).

LaRoche is frequently pictured in the programs and route books of the Barnum & Bailey Circus during his American and European tours with the show. In 1896 LaRoche appeared in Koster and Bial's Music Hall in New York's Herald Square. A poster of LaRoche performing for the Strassburger Circus was struck by Friedlander in Hamburg. He is also pictured, without name, under the caption of "Die geheimnisvolle Kugel" in a lithograph done in Berlin for the Wandercircus of Blumenfeld. *La Science au theatre* by Vaulabelle and Hemardinquer (Paris, 1908) attempts to explain the working of his act.

American circus historian Richard Flint graciously opened his files to me and supplied material on "Nevada" from the 1897 Barnum route book and on Don Oscarez from the September 30, 1956, issue of *Der Komet*.

Geroku recently performed with Fosset's Circus in Ireland and on the Paul Daniels television show in London.

13. ARTHUR LLOYD: THE HUMOROUS HUMAN CARD INDEX

Much of the material in this chapter (actual cards, lists, reviews, and manuscript notes of Lloyd) was provided by Chet Karkut and is gratefully acknowledged. Karkut contributed an article about Lloyd to a pamphlet entitled *Charlie Miller on the Card Index* (Chicago, circa 1980). Lloyd's act is described in Max Holden's *Programs of Famous Magicians* (New York, 1937).

Lloyd appeared on the cover of the May 1920 issue of *The Sphinx* magazine and was an occasional contributor to conjuring periodicals. He was featured in a June 14, 1936, column of Ripley's "Believe It or Not."

Witnesses of Herbert Brooks' marvelous presentation of producing chosen playing cards from his pockets were often unkind to Lloyd. In the *Paul Fleming Book Reviews*, volume III (Oakland, Ca., 1979), the author notes: "This exceptionally brilliant trick was promptly taken over by other magicians, some of whom 'improved' upon the Brooks procedure by undertaking not only to produce chosen playing cards but also postcards, automobile licenses, menus and various kinds of placards—and thus destroyed the charming simplicity of the effect and robbed it of all its mystery. In at least one instance the performer carried on his person so huge a load of cards that his attire literally abounded in suspicious bulges, and what should have been a baffling piece of deception was reduced to an absurdity."

In Lloyd's defense, his demystification of the act was a conscious decision to feature his remarkable memory rather than any magical effect. Indeed, Lloyd often exposed his pockets to the audience at the end of his performance. It made his ability to produce a single requested card seem even more amazing.

On an undated notice in the Karkut collection appears this review: "Arthur Lloyd has a meritless and disinteresting turn in which he displays old sleight-of-hand tricks and goes through some rigamarole with cards." Handwritten on the page was a note from Lloyd: *Do not fail to read this one. It made me sad, then happy. I sued for damages and won.*"

Critics of Lloyd, however, were few and far between; he had a remarkably long and successful career from his debut in 1907 to impressive club engagements in the late 1940's. In the 1950's, he served as an entertainment director on the Holland-America line and often performed for the passengers. His last years were spent alone, sadly, in a New York apartment.

14. ENTEROLOGY: GETTING INTO BOXES, BOTTLES, AND TROUBLE WITH SEAMUS BURKE AND OTHERS

The autobiography of Burke, *From the Earth to a Star* (County Wicklow, Ireland, 1959), is a surprisingly scarce work. It was first brought to my attention by Robert Lund, who insightfully anticipated my enjoyment of the material. The book lists thirty-six "plays" authored by Burke. (Actually, most were short music hall sketches.) Additional references may be found in the National Union Catalog.

Brunel White's columns in the *World's Fair* on February 5, 12, and 26; April 30; May 7 and 28; and June 4, 1938, all contain material on Burke.

Cazeneuve, the Davenport Brothers, and Houdini are all well documented in magic histories. Particularly helpful were original programs and materials in the Mulholland collection. The "Balch" test is documented in *Houdini's History of Magic in Boston* by H. J. Moulton (Glenwood, Ill., 1983). Interesting early versions of the trunk trick were also done by J. N. Maskelyne, E. Cooper Taylor, and Oscar Eliason. The article on Del Monte was provided by Claude Crowe. King Brawn was witnessed by the august magic collector and historian H. Adrian Smith, who graciously provided me with a first-hand account of his act. A playbill of Major Zamora appears in Christopher's *Panorama of Magic* (New York, 1962).

Dunninger's meetings with Pecoraro are chronicled in his *Inside the Medium's Cabinet* (New York, 1935). Additional information was provided by New York magic historian Stanley Palm through conversations with Dunninger.

The story of the bottle conjurer has been retold countless times. This account is taken from clippings in the contemporary London press. Information regarding the numerous prints on bottle conjuring may be found in D. M. George, et al., *Catalogue of Political and Personal Satires Preserved in the Department of Prints and Drawings in the British Museum.*

15. INCOMBUSTIBLE MEN AND FIREPROOF WOMEN

I believe I have been able to offer a comprehensive look at the long career of Chabert. This has been made possible by cuttings and playbills in the Mulholland Library, the Harry Price collection at the University of London, the Lysons' scrapbooks at the British Library, the author's materials, and a wonderful bound volume of Chabert material in the Humanities Research Center at the University of Texas at Austin. Also helpful were the writings of Christopher, Dawes, Altick, and Houdini, already cited, and an important account in Hone's *Every Day Book* (volume II, London, 1835).

The material about Chabert's early career and the quotes on page 240 are from *The Wonderful Life and Extraordinary Exploits of Monsr. Chabert the Fire King . . .* (London, circa 1830), which must be read with caution. The letter from Leicester Fields is also at the University of Texas, but among the materials originally collected by Houdini. Quotes not credited in the text are from unidentified contemporary accounts.

Material on the Indian Chief may be found in Chabert's *A Brief Historical Account of the Life and Adventures of the Botocudo Chieftain* (London, 1822) and in various editions of his similar work, *An Historical Account of the Manners and Customs of the Savage Inhabitants of Brazil Together with a Sketch of the Life of the Botocudo Chieftain and Family* (Birmingham, 1823; Exeter, 1823; and Edinburgh, 1823). Chabert's career in America is mentioned by Odell in *Annals of the New York Stage* (New York, 1927–1949), Pecor, *The Magician on the American Stage* (Washington, D.C., 1977), and Moulton's *Houdini's History of Magic in Boston* (Glenwood, Ill., 1983). Also helpful was a booklet of his drugstore recipes in the collection of Dr. J. H. Grossman in Connecticut.

Exploits of Richardson and other early fire-eaters are discussed by Beckmann in *A History of Inventions and Discoveries* (London, 1846) and by Houdini in *Miracle Mongers and their Methods* (New York, 1920). Dr. Panthot was a Professor of Physics at the College of Lyon; his report appeared in the *Journal des Scavans*, and subsequently in the *Gentlemen's Magazine*, 1755. The Voltaire quote appears in an undated account from the *Weekly Magazine* in the MacManus-Young collection at the Library of Congress. Powell quotes are from the Lysons' scrapbooks.

The German exposé of Herr Roger (Bremen, 1809) was made available to me by Volker Huber. The material on Chacon is from a playbill in the collection of Jacques Voignier. Chylinski and Lionetto are mentioned by Houdini and in the materials at the Humanities Research Center at the

University of Texas. Brooks' letter is quoted by Houdini. Kowalsky, Baly, and Leitsendorfer are discussed by Pecor. Potter, a very important early magician, is frequently discussed in magic histories.

The Buono Core–Fillipino controversy is explored in an undated cutting in the Leslie Cole collection. D. D. Home's fire tests are mentioned in Carrington's *The Physical Phenomena of Spiritualism* (Boston, 1907) and in Volume VI of the *Proceedings of the Society for Psychic Research*. An unusual and interesting study, recently published, is *The Enigma of Daniel Home* by Trevor Hall (Buffalo, 1984).

Rivalli is mentioned in *The Era*, February 24, 1900, in Houdini's *Miracle Mongers*, and in playbills in the author's collection. Mr. Kluganek's Russian bill is in the Humanities Research Center at the University of Texas. A brief biography and cover portrait of Barnello appear in the May 1912 issue of the *American Magician* magazine.

16. STONES, SWORDS, SNAKES, AND OTHER ENTRÉES

Many of the cuttings cited in this chapter appear in the scrapbooks of the Reverend Daniel Lysons housed in the British Library. The automaton stone-eater is listed (item #23, "The Bust of a Turk who will chew and swallow an artificial stone as often as any of the company choose to put one into his mouth") in the catalog entitled *Morning and Evening Amusements at Merlin's Mechanical Museum* (London, circa 1790).

Charles Hogan's note on O'Keefe appears in *The London Stage 1660–1800* (Carbondale, Ill., 1960–1968). Cummings' story is related in Wilson and Caulfield's *The Book of Wonderful Characters* (London, 1869), which also contains material on Battalia and other early stone-eaters.

There are many playbills and pamphlets relating to the appearance of Eastern jugglers in England in the second and third decades of the nineteenth century, but, to my knowledge, no major study of their activities exists. Ramo Samee and Khia Khan Khruse are the leading figures to emerge from this group. The great English clown Joey Grimaldi mimicked the antics of the Indian sword-swallowers by pretending to down a gigantic blade.

The sword-swallowers Cliquot, Fritz, Clifford, the Victorinas, and Dufour are mentioned by Houdini in *Miracle Mongers*. Additional material on Fritz and Clifford may be found in various route books and programs of the Barnum & Bailey Circus. Much original memorabilia of the Hallworths is in the Strong Museum in Rochester. *Step Right Up* (1977), a catalog of an exhibition of show business at the turn of the century, featuring Hallworth material, was prepared by Richard Flint, who was most helpful to me.

Leslie Fiedler's discussion of geeks and much else of interest to readers of this book is in *Freaks: Myths and Images of the Secret Self* (New York, 1978).

Mac Norton is mentioned by Jacques Garnier in his *Forains d'hier et d'aujourd'hui* (Orleans, 1968) and by Pete Collins' *No People Like Show People* (London, 1957). He is the subject of at least three Friedlander lithographs. Material on early spouters is to be found in Caulfield's, Kirby's, and other compilations of "wonderful characters" and in already mentioned works of Christopher, Dawes, and Clarke.

Works on the technical aspects of glass eating, sword swallowing, etc., not recommended but noted, are Leonard Miller's *Thrilling Magic* (London, 1946) and Sam Dalal's *Swami Magazine* (Calcutta, January 1972).

17. LE PÉTOMANE: THE END

The standard biography of Le Pétomane is Nohain and Caradec's *Le Pétomane, 1857–1945, Sa Vie—Son Oeuvre* (Paris, 1967). I am grateful to M. Caradec for supplying me with original photographs for use in this book. An English translation by Warren Tute appeared in London in 1967; and an American edition was done in Los Angeles, 1968. There are also pirated editions of the work in circulation.

Early references to the literature of flatulence may be found in D. F. Foxon's *English Verse, 1701–1750* (Cambridge, 1975). The *Bibliographie des ouvrages relatifs a l'amour, aux femmes, au mariage, et des livres facetieux, panta-grueliques, scatologiques, satyriques, . . .* (San Remo, 1873) and the *Bibliotheca Scatologica*, a curious catalogue of related articles compiled by Pierre Janet, J. F. Payen, and A. A. Veinant (Scatopolis, [Paris] 1849), provide later sources. Material on La Mère Alexandre is in Garnier's fascinating *Forains d'hier et d'aujourd'hui* (Orleans, 1968).

Those desirous of more information on Honeysuckle Devine should consult an article by Bruce David in the February 1975 issue of *Gallery* magazine.

Two entertaining books have recently explored the mythos: *Fee, Fie, Foe, Fum: A Dictionary of Fartology* by "E. Slove Prombles" (Brockport, New York, circa 1981, by Bruce Pennington) and *The Bean Report* (New York, 1984), the latter published anonymously by an erudite and amusing former editor of a national humor magazine.

The Japanese connection was inspired by conversations with John Solt, chairman of the East Asian Language Colloquium at Harvard University. As a scholar of "misemono," he led me to three works: the narrative of Gennai, translated by William Sibley of the University of Chicago, an excellent paper on misemono by Andrew L. Markus of the University of Kansas, and a translation of *L'art Péter* by Sumie Jones of Indiana University. The story of Fukutomi appears in *Narrative Picture Scrolls* by Hideo Okudaira (New York and Tokyo, 1973).

Acknowledgments

My interest in the unusual entertainers described in this book has been kindled largely by Jay Marshall in Chicago and Patrick Page in London. These men, themselves curious characters, are wonderful performers and encyclopedic sources of crazy and bizarre acts.

Persi Diaconis was instrumental in my transition from a casual reader and collector of occasional things historical into an uncontrollable and avaricious acquisitor of artifacts and academic trivia. I am not sure whether to thank or to curse him. I am most grateful for his encouragement and friendship.

My research took me to numerous collections. The institutions and individuals therein who have been particularly helpful are:

The American Museum of Magic, Marshall, Michigan: Bob and Elaine Lund, Proprietors

The Harry Price Library at the University of London Library: A. H. Wesencraft, Curator

The British Library: Nicolas Barker, Head of Conservation, A. D. Sterenberg, ESTC, and Jean Archibald

The Library of Congress: Leonard Beck, Curator of the Houdini and MacManus-Young collections, and Elena Millie, Curator of the poster collection

The Harvard Theatre Collection

The New York Public Library

The New York Historical Society

The Henry E. Huntington Library, San Marino, California: Carey Bliss, former Curator, Alan Jutzi, Curator of Rare Books and Thomas Lange

Guildhall Library, London: Ralph Hyde, Keeper of Prints and Maps

The University of Southern California Theatre Department

The Magic Circle of London: Leslie Cole, Executive Librarian

The Magic Castle, Hollywood, California

Egyptian Hall, Brentwood, Tennessee: David Price, Proprietor

The Cleveland Public Library

The Library Company of Philadelphia: Edwin Wolf II, Librarian, and Ken Finkel, Curator of Photographs

Museum of Opera, Santiago, Chile

The National Variety Theatre Museum, Tokyo, Japan

The Circus World Museum, Baraboo, Wisconsin: Robert L. Parkinson, Research Center Director

The Harry Ransom Humanities Research Center, the University of Texas at Austin: Paul Bailey, Tim Spragens, and Cathy Henderson

The William Andrews Clark, Jr., Memorial Library, University of California at Los Angeles: Thomas Wright, Librarian, who generously provided me with an office, where a considerable amount of this book was written, and I was aided by a wonderful research staff, including John Bidwell, Carol Briggs, and Susan Green.

The Mulholland Library of Conjuring and the Allied Arts, Los Angeles: This magnificent collection was started by the well-respected magician and author John Mulholland in the second decade of this century and added to until its owner's death in 1970. Since 1966 it had been housed at the Players Club in New York as part of the Walter Hampden Memorial Library. When a decision was made to put the collection at auction, an anonymous benefactor decided to keep the library together and asked me to be its curator. I am most grateful to him.

Private collections are often as important as holdings in public institutions. Their owners are usually passionate and frequently extremely knowledgeable about the materials they possess. Those whom I visited personally and who provided me with both hospitality and information are:

In the United States

H. Adrian Smith, Byron and Barbie Walker, Jay and Frances Marshall, Persi Diaconis, John Henry Grossman, David Meyer, Ron Wohl, Chet Karkut, Al Guenther, Ron Taxe, Walter Gydesen, Tim Felix, Jeffrey Hirsch, John Gaughan, and Milbourne Christopher

In England

Leslie Cole, Edwin Dawes, Peter Lane, John Fisher, Peter Jackson, Kay Robertson, Pat Page and Bob Read

In Scotland

Gordon Bruce, Stuart MacMillan, and the late Duncan Johnstone

In France

Jacques Voignier and Georges Proust

In Germany

Volker Huber and Peter Hackhofer.

I have also been assisted by a great number of people who have shared knowledge and provided paths of exploration and personal encouragement. I am most grateful to them and apologize to any I may have inadvertently overlooked. They are: Deborah Baron, Saul Bass, Gerald Bentley, Jr., Allen Berlinski, Lois Bianchi, Gaetan Bloom, Bob Bramson, Andrea Braver, Howard Caplan, François Caradec, Mike and Tina Caveney, Maurine Christopher, William and Victoria Dailey, Andrew Edmunds, Chuck and Hilda Fayne, Steve Finer, Jules Fisher, Richard Flint, Arthur Freeman, Steve Freeman, Angela Freytag, Barbara Gannen, Nat Gorham and Jan Shuler, Sabine Hake, Peggy Kahn, Frances Kean, Bill Liles, George and Judy Lowry, Oziar Malini, Tavo Olmos, Stanley Palm, James Randi, Tom Ransom, Patrick Reagh, Charles and Regina Reynolds, Carl Rheuban, Arthur Saxon, John Solt, Jim Steinmeyer, George Theofiles, Marcello Truzzi, Dai Vernon, T. A. Waters, Alain Weill, Steve Weissman, and Clarence Wolf.

I am grateful to my patient and indefatigable literary editor Peter Gethers and to the rest of the Villard/Random House staff who so conscientiously helped in the preparation of this book, and to my longtime literary agent and friend Candace Lake.

I have been saddened by the deaths of a number of people who have been most helpful to me in the preparation of this book: Al Flosso, the great magician and dealer in rare memorabilia, who provided me with some of my first treasures; Orson Welles, who, although we met infrequently, fascinated me with his passionate accounts of magic performances; Kuda Bux, the fire walker and "Man with the X-Ray Eyes," a marvelous performer and longtime friend; Manny Kean, the proprietor of the Kean Archives in Philadelphia, who generously provided me with materials for research; Walter Gibson, the prolific author on magic and a myriad of subjects, who was always willing to share his knowledge; Raymond Toole Stott, whose bibliographies of circus and magic are the starting points for any serious work in this area; and, finally, Milbourne Christopher, the pre-eminent magician-historian, who provided me always with assistance and encouragement. Though I had known Chris since I was a small boy, recent years and mutual interests had brought us together more and more frequently. His death was sudden and unexpected and is a great loss to the magic community and to me personally.

Index

Ricky Jay

Mr. Jay is a renowned sleight-of-hand artist whose one-man show *Ricky Jay & His 52 Assistants* was a critical and popular success, receiving the Lucille Lortel and Obie awards.

Mr. Jay is a historian in the fields of deception, unusual entertainment, and conjuring and has defined the terms of his art for *The Cambridge Guide to American Theater* and the forthcoming edition of the Encyclopaedia Britannica. He is the author of *The Magic Magic Book, Many Mysteries Unraveled, Cards as Weapons*, and the ongoing fine-press quarterly *Jay's Journal of Anomalies*. He has written and hosted his own television specials for CBS, HBO, A&E, and the BBC.

He established the firm "Deceptive Practices," which provides consultation for films, television, and the stage. As an actor, Mr. Jay is most recognizable from his roles in David Mamet's films *House of Games, Things Change, Homicide*, and *The Spanish Prisoner*. He has also appeared in *Boogie Nights* and the James Bond film *Tomorrow Never Dies*.